QUEER TIMES, BLACK FUTURES

SEXUAL CULTURES

General Editors: Ann Pellegrini, Tavia Nyong'o, and Joshua Chambers-Letson
Founding Editors: José Esteban Muñoz and Ann Pellegrini

Titles in the series include:

Queer Times, Black Futures

Kara Keeling

NEW YORK UNIVERSITY PRESS

New York

NEW YORK UNIVERSITY PRESS
New York
www.nyupress.org

References to Internet websites (URLs) were accurate at the time of writing. Neither the author nor New York University Press is responsible for URLs that may have expired or changed since the manuscript was prepared.

Library of Congress Cataloging-in-Publication Data
Names: Keeling, Kara, 1971–   author.
Title: Queer times, black futures / Kara Keeling.
Description: New York : New York University Press, [2019] | Series: Sexual cultures |
Includes bibliographical references and index.
Identifiers: LCCN 2018026983| ISBN 9780814748329 (cloth : alk. paper) |
ISBN 9780814748336 (pbk : alk. paper)
Subjects: LCSH: African American sexual minorities. | Queer theory. |
African Americans in mass media.
Classification: LCC HQ76.27.A37 K44 2019 | DDC 306.76089/96073—dc23
LC record available at https://lccn.loc.gov/2018026983

New York University Press books are printed on acid-free paper, and their binding materials are chosen for strength and durability. We strive to use environmentally responsible suppliers and materials to the greatest extent possible in publishing our books.

Manufactured in the United States of America

10 9 8 7 6 5 4 3 2 1

Also available as an ebook

CONTENTS

Another Litany for Survival

> Thinking thought usually amounts to withdrawing into a dimensionless place in which the idea of thought alone persists. But thought in reality spaces itself out into the world. It informs the imaginary of peoples, their varied poetics, which it then transforms, meaning, in them its risk becomes realized.
> —Édouard Glissant, "Imaginary"

"We were never meant to survive"; we become or we are unbecoming.[1] We change. We are no longer who we were or who we would have been. When something happens differently than it has before, when something affects us, we reforge ourselves in response. Every *now* harbors chaos and, therefore, a capacity for change. When survival is posed as enduring *as such*, we miss how that task calls for its own undoing in time. None of us survives as such; indeed, perhaps, freedom requires we give way to other things. Now. And perhaps again.

If we were never meant to survive *as such*, what do we do with "the time that remains," while we suffer, while we rejoice, while we exist within conditions not entirely of our own making, yet still open, currently defined by, but not simply confined by, flesh that dies and lives in its time?[2] What survives? What do "we" become in that survival, which was perhaps never meant to be? What of us should we invest in it? This book takes seriously the generative proposition *another world is possible*, the insistence that such a world already is here now and it listens, with others, for the poetry, the refrains, the rhythms, and the noise such a world is making.

Queer Times, Black Futures engages with some of those theories and ideas that I find currently offer roads through and perhaps beyond the most violently stubborn and persistently rationalized organizations of things: the imbrication of unequal relations with capitalist exploitation and the attendant logics of profit, calculation, and valuation.[3] One of the most recently articulated theories of interest to the present project is today called "new materialisms," the name given to a set of "theoretical turns" that draw (whether acknowledged or not) on old ideas and lines of inquiry hidden within Western thought, but kept perceptible by subjugated knowledges, discredited movements, everyday experiments in freedom, and counterhegemonic tendencies within Western philosophy.[4] Other theories and ideas animating this book include: various theories of time and temporality; "Bartleby" and selected other works by Herman Melville; critiques of US settler colonialism and strategies of radical refusal in the face of it; accounts of the potency of poetics; theories of technology and technē; Afrofuturisms; and formulations of finance capital and financialization.

Queer Times, Black Futures engages at-times-contradictory conceptual systems, assembling them nonetheless into a theoretical apparatus that, though doubtless constrained by this work's time and place of creation, might prove a humble offering to and for another world breathing here now. Since "Black futures" requires acting as if that other world were here now, the audience *Queer Times, Black Futures* imagines is cosmic. In other words, Black futures requires (re)creation and imagination, what Frantz Fanon referred to as "a real leap":

> I should constantly remind myself that the real leap consists in
>   introducing invention into existence.
> In the world through which I travel, I am endlessly creating myself.
> I am a part of Being to the degree that I go beyond it.[5]

In my own small endeavors to introduce invention into existence, I have been inspired by the currently available examples of Afrofuturism and surrealism, which, while not the same, are most compelling when they reveal what surrealist André Breton and others referred to as "the Marvelous."[6] For many surrealists, encountering the Marvelous anchors one in one's present in such a way that the magic in the world, the magic of the world, can be perceived, if only intuitively. As a way to combat "miserablism," or, as Franklin Rosemont defines it, "the rationalization of the unlivable," surrealism's insistence upon encountering the Marvelous includes an embrace of poetry and poetics.[7] Rosemont writes, "For surrealists, poetry is the fundamental experience, the root of all knowledge, the most certain guide to action. . . . For surrealism, poetry is . . . an immeasurably intensified awareness that involves an electrifying perception, an all-encompassing sense of the wonder and magic of things. It is the revelation of the world of our deepest internal desires and their unceasing interplay with external reality."[8]

Our deepest internal desires can be violent and cruel, as well as expansive, generous, and delightful. Still, Rosemont's formulation of poetry echoes that of Audre Lorde, for whom poetry is a way of thinking the space/time of politics for those deemed disposable or socially dead within the contexts of heteropatriarchy and white supremacy. As many scholars, activists, artists, and others have pointed out, Lorde, who was born in 1934 and died in 1992, has something significant to offer those of us gathered here in one of her futures. She was a Black lesbian feminist who was a poet, librarian, and activist. Her "woman of color" activism was influenced by and in many ways in contention with the broader, predominately white, feminist movement in the United States during the 1960s.

Lorde's theories about poetry undergird *Queer Times, Black Futures*. In this regard, this book participates in the broader contemporary reassessment of the insights and theories produced in the crucible of engaged struggle with, and in, the academy by Black and women of color feminists in the 1960s, 1970s, and 1980s. Their contributions might be understood as motivated by the kinds of critical impulses that would come to be known as "poststructuralist." Like other intellectuals, including artists and activists, I return to Lorde's work today in order to look after it, reading her theory about poetry, even against its grain, and participating in the ongoing excavation and reframing of her work within the terms and according to the demands of our time.

Throughout her writings, Lorde insistently returns us to the stubborn spatiotemporalities of our senses as a way to intervene in the smooth and seductive assertions of capitalism's inevitability, issued from Capital's predictable futures. Insofar as how we matter in the world is irredeemably here now, the stubborn facticity of what we understand to be our bodies and their senses renders them as sites not only of the application of power but also of power's transvaluation or redirection.

They are how we matter in this world—mechanisms from which futures are carved.

If the senses are a source of knowledge about the workings of power for Lorde, they also might be a nexus for the transduction of feelings through poetry into modes of resistance to the alienation characteristic of Capital. In her essay entitled "Poetry Is Not a Luxury," Lorde presents feelings as not just emotions, but as intimations that must be accessed and crafted into embodied knowledges capable of combatting the estrangement of the senses by Capital. Lorde asserts, "For within living structures defined by profit, by linear power, by institutional dehumanization, our feelings were not meant to survive."[9] Importantly, the feelings to which Lorde directs our attention are singular rather than collective. They surface in dreams or in sensuous experiences. "Feelings," not yet "emotions," are simply matter's capacity to be affected. Relations are forged through the work of poetry. The proliferation of connections through difference spreads through poetry. Lorde states, "Poetry is the way we give name to the nameless so it can be thought."

Lorde writes, "Each one of us holds an incredible reserve of creativity and power, of unexamined and unrecorded emotion and feeling. . . . As they become known to and accepted by us, our feelings and the honest exploration of them become sanctuaries and spawning grounds for the most radical and daring of ideas."[10] It could be said that, for Lorde, "poetry" is a vessel for making queerness communicable. Language is a vehicle through which sensory knowledge is parsed into common senses, and poetry has the capacity to deterritorialize language, making uncommon, queer senses available to thought. Poetry is a way of entering the unknown and carrying back the impossible; it is productive of ideas or knowledges that were incomprehensible and unacceptable before their distillation as such via poetry.

Lorde's thinking attends to what is now emergent in the past, even when what is emergent is not easily assimilated into a celebratory politics. Lorde's formulation of poetry acknowledges a situation in which a critical political investment in foreseeable futures has been lost. Although she is deeply invested in protecting "our worlds" from what she foresees as the possibility of their extinction, she understands those worlds to be born anew in each moment. Given the constant rejuvenation of future worlds in her thinking about poetry, Lorde's writing consistently records its own confrontation with fear and vulnerability because it is those feelings that preclude the becoming of other worlds that are "ours," but whose contours, details, logics, and so on are unforeseeable to us. In other words, Lorde's feminism, which is also a queer theory, requires a deterritorialization of gendered bodies (even as she insists on the difference gender makes) and a confrontation with the fear on which capitalism and heteropatriarchy rely for the reproduction of the logics and inscriptions through which they order our bodies.

Lorde is invested in "queer futures," but that investment is in renewal and creative invention, animated by difference in a way that seeks to safeguard the Diverse, rather than in what is foreseeable, programmatic, and rational. Where some Afrofuturism encourages speculation on possible futures, even if those futures are presently impossible, Lorde cautions against foreclosing on queer futures. What is of most interest to me about Afrofuturism throughout this book, then, is where Afrofuturism invests in Black futures, which are characterized by a type of wealth that cannot be measured by a predetermined yardstick, wrenched open in utterly unpredictable queer times that refuse foreclosing on queer futures. This is an Afrofuturism wherein aliens and others organize social life. There is partying on the Mothership.

Rosemont's formulation of surrealist poetry as an opening onto the sense of "the wonder and magic of things" expands this notion of the queer times of Black futures further by calling attention to things' agency: how things act on the environment. For Rosemont, matter is vibrant. For Rosemont's surrealists, agency resides in a perception and awareness that poetry, not formal knowledge, is "the most certain guide to action," wherein "poetry" itself might be a property of things, rather than simply a human capacity. When wrested from human desire, the poetry and poetics of things commingle with desire; and things desire.

In this regard, surrealism is compatible with the concept of "vibrant matter" as articulated by Jane Bennett and lends itself to an engagement with emergent theories that consider the agency of things.[11] Rosemont's formulation of surrealism offers an opportunity to enrich that body of scholarship by calling attention to living beings that have been relegated to the status of things within existing political, ontological, and social systems. Those beings have fashioned movements and cultural forms, including philosophies, out of their sustained engagement with other matter over time. A study of these movements and cultural forms can offer insights into the significance of existing modes of social life (some of which might be perceived as forms of social death) to emergent theories about the ontology of objects, race, and subjection.[12] In addition to surrealism and its investment in poetry and poetics, *Queer Times, Black Futures* looks to Afrofuturism, which combats miserablism by calling attention to the systematic rationalization of the unlivable, often imagining scenarios and sometimes movements that (re)turn to the cosmic, where "life" perhaps can be perceived, even (re)conceived, as existence beyond measure.

One of *Queer Times, Black Futures'* leaps is its serious scholarly engagement with philosophical questions of space and time, punctuated, poetically, by (ir)regular interruptions from Herman Melville's short story "Bartleby, the Scrivener: A Story of Wall Street" and the "Bartleby industry" it inspired.[13] Following the commercial failure of *Moby Dick* (now considered a classic American novel), Melville wrote several short stories and one more novel. Written in 1853, "Bartleby, the Scrivener" was one of these later pieces of fiction, whose titular character is best known for the refrain: "I would prefer not to."

Queer Times, Black Futures turns to Melville's story to offer a series of provocations about power, language, space, time, and resistance. "Bartleby" repeatedly interrupts the book's consideration of futures, futurity, speculation, disciplinarity, and technology to meditate on the (im)possibility of a politics of radical refusal.[14]

In tension with, but not antagonistic to, radical refusal, this book explores the limits and possibilities for producing a set of "freedom dreams" that issue from Afrofuturist imaginations. It seeks to explore where they open to another world (versus where they simply make compromises with what we currently know), yet not to define those dreams and render them knowable (though that may occur herein), nor to colonize the terrain they open onto (though like imagination, this book spatializes and fixes even as it seeks to unmoor what is familiar).[15] Rather, this book traverses such freedom dreams so that those of us living today who are forging logics and material relations and organizing things in support of that other world we believe is (im)possible can consider what in those freedom dreams might survive us and our limited perceptions, taking flight beyond what is presently imaginable.

There is no roadmap to freedom. Freedom dreams do not need roads even though it could be said that they make the roads as they move, laying them as common utilities for those who would follow.[16] While I (if there is such a thing) certainly strive to communicate well throughout this book, *Queer Times, Black Futures* does not pretend to know where the insights it generates might lead. *Queer Times, Black Futures* affirms that today one can perceive desires and attempts for "liberation" from those human structures and phenomena that define, fix, mold, alienate, confine, and limit the living beings and other things they order. It seeks an alliance with others, generating concepts that can animate worlds like those in the "freedom dreams" discussed by Robin D. G. Kelley in *Freedom Dreams: The Black Radical Imagination*.[17] Kelley argues that, when measured according to whether they changed society's basic structures, none of the "freedom dreams" movements he discusses was successful; yet, when accounted differently, each generated visions of the world that continue to feed and inspire others. All of these dreams survive, even when they are rendered imperceptible as such.

Introduction

Black Futures and the Queer Times of Life: Finance, Flesh, and the Imagination

The mothership can't save you so your ass is gonna get left.
—Erykah Badu, "On and On"

The future is "terra incognita": although we may be able to guess the outcome of events that lie close to us, as we project beyond this we enter an unmapped zone full of uncertainty. Paradoxically, the range of options this reveals can seem paralysing.

No one can definitively map the future, but we can explore the possibilities in ways that are specifically intended to support decision-making. At Shell we use scenario building to help us wrestle with the developments and behaviours that shape what the future may hold and prepare ourselves more effectively. We also believe it can inspire individuals and organisations to play a more active role in shaping a better future—for themselves, or even on a global scale.

In this book, we use a metaphor of exploration and map-making to describe how we think about building scenarios. Like a set of maps describing different aspects of a landscape, scenarios provide us with a range of perspectives on what might happen, helping us to navigate more successfully. Exploration—of a territory or the future—involves both analytical thinking rooted in whatever facts are clear, and also informed intuition.
—Shell International BV, "Shell Scenarios:
An Explorer's Guide"

Imagine that a man hails a taxi and instructs the driver to take him to a sustainable energy future. The taxi driver punches "sustainable energy" into the car's GPS and steps on the gas pedal. Glancing at his passenger in the rearview mirror, the driver asks, "Do you believe in aliens?" For the rest of the ride, the taxi driver tells a tale of outer-space creatures who have been watching human development on earth. They notice that human actions have rendered the earth's ecosystem increasingly tenuous and unsustainable and have depleted its energy supply. Speculating about the earth's future and the potential of earthlings to participate in an intergalactic community, the space aliens in the driver's tale determine that humans are "a bit too haphazard" to be "invited up to the intergalactic party." The driver asserts, "We need to get better at seeing the bigger picture. We need to face the energy challenge."

He continues by explaining that, from his present vantage point, one of two likely futures will become manifest. The first is characterized by a disorganized and unsustainable "scramble" for resources, with governments prioritizing the day-to-day and delaying the big decisions necessary for long-term energy sustainability in an unceasing game of catch-up focused on producing more and more energy. The other entails the innovation of a cooperative "blueprint," created by people all over the world taking action, agitating for their governments to change laws, imagining new paths for sustainable living, and working in harmony with the planet while "we all continue to profit and grow." Clearly, the cooperative "blueprint" is the better plan for the future that the "we" invoked here desire; and, according to the taxi driver, it would earn humans an invitation to the aforementioned intergalactic party.

This narrative is offered in an animated YouTube video produced by the future scenarios team at Royal Dutch Shell plc (aka Shell).[1] "Join the Taxi Ride to a Sustainable Future" illustrates the multinational gas and oil company's recent efforts to "look into the future" with their "Shell Energy Scenarios to 2050" project. A pioneer in the development of corporate "future scenarios," Shell's investment in "the future" involves forecasting into and speculating about that future in order to maximize their profits. It is an investment in maintaining its present status as a profitable multinational corporation. Attending to *how and why* they produce knowledge about that future offers insights into the temporality that sustains present relations.

Royal Dutch Shell's website not only showcases a set of future scenarios reports; it also includes documents that explain the process of producing scenarios and the benefits to corporations of doing so. According to the introduction to "People and Connections: Global Scenarios to 2020," scenarios are "a tool for helping managers plan for . . . different possible futures." They are "alternative stories of how the world may develop," which "help us understand the limitations of our 'mental maps' of the world—and to think the unthinkable, anticipate the unknowable, and utilise both to make better strategic decisions."[2] The future scenarios offered in the 2050 project—"Scramble" and "Blueprints"—draw from the available quantitative and qualitative data that Royal Dutch Shell deems relevant to its present decision-making. Based on the literature accompanying the scenarios, including the ninety-eight-page publication "Scenarios: An Explorer's Guide," these speculative fictions inform decision-making aimed to maximize the corporation's profits and ensure its survival.

Contestations over "the future" and "futurity" have been central to formulations of time throughout the twentieth century and into the twenty-first: from the scientific inquiries into the relations of space and time carried out by physicists such as Neils Bohr, Albert Einstein, and others; to the theorizations of time offered by philosophers and artists such as Henri Bergson, Martin Heidegger, and Aimé Césaire (which often contradict those advanced by physicists); to the theories of modernity offered by political theorists; to the rise of financial derivatives as part of a shift away from the gold standard; and to the ways that film and other technologies have transformed lived experiences of temporality. Thus, the strategies and assumptions that inform Royal Dutch Shell's futures scenarios are antagonistic to those that animate *Queer Times, Black Futures*, which centers some of the cultural logics of Afrofuturism.

In 1994, Mark Dery tentatively defined Afrofuturism as "speculative fiction that treats African-American themes and addresses African-American concerns in the context of twentieth-century technoculture—and more generally, African American signification that appropriates images of technology and a prosthetically enhanced future."[3] Over the past ten years, an explosion of interest in Afrofuturism has transformed the category itself, pushing its cultural logics and political investments into the twenty-first century. Currently, Afrofuturism is a rich and growing area of critical inquiry and cultural production, which includes film and other visual cultural forms, literature, critical scholarship, and audio culture. Its early definition, which influential scholar Alondra Nelson, among others, credited to Dery, has been revised and debated. Recently, Ytasha L. Womack offered the following definition in her book *Afrofuturism: The World of Black Sci-Fi and Fantasy Culture*: "Afrofuturism is an intersection of imagination, technology, the future, and liberation."[4] One of the aims of *Queer Times, Black Futures* is to interrogate these four constitutive elements of Afrofuturism—imagination, technology, the future, and liberation—within the context of finance capital's stances toward (and investments in) the future.

Queer Times, Black Futures considers the implications of scholarly, artistic, and popular investments in the promises and pitfalls of imagination, technology, futurity, and liberation that have persisted in Euro-American culture since the beginning of the twentieth century. The Afrofuturisms of interest to *Queer Times, Black Futures* consist of cultural forms and logics through which creative engagements with Black existence, technology, space, and time might be accessed and analyzed. Their conceptualizations of futures differ from those through which Royal Dutch Shell and other transnational corporations like it aim to ensure their existence.

The corporate use of scenarios to support profitable decision-making affirms Kodwo Eshun's claim in his essay "Further Considerations on Afrofuturism" that "science fiction is now a research and development department within a futures industry that dreams of the prediction and control of tomorrow."[5] Eshun continues:

> Corporate business seeks to manage the unknown through decisions based on scenarios, while civil society responds to future shock through habits formatted by science fiction. Science fiction operates through the power of falsification, the drive to rewrite reality, and the will to deny plausibility, while the scenario operates through the control and prediction of plausible alternative tomorrows.[6]

For Eshun, the difference between the future scenarios produced through science fiction and speculative fiction genres and those produced by the interdisciplinary teams assembled by multinational corporations resides in the stance each takes toward the present. Science and speculative fiction writers often produce future scenarios that the range of data available today would deem impossible, or that fly in the face of reality and plausibility. Multinational corporations, conversely, produce "credible, relevant, and challenging alternative stories" that help managers make long-term decisions rooted in present realities.[7] By combining "different fields of knowledge and ways of knowing," corporate scenarios seek to ward off what John Maynard Keynes referred to as "uncertainty," and thereby mitigate the vulnerability and risks of unanticipated events caused by blind spots, at least some of which, as I discuss below, the Shell scenarios team attribute to the epistemological limitations of disciplinary knowledge.[8]

Royal Dutch Shell's existence is predicated on a system of racial capitalism that thrives on the dispossession and exploitation of Black people, Indigenous peoples (some of whom describe themselves as "Black"), and people of color. A future in which Royal Dutch Shell would continue to exist as such forecloses upon a future in which those groups of living beings we currently can identify as "Black people" and/or Indigenous peoples, have the resources to enjoy a sustainable and joyful existence on this planet. In order to grasp the significance of Shell's speculative fictions about the future, it is helpful to have a sense of its history, including the environmental and human costs of its "strategic decisions."

Royal Dutch Shell was formed in 1907 after a merger between the British Shell and the Royal Dutch companies. Shell began as a venture between Marcus Samuel and his brother Samuel Samuel to control the oil trade in East Asia; it was formally launched in 1897 as the Shell Transport and Trading Company Limited.[9] Royal Dutch was founded in 1890 by a Dutchman named Aeilko Jans Zijlker, who, as a manager of the East Sumatra Tobacco Company in the Dutch East Indies, found oil in northeast Sumatra in 1880 and convinced the Dutch authorities to support his efforts to extract it and bring it to market.[10] While Zijlker founded Royal Dutch, it was Henri Deterding, another Dutchman, who later made it a profitable enterprise.

Shell began operating in the United States in 1912 and claimed worldwide operation one year later with its expansion to Venezuela. Venezuelan oil became an especially significant aspect of Shell's holdings, and it "was with mostly Venezuelan oils that the Allies fought the Second World War" on the European continent.[11] The arrangement depended upon the oil company's good relationship with Venezuela's president at the time, a fascist dictator named Juan Vicente Gómez.[12] Although the Royal Dutch/Shell Group (as it was then known) helped the Allies during World War II, even offering their dual headquarters in England and the Netherlands (which remained neutral during the war) to bolster the Allies' war efforts, Deterding made no secret of his admiration for fascist dictators. He idolized Italy's Mussolini and backed Spain's Franco and Germany's Hitler. Deterding reportedly offered to cooperate with Hitler, a decision that ultimately led to his ousting from his long-time leadership position.[13] The history of Royal Dutch/Shell underscores the distance between the company's stated purpose with its futures scenarios and the reality of how their profit-driven activities have impacted the peoples and ecologies they use in the name of ensuring the future of Shell Oil. The history of Shell's flirtation and collaboration with fascist dictators is sediment within the present relations that sustain the oil giant's profitability. These dealings contributed to Shell becoming one of the most profitable oil companies in the world after World War II. By the 1950s and 1960s, when post–World War II "economic growth throughout the industrial world was powered by cheap oil," Europe was "the most competitive market in the world," and "Shell was the leading European marketer."[14]

During that time, Shell's explorers found oil in Nigeria after a roughly fifteen-year search and set up an operation to extract it. The infamous events that followed reveal the extent to which Shell's existence is predicated upon its ability to exploit land, lives, and labor. The future scenarios initiative at Shell began in 1970, when Shell was causing overwhelming ecological destruction in the Niger Delta and perpetuating violence against the Ogoni people who live there. Key staff on Shell's scenarios team explain in a short video available on Shell's website that in the 1970s, they predicted "volatility in the world would rise" as a possible result of the decision by Iran, Iraq, Kuwait, Saudi Arabia, Venezuela to form OPEC (the Organization of the Petroleum Exporting Countries) in 1960.[15] Their speculation about a possible future that came to pass enabled them to prepare for the volatility ahead of time and thereby minimize its negative effects on their operations. But the future scenarios did not prevent them from extracting resources from the Niger Delta. Royal Dutch Shell's operations in Nigeria demonstrate one example of how the company's industrial practices have harmed the planet's ecosystem across the world, especially on Black and other Indigenous peoples' lands. Some of Shell's "strategic decisions" over time have threatened the survival of both the land from which Shell extracts its oil and those who live on it.

By 1995, the Ogoni people had organized themselves to use nonviolent means to achieve justice. One of the most visible and outspoken Ogoni leaders was writer, journalist, and leader of the Movement for the Survival of Ogoni People (MOSOP), Ken Saro-Wiwa. About MOSOP's beliefs and motivations, Saro-Wiwa explained:

> MOSOP was intent on breaking new ground in the struggle for democracy and political, economic, social and environmental rights in Africa. We believe that mass-based, disciplined organizations can successfully revitalize moribund societies, and that relying upon their ancient values, mores, and cultures, such societies can successfully reestablish themselves as self-reliant communities and at the same time successfully and peacefully challenge tyrannical governments.[16]

MOSOP's effective nonviolent campaign drew international attention in the early 1990s. In 1990, Saro-Wiwa wrote the first draft of the Ogoni bill of rights. As Bronwen Manby describes: "In October 1990, MOSOP sent the Ogoni Bill of Rights to then–military head of state General Ibrahim Babangida, but received no response. In December 1992, MOSOP sent its demands to Shell, Chevron, and NNPC [Nigerian National Petroleum Corporation], together with an ultimatum that they pay back royalties and compensation within 30 days or quit Ogoniland."[17] By 1993, citing intimidation and attacks on its staff, Shell's operations in Ogoniland were suspended, and state-sponsored and extra-legal violence had been unleashed to stop MOSOP's nonviolent protests of Shell Oil's activities in the Ogoni area, which resulted in the deaths of "hundreds of unarmed Ogoni men, women, and children."[18]

After several previous detentions, Saro-Wiwa and other members of MOSOP were forced into a detention center in Port Harcourt in 1993. Writing from there, Saro-Wiwa claimed that Shell was sponsoring the violent attacks against MOSOP. To this day, Shell denies any involvement. On November 10, 1995, after a trial that has been widely criticized as unfair, Saro-Wiwa and his eight co-defendants were hanged in Port Harcourt Prison. Shell Oil condemned the executions. In 2009, "before the start of a trial in New York that was expected to reveal extensive details of Shell's activities in the Niger Delta," Shell settled with Saro-Wiwa's son, Ken Saro-Wiwa Jr., for $15.5 million dollars, claiming that it was a humanitarian gesture.[19]

As of August 2018, Shell Oil is worth US$306.5 billion,[20] and the company has been widely regarded as a leader in "corporate responsibility."[21] Yet, in 2004, Shell rocked the global financial market when it admitted that it had been overestimating its oil reserves by "2.1 billion barrels in Nigeria and Oman, 1.2 billion in Australia and Kazakhstan and 0.6 billion in other fields around the world."[22] Some commentators and observers placed partial blame for the deception on the company's massive bureaucratic structure.[23] The decision to overstate the reserves by 41 percent was attributed to the leadership at the time, and led to the replacement of three senior executives.[24]

Under international pressure from activists and humanitarians after the execution of "the Ogoni nine," Shell conducted an internal review and updated its business principals to include "specific references to human rights."[25] In their first social responsibility report, published in 1998, the company stated: "We engage in discussion on human rights issues when making business decisions. We have established a regular dialogue with groups which defend human rights."[26] Yet, Royal Dutch Shell's present existence has clearly depended upon their ability to wreak havoc on, if not destroy, the living conditions of those who inhabit the lands from which Shell extracts its profitable oil.

"Corporate responsibility" is another calculation to increase profit since Shell by no means plans to redistribute its wealth to account for the history that made it the one of the richest companies in the world. Under these circumstances, any likely future for Shell justifies the violences it has inflicted. The scenarios it predicts for the future, therefore, embed these violences and obfuscate present possibilities for redressing and preventing them. Moreover, Shell's futures assume that Shell will continue to extract whatever resources it needs. Presently, Shell's interest in futures and future scenarios evidences its investment in its survival as a corporate entity. While the taxi driver's tale blames government policies, Shell Oil's own survival also jeopardizes the survival of the planet and all living things insofar as its profits continue to depend upon the exploitation and appropriation of land and living labor.

Since Shell Oil's future scenarios are of course designed to speculate on futures wherein the company will continue to generate profits, they do not include situations in which Shell Oil itself no longer exists, is rendered obsolete, or has redistributed its wealth. As such, Royal Dutch Shell's continued existence (since its inception in the late 1800s) can be understood as part of the longue durée of a modernity that, as I will discuss later in this introduction, was inaugurated by the colonization of the so-called New World, the attendant enclosure of land, and the transatlantic slave trade. Their future scenarios are part of a knowledge project that has been calibrated to reproduce existing relations.

The Interdisciplines and Societies of Control

The mode of knowledge production that animates Shell's future scenarios hinges upon its understanding of the value of interdisciplinarity. Shell presents interdisciplinarity as a significant method for fulfilling the role played by speculative scenarios in its decision-making process, as explained in its publication, "Scenarios: An Explorer's Guide":

> Scenarios address blind spots by challenging assumptions, expanding vision and combining information from many different disciplines. Our experience, training, current fashions and familiar ideas can strongly influence what we notice and how we interpret the world. The positive view of these influences is that they help us focus, but they can also create blind spots—whole areas we know nothing about—leaving us exposed to unanticipated developments. Expertise itself can, paradoxically, help to create these blind spots. Information acquired from discipline-based research can create fragmented learning.[27]

The value for Royal Dutch Shell of assembling "interdisciplinary" scenarios teams consisting of experts from a variety of fields, combined with their interest in using the story form to include relevant qualitative, nonquantifiable information in their scenarios, calls attention to the convergence of the knowledge-production apparatus of a controversial transnational corporation with current academic discourses and practices. Those include interdisciplinarity and collaboration, the tropes and creative operations of speculative and science fictions, and the range of interests currently animated by imaginative speculations on the future. Here, "interdisciplinarity" marks a mode of knowledge production that can meet the challenges and demands of contemporary capitalism. Heralded in some academic quarters as a way to resist the governance of traditional disciplines, "interdisciplinarity," according to Shell Oil's future scenarios team, is also an emergent logic that serves the current needs of Capital by calling attention to existing "blind spots" created by disciplinary assumptions and their attendant methods of knowledge production. As a way to engage with the world that might direct attention to what Capital has not (yet) taken into account, interdisciplinary and collaborative scholarship emerges in accordance with the needs of finance capital.

Yet the difference between assembling a team of cross-disciplinary experts and producing interdisciplinary fields and areas of study is worth considering here. Talking specifically about the discipline of economics, Lawrence Grossberg has argued that Cultural Studies ought to take seriously the ways that interdisciplinary scholarship works to transform disciplines.[28] Grossberg asserts that scholars in Cultural Studies have become "lazy" as a result of "the increasing tendency to tame interdisciplinarity by incorporating it into and delimiting it within the disciplines. Rather than taking on other disciplines," Grossberg writes, "we grab onto a body of literatures and paradigms that have become transdisciplinary, so that they appear to liberate people from disciplinary canons to some extent."[29] It is debatable whether or not this tendency can be diagnosed as a symptom of laziness, rather than, say, the myopic modes through which scholarship is rewarded, at least in the United States, if not elsewhere, through publishing protocols and merit reviews that privilege the reproduction of existing scholarly methods, paradigms, and assumptions. Such a debate would not detract, however, from what is to be gained by pointing out, following Grossberg, that the interdisciplinarity of Cultural Studies historically has been predicated on a different model than the interdisciplinarity that informs the assembly of Shell Oil's scenarios team.[30]

The interdisciplinary drive of Cultural Studies, at its most impactful, has been consistent with how Stuart Hall retrospectively described the interdisciplinary activities of the Centre for Contemporary Cultural Studies (CCCS), founded at the University of Birmingham, England in 1964 by Richard Hoggart. The CCCS, which closed in 2002, was the institutional home of "the Birmingham School of Cultural Studies," which notably included Stuart Hall. In an essay entitled "The Emergence of Cultural Studies and the Crisis of the Humanities," also quoted in Grossberg, Hall writes:

> Serious interdisciplinary work involves the intellectual risk of saying to professional sociologists that what they say sociology is, is not what it is. We had to teach what we thought a kind of sociology that would be of service to people studying culture would be, something we could not get from self-designated sociologists. It was never a question of which disciplines would contribute to the development of this field, but of how one could decenter or destabilize a series of interdisciplinary fields. We had to respect and engage with the paradigms and traditions of knowledge and of empirical and concrete work in each of these disciplinary areas in order to construct what we called cultural studies.[31]

The interdisciplinary work described by Hall involves a sustained engagement with existing literatures in order to construct another field. It could be characterized as a mode of scholarly production that imaginatively, yet seriously, engages with disciplinary and interdisciplinary areas' "existing paradigms and traditions of knowledge" and "empirical and concrete work" to construct a new scholarly terrain. Such an endeavor is calibrated to "be of service to people studying" a particular object or set of objects, or to those interested in specific questions; it creates ways to do that work. It is animated by a scholarly imagination. As Hall explains, after the critical, negative work that those who formed the CCCS did to distance themselves and their work from some of the ongoing traditions in the humanities, "the positive work one then went on to do in the Centre had still to be invented."[32]

The pulls toward interdisciplinarity can be situated within a broader transformation, described by Gilles Deleuze, away from disciplinary societies and toward "societies of control." In a short essay published in

1992 and entitled "Postscript on the Societies of Control," Deleuze argues, "We are at the beginning of something." He describes it as a widespread "substitution" of "mechanisms of control" for the "disciplinary sites of enclosure" that characterized the prior formations of power described by Michel Foucault as those of "disciplinary societies." The struggle over the transformation or destruction of the traditional academic disciplines in order to develop interdisciplinary sites of knowledge production can be understood as part of the broader struggle against disciplinary societies, which are animated by the same logics of enclosure.[33]

The logics of interdisciplinary knowledge production, however, also are consistent with aspects of the mechanisms of control discussed by Deleuze in 1992. According to him, in place of the enclosed spaces of disciplinary societies, which "reached their height at the outset of the twentieth" century, mechanisms of control have been accelerating since the end of World War II to become the dominant logic of power. Deleuze writes, "Enclosures are molds, distinct castings, but controls are a modulation, like a self-deforming cast that will continually change from one moment to the other, or like a sieve whose mesh will transmute from point to point."[34] As the logics of disciplinary societies are increasingly eclipsed by those of control societies, institutions are being transformed, and the protocols and methods through which a variety of disciplines, including disciplinary knowledge production, have been maintained over time are subjected to modulation and fluidity.

Under present conditions, interdisciplinary modes of knowledge production can work as a mechanism of control.[35] As such, they encapsulate a confrontation between liberating and enslaving forces. Based on our examples of Shell Oil's scenarios team and considering the importance of interdisciplinarity to neoliberal university management logics, it could be argued that control societies are substituting interdisciplinarity (practiced as what Grossberg characterizes as transdisciplinarity, or assembling experts in different disciplines in order to produce knowledge across those disciplines) for disciplinarity.[36] The logics and methods of interdisciplinarity do not guarantee, nor do they inherently express, liberatory or radically transformative knowledges. Yet, as Deleuze asserts, "There is no need to fear or hope, but only to look for new weapons."[37] Because "the different control mechanisms are inseparable variations," it must not be assumed, however, that the weapons available to be found may not also be used to build the societies of control themselves.[38] In other words, interdisciplinary knowledge—that is, knowledge that transforms the disciplines while creating other forms of knowledge—might still be fashioned into a weapon directed against the investment in interdisciplinarity as a strategy of control.

The Imagination

The imagination is among the weapons on offer in societies of control. "Invention," "innovation," and "creativity" are buzzwords in many of today's corporate cultures, in large part because they are thought to be living, human engines of capitalist growth and expansion. Entrepreneur, best-selling author, and marketing expert Seth Godin, for example, argues in his book *Linchpin: Are You Indispensible?* that, unlike the Fordist mass production–mass market economy for which Americans have been trained, today's economy requires people who are willing to "draw their own maps" and make "each day into a kind of art."[39] The art-ification of labor not only points to the significance of affective labor to contemporary capitalism, something about which Godin comments in his book, but also highlights one of the ways that, as Franco Berardi (aka Bifo) puts it, the imagination currently is being "blackmailed" by the economy and epistemologically dominated by economics.[40]

Berardi explains that he can see no way out of "the present catastrophe," in which "capitalist rule is liquidating modern civilization," except by going through it. He writes:

> My knowledge and my understanding do not show the possibility of any acceptable development out of the present catastrophe. But catastrophe, a word whose etymology stems from the Greek Kata (for "moving") and Strophein, (for "beyond"), is exactly the point where we "move beyond" the present and a new landscape is revealed. I do not see that landscape because my knowledge and my understanding are limited, and the limits of my language are the limits of my world.
>
> My knowledge and understanding are missing the event, the singularity that might open onto that new landscape.
>
> So I must act "as if."

> As if the forces of labor and knowledge may overcome the forces of greed. As if the cognitive workers may overcome the fractalization of their life and intelligence. I must resist simply because I cannot know what is happening after the future, and I must preserve the consciousness and sensibility of social solidarity, of human empathy, of gratuitous activity, of freedom, equality and fraternity. Just in case, right?[41]

For Berardi, acting "as if" is a way of holding in reserve a radical imagination that approaches the limits of knowledge, not as a problem to be overcome, but as the condition of possibility for a "new relationship between the environment and the human organism" to be called forth by "the radical imagination."[42]

Today, as universities slash the budgets of those humanities programs and disciplines that have been (incompletely) transformed by Cultural Studies (as a result of the current accounting logics of university administrators in the United States and elsewhere), many of the methods and knowledges generated in those programs and disciplines remain a crucial part of a collaborative and interdisciplinary scholarly engagement with the world. As Shell Oil's explanation of how scenarios can address the blind spots created by disciplinary expertise describes, the scenarios' story form is valuable precisely because it might introduce qualitative elements that cannot be neatly quantified and measured; the use of the story form also might serve as one of the elements in what Berardi identifies as "the new space of activism," namely, "in the meeting point of poetry and theory and creation of new paradigms."[43]

Arts and humanities concepts and practices in and of themselves are not a defense against the survival strategies of a corporation like Shell Oil and the attendant logics of exploitation on which they rely, which also include listening for—and to—a certain "poetry from the future."[44] Such concepts and practices have been conscripted into Shell's survival strategies in order to shed light on the presently unknowable so that existing blind spots might more effectively be navigated by those who seek to "explore" and "map" the future by tethering it to the present.

Nonetheless, humanities-based practices and ways of knowing also introduce additional uncertainty into calculations because they work with and through the unpredictable and imaginative activities that are part of what Karl Marx refers to as "the absolute working-out" of the "creative potentialities" of those living beings currently recognizable as "human."[45] To the extent that they do so while holding uncertainty open, critical theory, poetry, dance, literature, philosophy, music, and other creative sonic phenomena can each continue to feed thought (and the capacity for thinking) in ways that touch and inform not only the rational decisions of corporate leaders and managers but also, as Édouard Glissant put it, "the imaginary of peoples, their varied poetics."[46]

For Glissant and Berardi, efforts to think thought carry the capacity to transform "the imaginary of peoples" and "their varied poetics"; in them, the risks of efforts to think thought become realized. Berardi's and Glissant's insights about the capacity of thought and "the thinking of thought" to affect the imaginary and poetics of peoples are a call for those of us for whom the production of knowledge matters, those whose intellectual labor seeks to be an operation of, through, and on the material realm, to assess the stakes involved in struggles over meanings, over the significance of things, and to participate in the collective production of shared senses of possibilities, of bodies and pleasures, of eccentric and errant affiliations, of matter, of times, and of worlds.

Attending to the ways that thinking matters calls for a reinvigorated concept of knowledge production—as an imaginative, scholarly enterprise characterized by an engagement with existing thought that eschews any version of "thinking thought" that simply withdraws into a "dimensionless place in which the idea of thought alone persists."[47] It calls for scholarly practices that engage with existing academic work and other knowledges and that involve the body as well as the mind. Such practices space themselves out into the world, recruiting matter(s) that perhaps have not participated in previous knowledge projects, or that have not been recognizable as ways of knowing, and finding out what those can do in thought now.

As the antithetical interests of Shell Oil's energy scenarios, on the one hand, and projects invested in Black liberation and Indigenous sovereignty, on the other, make clear, the politics of imaginative knowledge production are by no means guaranteed. Yet, imaginative modes of scholarly production that both embrace the demands of "rigorous scholarship" and challenge the interests served by existing measures of academic rigor might work to transform existing knowledges (much as Hall claims the early intellectuals in the CCCS worked to do) and communicate their findings in ways that could inform "the imaginaries of people, their varied poetics."[48] In addition to the traditional intellectual stances and methods of committed research in the pursuit of "truth," they also might work affectively, telling relevant stories and seeking to affect matter—to spark and authorize additional creative engagements within matter.[49] The imaginative scholarly production sketched here tarries with Utopia as a horizon but does not fix its sights on it. Instead, it sinks deeply into matter and existing material relations in a world in which horizons shift depending upon whether one has power to delimit them. "The imagination of people, their varied poetics," also become enmeshed in such a scholarly imagination even as it is affected by them.

The understanding that undergirds this description of imaginative scholarship is not new. Indeed, it is inherited from Romantic and Enlightenment thought and has served as one motor of prevalent understandings of both modernity and postmodernity. Other commentators have pointed out that renewed attention to the imagination in the twenty-first century is not surprising; from claims that finance is capital's imagination to corporate slogans to "think differently," to conceptualizations of a variety of "radical imaginations," to the rallying cry "another world is possible," the imagination today is called to do dramatic, urgent work toward divergent ends.[50]

In the present project, the imagination also plays a central role: it animates the mode of knowledge production for which this project invested in Black futures calls, and it anchors a spatiotemporal organization in which "queer remains" are generative, deterritorializing forces. Thinking with and through a vibrant concept of the imagination opens onto this project's perceptions of queer times and Black futures, and of the spatial politics that might be associated with them. Throughout this book, I call attention to the quotidian violence that secures the existing organization of things. The quotidian violence that holds existing reality in place does so in part by making the concepts "queer" and "Black" appear as aberrations while at the same time generating those concepts as sutures through which existing reality disavows its founding genocidal wars against Black and many other native peoples.

What I call "quotidian violence" is the violence that the reproduction, reinscription, and survival of what exists relies upon and enacts in order to manage what Octavia Butler's character Lauren Olamina from her novel *Parable of the Sower* calls "the only lasting truth": change.[51] In other words, quotidian violence names the violence that maintains a temporality and a spatial logic hostile to the change and chance immanent in each now; a quotidian violence presently holds in place a spatiotemporal logic that is hostile to the queerness in time.[52]

Yet, it could be argued that the queerness in time is part of what facilitated such violence to accumulate in, and as, our present. To the extent that queer is perceptible at this point in our analysis, it appears as a structuring antagonism of the social, and therefore of all those institutions, practices, traditions, and so on that seek to govern sociality and regulate the terms of sociability, including the management of time and space. As a structuring antagonism of the social, "queer" anchors social orderings as their negative. The use of "queer" throughout this book builds on the definition offered by Eve Sedgwick in "Queer and Now," her introduction to the 1993 collection *Tendencies*. She writes, "One of the things that 'queer' can refer to: the open mesh of possibilities, gaps, overlaps, dissonances and resonances, lapses and excesses of meaning when the constituent elements of anyone's gender, or anyone's sexuality aren't made (or can't be made) to signify monolithically."[53]

In my usage of the term, "queer" is not an ontological category—it is not what one is; rather, it is an epistemological category—one that involves life and death questions of apprehension and value production. "Queer" involves how one signifies or how groups of living beings are made to signify within a given set of significations. It may include what one does, how one does it, and where those actions place one in relationship to the maintenance of the present organization of things, including the groupings and affiliations of living beings constitutive of social, political, and economic relations. Recent scholarship in Transgender Studies has enabled a productive engagement with and critique of the ways "queer" has been conceptually allied with the politics of sexuality and the activism that seeks to address inequalities among people of different sexual orientations. Salient critiques of the extent to which "queer" has been domesticated and fixed along lines of sexuality, gender, class, ethnicity, and race in various national contexts remain important because they address how the politics that grow out of the disturbances through which "queer" has become perceptible might be responsible to those who presently might claim and/or be claimed by that category. Here and now, "queer" indexes shifting sets of references, produced in dynamic ways through material sociopolitical processes. Challenges to attempts to fix its significations into an identity are salutary because "queer" remains a constitutive logic of the present reality commonly perceptible in many geographic locations.

The production of "queer" is violent, material, and excessive to the management and control of sociability. "Queer" is palpable, felt as affect. It is also not only an imposition but simultaneously a becoming.[54] Queer fluidly anchors and defines the normative. It flows through Capital itself. Queer might be felt as utopian or dystopian, quotidian, banal, spectacular, public, private; yet, in each of its material operations on and through bodies, it carves out our relations temporally and spatially and proliferates connections within difference. Take, for example, the beginning of the collection of stories of queer Kenyans compiled by the Nest Collective, "a multidisciplinary arts collective living and working in Nairobi." Formed in 2012, the Nest Collective explains about its work: "Together we explore our troubling modern identities, re-imagine our pasts and remix our futures."[55] The subtitle of the Nest Collective's book, *Stories of Our Lives: Queer Narratives from Kenya*, illuminates that "queer" remains available as a relational axis of affiliation through sexuality in Kenya, where homosexual acts are outlawed. Toward the beginning of *Stories of Our Lives*, the Nest Collective writes:

> Dear Kenyan Queer:
> You are not alone. Whether you're a man or a woman, whether you're somewhere in between or somewhere beyond; you exist. You might feel small and fragile in the face of Statutes, Laws, Caucuses, Stones, Insults, a Church-State and Family that tries to deny your existence, but you exist. You must never let them take that away.
> Exist. Breathe. Love and Be Loved. Fuck. Thrive. Apologize to no one for your existence.
> Even though we do not know you, and even though we didn't get to meet you and hear your story, understand what we mean when we say: you are not alone, and this is your story, too.
> With all our hearts,
> The Nest Collective
> May 2015[56]

"Queer" is a long-haul proposition available in any-instant-whatever. Queer's proliferation of connections among disparate, qualitatively different things piles up, indifferent to its ability to measure or completely capture them. Capable of being modulated according to the demands of Capital, queer nonetheless stubbornly works on and through bodies, establishing relations between them and thereby connecting them across space and time. It might be said that queer is endogenous to time. Along the axis of the social, Capital must manage queer's proliferation of errant, irrational, and unpredictable connections in the interests of objectifying and delivering reliable futures. That a particular historical trajectory of "queer" has been domesticated in the United States—contained through the affirmation of "gay marriage" and the increased visibility and recognition through which it was achieved—is simultaneously a sign of victory for a vivacious, bold, and heterogeneous movement for "LGBT rights," and evidence of a recent modulation of control vis-à-vis sexuality and the organization of social life. To the extent that the dreams and visions of the world for which queer and trans* Americans have struggled over time have not been exhausted in the acquisition of the right to marry, in the United States "queer" remains an active and energetic reservoir for connection, affiliation, and experimentation.[57]

As Deleuze said about control societies in general, "There is no need to fear or hope, but only to look for new weapons."[58]

"Queer temporality," in my formulation, names a dimension of time that produces risk. In terms of financial management, it is well known that "time" itself produces risk. Here, "queer temporality" names that dimension of the unpredictable and the unknowable in time that governs errant, eccentric, promiscuous, and unexpected organizations of social life. The complex equations for managing risk in stock investment profiles attempt to contain risk, accounting for it through calculations and algorithms devised to predict and control for randomness. In relationship to queer temporality, these calculations' efforts to anchor the future to the knowable present miss the ways "queer" remains here and now in both recognizable and imperceptible forms. Insofar as some of those present forms are imperceptible to existing modes of knowledge production, they remain unaccountable to or within, for example, Shell Oil's scenarios team's plan to alleviate the risks posed by "blind spots" by telling stories crafted through interdisciplinary knowledges. Yet, even imperceptibly, queer stubbornly persists in present relations. Now.

In this regard, the queerness that is endogenous to time animates what Nassim Nicholas Taleb refers to as "Black Swan" events in his book *The Black Swan: The Impact of the Highly Improbable*. The name "Black Swan" derives from the tale that holds that before Europeans discovered Australia, they were convinced that all swans were white. This story, for Taleb, "illustrates a severe limitation to our learning from observations or experience and the fragility of our knowledge."[59] Taleb explains that what he refers to as a "Black Swan" has three attributes:

> First, it is an outlier, as it lies outside the realm of regular expectations, because nothing in the past can convincingly point to its possibility. Second, it carries an extreme impact (unlike the bird). Third, in spite of its outlier status, human nature makes us concoct explanations for its occurrence after the fact, making it explainable and predictable.[60]

"Black Swan" events are characterized by "a combination of low predictability and large impact."[61] The most important aspect of this concept for Taleb, and for our purposes here, is "the fact that we tend to act as if it does not exist!" To clarify his "we," Taleb continues, "I don't mean just you, your cousin Joey, and me, but almost all 'social scientists' who, for over a century, have operated under the false belief that their tools could measure uncertainty."[62] Taleb's primary target in his analysis is the science of economics and finance, in which measurements of "risk" purportedly account for future possibilities. Yet, according to Taleb, their measurements exclude the possibility of the Black Swan, evincing a "blindness with respect to randomness" because they focus on the minutiae instead of accounting for the big unforeseeable Black Swan events.[63] According to Taleb, "Black Swan logic makes what you don't know far more relevant than what you do know. Consider that many Black Swans can be caused and exacerbated by their being unexpected."[64]

In *The Physics of Wall Street: A Brief History of Predicting the Unpredictable*, James Owen Weatherall contends that Taleb himself overlooks that a recognition of the flawed nature of building and revising mathematical models is built into the methodologies behind the models currently used in financial markets. For this reason, Weatherall argues, rather than condemn mathematical modeling in financial markets (after all, the methods behind those mathematical models were also used to achieve engineering feats on which we regularly rely, such as air travel or the George Washington Bridge), one ought to recognize the value of trying to "domesticate as many unknown unknowns as possible," regardless of the fact that one can argue that any particular model is flawed.[65] For Weatherall, in other words, financial modeling's methods are convincing enough to warrant their use even though catastrophically unforeseen Black Swan events can and will happen in any arena. Weatherall further argues, "It is important to distinguish between the impossible and the merely very difficult. There is little doubt that mastering financial risk is extremely difficult, much more difficult . . . than solving problems in physics." Yet Weatherall insists that the scientific method through which the mathematical models governing financial markets have been developed "is the best way we have ever come up with for addressing our biggest challenges," and he asserts, "We shouldn't abandon it here."[66]

To further clarify his own position, Taleb offered the concept of "antifragility" in his next book, *Antifragile: Things that Gain from Disorder*. There, Taleb asserts:

> By grasping the mechanisms of antifragility we can build a systematic and broad guide to nonpredictive decision making under uncertainty in business, politics, medicine, and life in general—anywhere the unknown preponderates, any situation in which there is randomness, unpredictability, opacity, or incomplete understanding of things. It is far easier to figure out if something is fragile than to predict the occurrence of an event that may harm it. Fragility can be measured; risk is not measurable (outside of casinos or the minds of people who call themselves "risk experts"). This provides a solution to what I've called the Black Swan problem—the impossibility of calculating the risks of consequential rare events and predicting their occurrence. Sensitivity to harm from volatility is tractable, more so than forecasting the event that would cause the harm. So we propose to stand our current approaches to prediction, prognostication, and risk management on their heads. In every domain or area of application, we propose rules for moving from the fragile toward the antifragile, through reduction of fragility or harnessing antifragility. And we can almost always detect antifragility (and fragility) using a simple test of

asymmetry: anything that has more upside than downside from random events (or certain shocks) is antifragile; the reverse is fragile.[67]

Over the course of an argument that spans three books, *Fooled by Randomness*, *The Black Swan*, and *Antifragile*, Taleb's concept of "antifragility" emerges as a central attribute of entrepreneurs and risk-takers who have "flesh in the game." While Taleb mentions popular, ground-up movements and innovations as wellsprings of antifragility, his project valorizes entrepreneurial capitalists and not radically visionary freedom dreamers. Nonetheless, the concept of "antifragility" offers the following to the present project and its investments in freedom dreams: (1) a critique of finance capital's construction of "futures" that complements the analysis I advance herein; and (2) another way of thinking about the queerness in time as an ally in building the antifragility of freedom dreams, the obsessive love that sustains them, and those who advance such dreams within, without, and through love.

Within the calculations of the colonization of the Americas, the Atlantic slave trade, and the logics of white supremacy, the Haitian Revolution was a Black Swan event. It proved that Black belonging, anchored in love of freedom and of Black people, could be an antifragile revolutionary force at the same time that it demonstrated the robustness of European settler colonialism and white supremacy tethered to capitalist exploitation throughout the Western world. Explaining that Napoleon's army's inability to defend its territories in Louisiana lead to the defeat of the French in Saint-Domingue (now Haiti), historian Edward E. Baptist states in *The Half Has Never Been Told: Slavery and the Making of American Capitalism*:

> Even today, most US history textbooks tell the story of the Louisiana Purchase without admitting that slave revolution in Saint-Domingue made it possible. And here is another irony. Haitians had opened 1804 by announcing their grand experiment of a society whose basis for citizenship was literally the renunciation of white privilege, but their revolution's success had at the same time delivered the Mississippi Valley to a new empire of slavery. The great continent would incubate a second slavery exponentially greater in economic power than the first.[68]

The events and significance of the Haitian Revolution have been studied, narrated, assessed, and debated by many others.[69] What is important here is that it happened, and, in happening, it affirmed that what appears to be a random, unpredictable, outlier "Black Swan" event from within one conception of the world might emerge as the result of planning, visioning, risk-taking, and radical love rooted in another conception of the world, one that is simultaneously antagonistic to, incommensurable with, and indifferent to the first. Susan Buck-Morss, citing Michel-Rolph Trouillot's book *Silencing the Past: Power and the Production of History*, writes that the Haitian Revolution "entered history with the peculiar characteristic of being unthinkable even as it happened."[70] The Haitian Revolution can be understood as the production of an expansive conceptualization of Black belonging as an expression of obsessive love, which was unforeseeable from within Euro-American conceptions of the world.[71] After the Haitian Revolution, the possibility that slaves could end slavery through violent revolt was no longer unthinkable; for Britain and France, the Haitian Revolution marked the beginning of the end of the slave trade. In the Americas, potential slave uprisings were managed and assumed as an inherent risk of the slave trade. The Haitian Revolution played a role in transforming chattel slavery as it had existed until that time. In this regard, it is a manifestation of one of the "risks" assumed by the entrepreneurs who innovated within chattel slavery.

Ian Baucom explains in *Specters of the Atlantic: Finance Capital, Slavery, and the Philosophy of History* that a modern system of speculative finance capital developed with and through the Atlantic slave trade and has come to characterize global capital accumulation in the late twentieth and early twenty-first centuries. Since at least the sixteenth century, when options were used to buy and sell commodities in Antwerp and Amsterdam, economies have relied upon some mechanism to hedge against the uncertainty carried in time.[72] According to Baucom, the struggle between the slave traders and the abolitionists in the late eighteenth century

> both extends and replays what scholars in recent years have taken to be the central epistemological drama of the long eighteenth century, the drama— emerging from the social rivalry of the old landed and new moneyed

classes—in which, as mobile property displaced "real" property, and the imaginary value of stocks, bonds, bills-of-exchange, and insured property of all kinds trumped the "real" value of land, bullion, and other tangibles, the concepts of what was knowable, credible, valuable, and real were themselves transformed. Such transformations, J. G. A. Pocock was one of the first to argue, generated a wide array of epistemological shifts in British public life, shifts in the ways that eighteenth-century Britons struggled to make sense of and devise new forms for these novel structures of knowledge.[73]

Michael McKeon and other scholars have identified the literary novel as among the most important new forms that emerged to meet the epistemological challenges of the eighteenth century for Britons. Baucom suggests that speculation arises as a new form that intensified and generalized throughout the world during the present phase of financialization. Baucom's argument enables us to encounter in our present conjuncture the genocidal calculations, both financial and moral, that animated the transatlantic slave trade. Chattel slavery and the ontological, epistemological, and social-material regimes of settler colonialism that supported and perpetuated it underwrite our present.[74] The wealth generated through chattel slavery, settler colonialism, and European colonialism in Asia, Africa, and the Americas provided the foundation for present relations of exploitation and domination to accrue their force and authority—in other words, for today's quotidian violence.

Due to the time and distances involved in the transatlantic slave trade, "the financial life of the trade and the theory of value that it made possible" produced a system of credit involving "a mutual and system-wide determination to credit the existence of imaginary values."[75] The spread of chattel slavery across what Western Europeans claimed as their "New World" occurred in the context of and, according to Baptist was a driving force behind, the innovation of new technologies (such as the cotton gin), a new division of labor, and the entrepreneurial development of new financial instruments. Fueled by the risk-seeking behavior of entrepreneurs who harnessed capitalism's capacity for "creative destruction," the markets for slaves in the Americas capitalized upon the queerness that is endogenous to time. At the same time, systems of credit and speculation emerged to manage the risks unleashed and assumed by those entrepreneurs who grew the slave trade.

Financial Derivatives and the Afterlife of Slavery

> Slavery had established a measure of man and a ranking of
> life and worth that has yet to be undone. If slavery persists
> as an issue in the political life of black America, it is not be-
> cause of an antiquarian obsession with bygone days or the
> burden of a too-long memory, but because black lives are
> still imperiled and devalued by a racial calculus and a politi-
> cal arithmetic that were entrenched centuries ago. This is the
> afterlife of slavery—skewed life chances, limited access to
> health and education, premature death, incarceration, and
> impoverishment. I, too, am the afterlife of slavery.
> —Saidiya Hartman, *Lose Your Mother*

In today's global economy, the financial derivative has risen in prominence, and its contemporary logics have taken shape as part of the
organization of Capital into the forms of "globalization" and "financialization" that digital technologies have facilitated. Taken together,
derivatives today mark one of the largest swaths of finance capital. Yet,
as Dick Bryan and Michael Rafferty point out, derivatives also remain
one of the least understood elements of capitalism. Bryan and Rafferty explain that the primary function of derivatives is computation.
They write, "Derivatives are, within themselves, computational—they
embody systems of calculation that commensurate different forms of
capital according to notional competitive norms. They are, in this sense,
a universalizing force."[76] Commensurating different forms of capital,
derivatives are "themselves computations of relative values, embodying social relations of competition, not just trust, power, promises and
obligations."[77]

Drawing on Bryan and Rafferty's work, Lawrence Grossberg argues,
"The contemporary explosion and use of derivatives is at least in part a
response to, first, the move from gold to money as the universal equivalent on a global scale and second, the denial of the universal equivalent."
Continuing with reference to the global economic collapse of 2007 to
2009, Grossberg observes that "the current credit crisis can be seen, perhaps, as the failure of the derivative, which itself must be located within
a larger configuration of the contemporary impossibility of a universal

commensuration." For Grossberg, then, "the collapse/failure of the derivatives market" in the late 2000s "has itself to be related to crises of value in specific capital formations, such as commodity markets, which have had to confront the new hyper-differentiation of markets. One could argue, for example, that what is frequently dismissed as branding and niche-marketing signals a radical restructuring of value beyond our capacity to measure it. The result is, apparently, a situation of the increasing sense of the unpredictability of value itself."[78]

A "process of continual recalculation" is built into derivatives, endowing them with a capacity for self-transformation that also universalizes capitalist logics. Following Bryan and Rafferty, Grossberg reminds his readers that, while derivatives often have been grasped in their function as financial instruments that manage risk, their primary function is to commensurate value. Moreover, as Grossberg argues, one can read Marx's critiques of capitalism as "a critique of a particular form of mediation, of the social character of labor as a historically determinate social relationship."[79]

Bryan and Rafferty's and Grossberg's analyses are relevant to the present discussion about interdisciplinarity, futures, speculation, the concepts and affects that animate Black existence, queer temporality, and the imagination insofar as they renew our ability to bring analyses of class, labor relations, and political economy into ongoing engagements with cultural politics. Finance capital exists within a longer history of racial capitalism, itself undergirded by and maintained through the socioeconomic and cultural relations set in motion by the technological innovations and exploitation of risks that spread chattel slavery in the Americas. My attempt to bring the present political economy of finance into conversation with cultural politics is consistent with Randy Martin's call, writing in collaboration with Bryan and Rafferty, for an interdisciplinary scholarship calibrated to assess and address the changes wrought by financialization. Bryan, Martin, and Rafferty explain:

> Financialization, as a moment in the genealogy of capital, extends and refines accumulation, but it also elaborates mutual indebtedness as a more general feature of human sociality from labour to lived experience. More than a shift from one axis to another, it is one way that capital speaks its

social relations. Risk becomes not simply a form of calculation, a way of knowing, but also invites a kind of being. The boundaries between being and value, sheer quality and ceaseless quantity, have become blurred.[80]

Situating financialization in capital's genealogy, and, importantly, as subtended by "real relations" rather than the fictitious ones often attributed to finance capital because of its intimacy with speculation, Martin, Bryan and Rafferty conclude,

> Financialization . . . is not simply a stable object of inquiry that awaits bright lights, but an occasion of self-reformulation around an expanded political arena. In their profound interdisciplinarity, such politics might otherwise fall between the attentions of the domains of political and cultural economy—each bearing a potent conceptual lens that too frequently is tempted to look past what the other has in view.[81]

In much the same way as Shell Oil's desire to address the blind spots caused by looking into the future with only one disciplinary lens leads to their formation of interdisciplinary futures scenarios teams, the changes wrought by financialization call for attention by progressive and radical thinkers capable of interdisciplinary analyses. For instance, interdisciplinarity might be fostered by locating financialization in a longer history of credit and finance that acknowledges the central role that racial formation, the enclosure of land, and, importantly, anti-Black racism have played in credit and finance's rise to historical prominence.

In *Specters of the Atlantic*, Baucom argues that in the current conjuncture, the historically determinate social relationships between masters and slaves and colonizers and colonized rise to prominence as forms of mediation characteristic of finance capitalism: "As commodity capital is to the nineteenth century's intensification of the seventeenth, so finance capital is to the long twentieth century's intensification of the eighteenth."[82] Baucom focuses on the slave ship *Zong*'s 1781 voyage, when enslaved Africans were dumped overboard so that, instead of selling them into slavery, the slavers and the Liverpool merchants involved in the transatlantic slave trade could collect insurance on them as lost property. (Dear Reader, you might want to read the previous sentence a second time to allow the violences and pathologies it indexes to register with you affectively as well as intellectually. Or, take a break from this study, bookmark this page, and go read M. NourbeSe Philip's *Zong!*.)[83]

Presenting the *Zong* voyage as emblematic of the logics of the social character of finance capital, Baucom argues that, in Britain during the eighteenth century, the evidence of a slave trade shows up belatedly. He explains:

> The evidence came later: after a voyage was complete; after the slaves had been sold; after the record keeping, the account adjusting, and the other work of documentation upon which historians rely for their own imaginary reconstruction of events. But the value already existed, prior to and independent of the evidence that what was valued in fact existed. Time and distance are part of the explanation. The time it took to complete the vast triangular circuit of the trade dictated that merchants must conduct much of their business on credit. But for such a system of credit to operate both a theory of knowledge and a form of value which would secure the credibility of the system itself had to be in place. Central to that theory was a mutual and system-wide determination to credit the existence of imaginary values. Central to that form of value was a reversal of the protocols of value creation proper to commodity capital. For here, value does not follow but precedes exchange (not, to be sure, as the classical Marxist account has it, in the form of that use value that is held to preexist the moment of exchange, but as what Marx understood to be the end product rather than the originary moment of capital: as money value, value in the guise of the "general equivalent"). Such value exists not because a purchase has been made and goods exchanged but because two or more parties have agreed to believe in it. Exchange, here, does not create value, it retrospectively confirms it, offers belated evidence to what already exists.[84]

The *Zong* massacre reveals that the economy of the transatlantic slave trade was a speculative one, predicated on the belief that the future would confirm the present value of slaves and the other commodities of the trade. Baucom's analysis helps us to understand that certain of today's forms of finance capitalism intensify a speculative economy entrenched during the slave trade; while the spatiotemporal logics and the sociopolitical relationships are mapped differently today, the general geopolitical logics and material relations remain present. The African slave of the sixteenth to nineteenth centuries, and the colonized subjects and nations of the sixteenth through twenty-first centuries, are sedimented within present relations of precarity, haunting them in different ways in different settings. The crisis of value that the financial derivative today resolves (however clumsily) extends back through centuries of temporal accumulation, piling up on the bodies of Africans and Indigenous peoples (some of whom are Black and/or Africans), present in "modernity's most violent scenes of exchange."

This is the context in which discussions of modernity and political economy can unfold in ways that might remain attentive to the central issues of this book: queer temporality, the fact of Black existence and its potentialities, the imagination, and technological mediation. In this context, our discussion of financial derivatives is in conversation with Saidiya Hartman's statement (offered above) that slavery

> had established a measure of man and a ranking of life and worth that has yet to be undone. If slavery persists as an issue in the political life of black America, it is not because of an antiquarian obsession with bygone days or the burden of a too-long memory, but because black lives are still imperiled and devalued by a racial calculus and a political arithmetic that were entrenched centuries ago.[85]

Computation meets flesh and culture in the ongoing production and reproduction of Black existence.[86]

In Grossberg's analysis of finance capital, the financial derivative "proposes a mechanism of commensuration, of establishing equivalences and relations, among disparate and different elements, without appealing to the existence of a third standard term." Grossberg asserts that the "derivative is not simply another expression of the commodity form, a binary structure holding together abstract and concrete risk, but the re-invention or at least the re-imagination of another form of economic exchange, one that refuses the need for such a binary structure grounded in a stable abstract term, in favor of an infinitely changing process of calculation."[87]

Within the capitalist system, derivatives remain tied to a conception of "wealth" that grows out of and perpetuates exploitative capitalist rela-

tions. Although it remains debatable to what extent the rise of derivatives marks the incorporation of everything into the logics of capital,
it seems clear that derivatives exert a centripetal force, striving to pull
everything into the orbit of capitalist commensuration. Bryan and Rafferty explain,

> Each derivative product is a package of conversion of one form of capital
> to another—whether this is a simple commodity futures contract or a
> complex conversion of a particular currency index to a particular stock
> market index. When all these products are taken together, they form a
> complex web of conversions, a *system of derivatives*, in which any "bit" of
> capital, anywhere and with any time or spatial profile, can be measured
> against any other "bit" of capital, and on an on-going basis.[88]

Though Bryan and Rafferty do not pursue it, their use of the phrase "'bit'
of capital" recalls the significance of digital technologies, and of computation in particular, to derivatives. The connection between them is
historical: that is, the rise to prominence of derivatives in contemporary
finance has been facilitated by digital technologies, and computation
enables both derivatives and digital technology, but neither derivatives
nor digital technologies determine the other or are necessary to each
other. Both financial derivatives and digital technologies could exist without calling for the other. However, as Bryan and Rafferty and Grossberg
suggest, derivatives are part of "a complex web of conversions . . . in
which any 'bit' of capital, anywhere and with any time or spatial profile,
can be measured against any other 'bit' of capital, and on an on-going
basis."[89] Significantly, derivatives also "bind the future to the present or
one place to another."[90] This perspective illuminates the shared logics
between derivatives and digital technologies, and underscores the ways
that finance capital itself sometimes exists simply as digital units, bits, in
an economic system that is no less material because of it.

In Cinema and Media Studies, the rise of digital mediation technologies is assessed and analyzed in a variety of ways, including, among
other approaches, formulations of "the death of cinema" and an attendant eclipse of "Film Studies" or "Cinema Studies" by "Media Studies"
(marking a relative indifference to, or, alternatively, a heightened interest
in, the difference the specific medium of mediation makes), an incorpo-

ration of "Science and Technology Studies" into Media Studies, and the development of "New Media Studies" as a subfield within Media Studies. Analyses and theories of the specific role played by computation in digital media are of particular interest here because they help explain how digital cultural productions interface with the processes of computation and calculation that enable digital technologies. Any interface between digital cultural productions such as films, music, and digital art and those computations and calculations through which finance capital functions is an opportunity for contemporary demands for commensuration amidst various crises of value to be challenged by what Glissant has referred to as "a right to opacity."

As it has been formulated in Glissant's oeuvre, "opacity" names a politicized cultural strategy. Opacity is part of Glissant's philosophy of "Relation." It might be calibrated to secure an investment in what I will call "Black futures" (which may not look like an "investment" at all) through a reliance on a queer temporality. For Glissant, opacity is a mode through which one person or a group of living beings might resist Western thought's "requirement for transparency." Glissant explains that, from the perspective of Western thought, "in order to understand and thus accept you, I have to measure your solidarity with the ideal scale providing me with grounds to make comparisons and, perhaps, judgments. I have to reduce."[91] He suggests that perhaps "we need to bring an end to the very notion of a scale. Displace all reduction."[92]

To insist upon a group's "right to opacity" in sociocultural terms, therefore, is to challenge the processes of commensuration built into the demand for that group to become perceptible according to existing conceptions of the world. It is a way of asserting the existence in this world of another conception of the world, incomprehensible from within the common senses that secure existing hegemonic relations and their "computations of relative value."[93] Elsewhere, I have described cinematic images as images of value in process.[94] If, as I have argued, cinematic images index existing relations in ways that most often make perceptible "common sense" as the content of those images, then the eclipse of celluloid by digital video (and the attendant collapse of any claim to what film theorists have referred to as "profilmic reality") reveals that the so-called crisis of the index in the digital regime of the image is merely an intensification of a crisis that has been constitutive of cinematic reality since the invention of cinema: namely, the unmooring of an appearance from its material referent.[95] What was perceptible as a particular crisis of the image, the failure of images of Black people to empirically and positively represent Black people, has become a general crisis of representation that is emerging today, in part because digital media is explicitly indifferent to the truth claims undergirding appeals to a profilmic reality.[96]

As I discuss in greater detail in chapter 3, as the digital regime of the cinematic image rises to prominence within the cinematic, digital cinematic images become perceptible as images that abstract existing relations through modes of commensuration (such as "common sense") rather than through a claim, however false and contested, to some pro-filmic reality (and its attendant politics of correspondence and recognition). They do so according to calculations, mutability, fluctuations built into them. Retaining the opacity of certain cinematic images therefore offers one way to enhance the queer temporalities within the cinematic; it stalls (however momentarily) recognition of those images according to existing systems of evaluation and commensuration.[97] An insistence on opacity gives queer time for the conceptions of the world sedimented or, to employ a term offered by Baucom with a stronger economic sense, *accumulated* within existing relations to appear now.[98]

"Black futures" emerges here as a way of indicating an investment in the risk that already inheres in social life—an antifragile investment in the errant, the irrational, and the unpredictable, made by a political imagination that posits radical socioeconomic and geopolitical transformations. Where financial derivatives and their calculations seek to quantify risk, account for randomness in advance, and perform the endless computations necessary for commensuration between various things, "Black futures," animated in queer times and inseparable from queer relations, names what remains unaccountable to existing instruments of measurement and the interests those instruments presently serve. "Black futures" do so even when they are purportedly accounted for in advance through structures of anticipation that often miss that "Black futures" are here in every now. The ungovernable, anarchic here and now harbors Black futures. Black futures stall movements predicated on temporal deferral, problematically proclaiming "we are the ones we have been waiting for," while singing (also problematically) "we shall overcome one day," here, queer, in each now.[99]

Black Radical Imagination

Imagination makes temporality possible. A version of the oft-cited definition of the imagination (most often attributed to Immanuel Kant) is found in the first two entries for the word in the *Oxford English Dictionary*: (a) "the power or capacity to form internal images or ideas of objects and situations not actually present to the senses, including remembered objects and situations, and those constructed by mentally combining or projecting images of previously experienced qualities, objects, and situations"; and (b) "an inner image or idea of an object or objects not actually present to the senses; often with the implication that the idea does not correspond to the reality of things." These definitions are important to my project here because they underscore the extent to which the imagination participates in the construction of the present through a combination of past and present elements that are not necessarily attached to presently perceptible reality.

Max Haiven and Alex Khasnabish offer a helpful gloss on "imagination" in their co-written introduction to a 2010 special issue of *Affinities: A Journal of Radical Theory, Culture, and Action*. They write:

> We approach imagination as a process by which we collectively map "what is," narrate it as the result of "what was," and speculate on what "might be." It is cognitive and corporeal, intensely creative and utterly mundane all at once. And while imagination is a terrain of political struggle it is not merely reducible to "ideology" in any simplistic sense of "false consciousness" or "fetishism." Imagination represents a more rich, complex, agent-driven and ongoing working-out of affinity. It is a crucial aspect of the fundamentally political and always collective (though rarely autonomous) labour of reweaving the social world. Despite its problematic history as the fetish of the European "Enlightenment," we cannot let go of a radicalizing idea of the imagination because it speaks to our ability to create something else, and to create it together.[100]

The friction between the image of a thing, including an event, in its absence and a present image of that thing is what Robin D. G. Kelley is after when he writes in the preface to his book *Freedom Dreams: The Black Radical Imagination* that, by the measure of whether or not the visions that animated radical movements of the past were realized, "virtually every radical movement failed because the basic power relations they sought to change remain pretty much intact. And yet it is precisely these alternative visions and dreams that inspire new generations to continue to struggle for change."[101]

For Kelley, the theoretical underpinnings of radical movements continue to exert a force that exceeds those movements' practices and tangible outcomes. The imagination is central to the freedom dreams about which Kelley writes: surrealism, Black feminism, Black internationalism, Communism. It is what allowed those movements to reach through and beyond what exists, including the distracting demands of daily life, and make perceptible another organization of things. Insofar as imagination also entails, as Haiven and Khasnabish assert in the quotation above, "a more rich, complex, agent-driven and ongoing working-out of affinity," it might also be a motor of errant connections and affiliations enabled by the queerness in time.

The radical imagination works with and through what exists in order to call forth something presently absent: a new relationship between and within matter. It is radical because it goes against the root, taking aim at the very foundations of a shared reality. As Kelley's work underscores, the Black radical imagination recombines the contents of the long arc of Black existence in ways that call forth new relations for all. A marker of a historical mode of existence that exerts pressure on, and indeed has been perceived as antagonistic to, the ontology of the human, Black existence is a condition of possibility for moving beyond what is. At the same time, it presently anchors a set of possibilities for "something else to be."[102]

To use Berardi's formulation, it might be said that the modes of Black belonging generated by the Black radical imagination lie "after the future." In the long quotation cited earlier, Berardi claims that he must resist what is because he cannot know what will happen "after the future." His formulation of "after the future" acknowledges that the political mode of investing in and acting to affect the future that has characterized the twentieth-century's dominant approach to the temporality of movements and change now only reproduces present logics. In his *After the Future*, he writes:

When the punks cried "No Future," at the turning point of 1977, it seemed like a paradox that couldn't be taken too seriously. Actually, it was the announcement of something quite important: the perception of the future was changing. The future is not a natural dimension of the mind. It is a modality of projection and imagination, a feature of expectation and attention, and its modalities and features change with the changing of cultures. . . . We don't believe in the future in the same way [as the Futurists whose artistic movement encapsulated the twentieth-century's belief in the future]. Of course we know that a time after the present is going to come, but we don't expect that it will fulfill the promises of the present.[103]

Beradi's formulation "after the future" is thus anchored in an epistemological mode that embraces opacity. Recently, David Scott, Gary Wilder, and other scholars have advanced theories of temporality characterized by a notion of "futures past." About his 2015 book *Freedom Time: Negritude, Decolonization, and the Future of the World*, an intellectual history of Aimé Césaire and Léopold Senghor between 1945 and 1960, Wilder explains, "I am not primarily concerned with futures whose promise faded after imperfect implementation nor with those that corresponded to a world, or to hopes, that no longer exist but instead with futures that were once imagined but never came to be, alternatives that might have been and whose unrealized emancipatory potential may now be recognized and reawakened as durable and vital legacies."[104] Wilder's study reminds us that the long arc of Black existence contains within it imaginative formulations of "futures past" that might be accessed now, in these queer times.

Persistent anti-Black racism continues to delimit otherwise visionary movements and possibilities, shaping existing geopolitics and other present realities. In this context, the long arc of Black existence contains vital elements that might be recombined to call forth new relations for all. Black existence has called modernity-as-progress narratives into question since the dawn of modernity during the transatlantic slave trade and the European colonization of African, Asian, Aboriginal, and other Indigenous peoples' lands. It carries within it alternative organizations of time in which the future, if there is such a thing, has not been promised; it has had to be created by reaching through and beyond what exists. It still does.

(Black) Existence beyond Measure

Two historical trajectories are imbricated in my use of "Black existence," though there are more available. One can be described as the residue of white Being, as that temporal and ontological "impurity" expunged from the (European) human for it to cohere as such, and violently ordered into racial difference by a variety of disciplines. The other trajectory is creative invention, wherein "Black belonging" organizes the sociocultural life that escapes the above trajectory's orderings and exclusions.[105] Both trajectories coexist within "Black existence" and contaminate each other.

Nonetheless, each does a different type of work in relationship to futures. Whereas Black existence indexes a residue of the consolidation of white Being, the present preordains or preempts the future—part of what Fanon called "a hellish cycle."[106] Whereas Black existence is generative of Black belonging, futures are animated by an invention that renders "the future" opaque—Black futures exist "after the future," blossoming in spite of what presently seems destined to be the future. Both of the trajectories named above harbor valences of risk to efforts to bind the future to the present, and both rely upon the difference between Black existence and individual Black people (or groups of people recognizable as Black in a given context). As a historical production open to both Fanonian invention as well as capture (some of which Fanon also elucidates brilliantly), "Black existence" anchors an opacity that invites and frustrates knowledge, transparency, and measure.

What I am after here is the provocative formulation with which Fred Moten ends his 2008 essay, "The Case of Blackness": the "fugitive being of 'infinite humanity,' or as that which Marx calls wealth." Moten refers to the following quotation from Marx:

> In fact, however, when the limited bourgeois form is stripped away, what is wealth other than the universality of individual needs, capacities, pleasures, productive forces, etc., created through universal exchange? The full development of human mastery over the forces of nature, those of so-called nature as well as of humanity's own nature? The absolute working-

out of his creative potentialities, with no presupposition other than the previous historic development, which makes this totality of development, i.e., the development of all human powers as such the end in itself, not as measured on a predetermined yardstick? Where he does not reproduce himself in one specificity, but produces his totality? Strives not to remain something he has become, but is in the absolute movement of becoming?[107]

The "real leap" about which Fanon reminds himself and his readers, the "wealth" that is characteristic of the "fugitive being of 'infinite humanity,'" calls for knowledges that might animate calculations that do not perpetuate existing relations but instead point beyond the bourgeois form to a concept of wealth that encompasses all matter.[108] It calls, perhaps, for a concept of "universal exchange" facilitated by opacity and incommensurability. Marx's notes in *The Grundrisse*, provided in the long quotation above, point toward one possible conception of wealth along these lines.

Marx's conception of "wealth" stripped of its "limited bourgeois form" is wrenched from temporal demands imposed upon labor by the workday, the extraction of surplus labor power, the attendant alienation of labor into a commodity form, and the use of labor power to create surplus value for the capitalist. Stripped of this limited form, "wealth" accrues because it no longer is generated by alienated labor; rather, it is produced by the widespread exchange of material and immaterial products of affective and necessary labor. In these admittedly brief, incomplete, and therefore problematically authoritative, yet suggestive, notes, Marx points to a concept of "wealth" in which the development of human capacities is the engine through which humanity creatively reproduces itself as other than it was. Such wealth is presented as "the universality of individual needs, capacities, pleasures, productive forces, etc., created through universal exchange . . . the development of all human powers as such" and as the "end in itself, not as measured by a predetermined yardstick."[109] This "wealth," which, in ways I elucidate in chapter 1, might be understood in Gilbert Simondon's terms as "preindividual," eludes calculation and measure.

For Moten, Marx's concept of wealth helps to illuminate the difference between "Blackness" and "Black people" by underscoring the ways "Blackness" itself is a historical becoming, tied to the human and therefore available to all. It both exceeds and supplements those who are called "Black people," but cannot be divorced from Black people without epistemological and ontological violence to both the concept and the material realities it currently participates in organizing.[110]

Moten's formulation of "Blackness" and "Black people" in relationship to Marx's concept of "wealth" stripped of its "limited bourgeois form" not only highlights the racial dimensions of "the human" to which Marx refers (reminding us that "the Black" in Western philosophical thought is, as James Snead argues, "always there already" before, within, after, and beyond "the human"); it might also animate a notion of Black belonging in which, among other things, a Black radical imagination is central to "the absolute working out" of humanity's "creative potentialities, with no presupposition other than the previous historic development."[111] "Wealth" is, in part, a feat of the imagination.[112] The imagination is entangled with finance capital in pursuit of the bourgeois form of wealth that is still operating according to the temporalities of capitalist exploitation, however accelerated. This entanglement can be understood, following Berardi's invocation of catastrophe in the quotation above, as not only a limit but also a condition of possibility for "a new relationship between the environment and the human organism" to be called forth by a "radical imagination" and its cosmic poetry.

Queer Times, Black Futures

In each of the chapters that follow, I consider a different constellation of the entanglements between racial capitalism, temporality, technology, mediation, and the imagination. Chapter 1, "'It's after the End of the World (Don't You Know that Yet?)': Afrofuturism and Transindividuation" takes the refrain from Sun Ra's film *Space Is the Place* (directed by John Coney, 1974) as an opening for a discussion about how the temporalities of particular Afrofuturist cultural productions participate in reorienting speculative imaginations toward the presently impossible, thereby emphasizing the salience of Gilbert Simondon's theory of "transindividuation" as an intervention into Western conceptualizations of Being.

In chapter 2, "Yet Still: Queer Temporality, Black Political Possibilities, and Poetry from the Future (of Speculative Pasts)," I discuss how four films, *Looking for Langston* (directed by Isaac Julien, 1989), *The Watermelon Woman* (directed by Cheryl Dunye, 1996), *Brother to Brother* (directed by Rodney Evans, 2005), and *The Aggressives* (directed by Daniel Peddle, 2005) involve related but different organizations of time. All of the films offer insights into the temporality of a present sense of political possibility, but whereas the first three evince a desire for a usable past that might work in the service of the present, *The Aggressives* organizes time idiosyncratically in a strategy that provides an opportunity to consider how queer temporality carries spatial implications that might anchor another orientation toward the past, present, and the future, one in which listening for "poetry from the future," without insisting that it be recognizable as such, is an ethical demand of and for our times.

Chapter 3, "Black Cinema and Questions Concerning Film/Media/Technology," focuses on the role technological considerations have played in the history of Black cinema, with a particular emphasis on the rise of technologies of digital mediation. In this chapter, I follow the interest in technē posited in the first wave of Afrofuturist cultural production during the 1990s and suggest that Beth Coleman's 2009 essay on "race as technology" can offer a conceptualization of Black existence that is attuned to the contested ontological status of Black being, if there is such a thing.

The following chapter, "'Corporate Cannibal': Risk, Errantry, and Imagination in the Age of Catastrophe," continues to develop a reading of Coleman's essay through an engagement with pop star Grace Jones's body of work. I discuss Édouard Glissant's conceptualization of "errantry" as a mode through which Jones navigates the historical imbrication of Black skin with questions of ownership, gender, sexuality, (im)propriety, and technē before turning to a consideration of Glissant's broader concept of "Relation" in the final chapter of the book, "'World Galaxy.'" In that chapter, Alice Coltrane's errant sonic experiments with Asian musical forms offer a way to think about a different constellation of Afrofuturism, one that turns not toward outer space, as in the case of Sun Ra's *Space Is the Place*, but toward an exploration of inner worlds as harbingers of another organization of things within the present. From Alice Coltrane's Afro-Asian imagination, I turn to Nnedi Okorafor's and Wanuri Kahui's recent speculations on Africa, in particular Okorafor's 2010 novel, *Who Fears Death*, and Kahui's short film *Pumzi* from 2009.

These fictional texts offer errantry, myths, and stories as generative strategies through which the dystopian speculations about Africa on which corporate scenarios rely might be resisted, and the worlds those dystopian imaginations work to suppress can be felt.

Bartleby

The chapters that comprise *Queer Times, Black Futures* are punctuated throughout by shorter meditations on Herman Melville's 1853 novella, "Bartleby the Scrivener: A Story of Wall Street." Though "Bartleby" was published in the decade leading up to the American Civil War, when the relationship between the United States and various Indigenous nations was being codified, I have not yet found evidence to suggest the story is explicitly about settler colonialism, slavery, or enslaved Africans or Black existence; however, the story is compelling to consider in the context of *Queer Times, Black Futures* for the following reasons: first, its setting (Wall Street, New York City) and title explicitly reference that center of finance; second, Bartleby's occupation as a legal copyist directly implicates his character and the story itself in questions of law and governance; third, Bartleby has inspired philosophical concepts relevant to the spatiotemporal entanglements of concern throughout this project; fourth, as I explain in the "Interlude," Bartleby calls attention to the interplay of sound and vision in ways that might be of interest to those who are thinking with and through the digital regime of the image in societies of control; fifth, like the rest of Melville's oeuvre, including *Moby Dick* (which I discuss in the "Intercession"), "Bartleby the Scrivener" raises questions about the American enterprise that might generate imaginative formulations of the errant possibilities it harbors; and finally, as we shall see in the following section, what Gilles Deleuze refers to as Bartleby's "queer formula"—"I would prefer not to"—rather than indicating a privileged disengagement with the ontological, epistemological, and hence material violences of the quotidian organization of things, can be understood as a mode of radical refusal, a de-creative, unaccountable, ungovernable, and errant insistence that confronts such violences head on in search of an expressive realization of existence beyond measure.

INTERREGNUM

The Unaccountable Bartleby

It is much too late for the accounts of death to prevent other deaths; and it is much too early for such scenes of death to halt other crimes. But in the meantime, in the space of the interval, between too late and too early, between the no longer and the not yet, our lives are coeval with the girl's in the as-yet-incomplete project of freedom. In the meantime, it is clear that her life and ours hang in the balance.
—Saidiya Hartman, "Venus in Two Acts"

Recombining the long arc of Black existence to call forth new relations for all is not a linear, progressive process. Rather, it relies upon a sense that the past is not done, and that futures still might be excavated from within it. Although the interval's temporality suggests it is too soon, too early, or too late to achieve new relations, such relations may still be immanent. We might think of the interval as the time that remains when "now" is both "too soon" and "too late."[1] It is another formulation of "after the future"—a time when we might do our work, without guarantees.

In the epigraph that begins this section, Saidiya Hartman refers to a girl she found in the official archives of slavery: "a *dead girl* named in a legal indictment against a slave ship captain tried for the murder of two Negro girls."[2] One of Hartman's chief concerns in that work is to query what the official archives of slavery make it possible for us to know and what they render unknown and unknowable except through speculation, and to insist upon reckoning with the ethico-political hold slavery has on the present.

Still, the archive that Hartman encounters as a historian does not allow for the ethical production of a story involving the two girls mur-

41

dered by the slave ship captain. Hartman writes: "Yet how does one re-cuperate lives entangled with and impossible to differentiate from the terrible utterances that condemned them to death, the account books that identified them as units of value, the invoices that claimed them as property, and the banal chronicles that stripped them of human fea-tures?"[3] Given this context, Hartman muses, "It would not be far-fetched to consider stories as a form of compensation or even as reparations, perhaps the only kind we will ever receive."[4]

As Sylvia Wynter insists, "story-telling" is a fundamental human ac-tivity.[5] Every story unfolds in time, and therefore carries risk. Since the extant facts about the girls confine imagination of the slave trade to the authority of its official archives, which foreclose on the possibility of hearing, seeing, or otherwise knowing the experience of those enslaved, Hartman chooses not to conjure a story about them in order to redress the violence of the archive. She decides it is better to leave them as she finds them: "two girls alone."[6] Instead of imagining a story that might redeem the lives of the two slave girls, Hartman chooses to describe "as fully as possible the conditions that determine" how they appear in the archive and "dictate" what we might hear from them.[7] Noting that our present can be understood as an "afterlife of property," by which she means, "the detritus of lives with which we have yet to attend, a past that has yet to be done, and the ongoing state of emergency in which black life remains in peril," Hartman offers the statements in the above epigraph.[8]

In and for the meantime, Hartman turns in that same essay to a novel by Octavia Butler, *Kindred* (1979), as "a model for practice."[9] Working with and against the generic conventions of fantasy fiction, *Kindred* con-veys the extent to which chattel slavery is inextricable from present reali-ties and the relations sustained within and animated by them. In Butler's story, Dana, an African American character living in the 1970s, must travel back in time to when slavery was legal to save her white ancestor who has enslaved one of her foremothers.

For Hartman, the "afterlife of property" marks a transition from the enslaved marked as property, legible as entries on antebellum financial ledgers, bills of sale, and inventories, to those who, though nominally free, are similarly perceptible according to postbellum capitalist in-stitutions' logics of legibility and accounting. In the present study, my attention to the long arc of Black existence involves examining how to-day's finance capital and its logics of financialization extend and replay (though with significant differences, as I explain below) epistemologies set in motion with the transatlantic slave trade and the colonization of the Europeans' new world. While *Kindred* provides Hartman with "a model for practice," in which the speculative fictional telling of events that take place before the Civil War in the United States might retrieve what "remains dormant" in the archives of slavery, a short story writ-ten in the United States during slavery, Herman Melville's "Bartleby the Scrivener: A Story of Wall Street," serves throughout this study to engage with the organization of racial capitalism into financialization, which has roots, as Ian Baucom and others point out, in the upheav-als and innovations of the transatlantic slave trade and European settler colonialism.

Although Melville wrote "Bartleby" in 1853, in the decade leading up to the American Civil War, there is little evidence to suggest that he had slavery or its abolition (the main cause of the Civil War) in mind.[10] My interest in Melville's short story throughout *Queer Times, Black Futures* is for the various insights it offers into the politics, possibilities, and pit-falls of opacity, incommensurability, radical refusal, and risk.

"Bartleby" is narrated by a lawyer around the age of sixty who de-scribes himself as "a safe man": "one of those unambitious lawyers who never addresses a jury, or in any way draws down public applause; but, in the cool tranquility of a snug retreat, do a snug business among rich men's bonds, and mortgages, and title-deeds."[11] This lawyer chooses to tell a tale about Bartleby, whom he describes as "a scrivener, the strang-est I ever saw, or heard of." He continues, "While, of other law-copyists, I might write the complete life, of Bartleby nothing of that sort can be done. I believe that no materials exist, for a full and satisfactory biogra-phy of this man. It is an irreparable loss to literature."[12]

The lawyer and his copyists work in an office that "not a little re-sembled a huge square cistern," wedged between "the white wall of the interior of a spacious skylight shaft, penetrating the building from top to bottom" and "a lofty brick wall, black by age and everlasting shade; which . . . was pushed up to within ten feet" of the office's window panes.[13] Before Bartleby arrives in the lawyer's office, the lawyer had employed two men, Turkey and Nippers, and a boy around twelve years old named Ginger Nut; these are nicknames, "mutually conferred upon each other by [the] three clerks, and . . . deemed expressive of their respective persons or characters."[14] The narrator explains that although each of his three employees has certain eccentricities that render them less efficient at certain times of the day than at others, all three of them are civil, and Nippers and Turkey are "very useful" men to him. Bartleby does not prove to be so civil, nor so useful.

Bartleby, Turkey, Nippers, and Ginger Nut become co-workers after Bartleby responds to an advertisement that the lawyer places when he determines that he needs another scrivener:

> In answer to my advertisement, a motionless young man one morning stood upon my office threshold, the door being open, for it was summer. I can see that figure now—pallidly neat, pitiably respectable, incurably forlorn! It was Bartleby.
>
> After a few words touching his qualifications, I engaged him, glad to have among my corps of copyists a man of so singularly sedate an aspect, which I thought might operate beneficially upon the flighty temper of Turkey, and the fiery one of Nippers.[15]

The lawyer arranges for Bartleby to sit beside him, with a screen between them that allows them to hear but not see each other. In this way, according to lawyer, "privacy and society were conjoined."[16] At first, Bartleby "did an extraordinary quantity of writing. As if long famishing for something to copy, he seemed to gorge himself on my documents." Yet, he does so "silently, palely, mechanically." On Bartleby's third day, the lawyer calls Bartleby to examine the lawyer's copy; in so doing, the lawyer appears to violate the terms of their previous agreement, which stipulates that Bartleby copies until he needs his documents to be examined. The lawyer, "being much hurried to complete a small affair . . . abruptly called to Bartleby." The lawyer explains, "In my haste and natural expectancy of instant compliance, I sat with my head bent over the original on my desk, and my right hand sideways, and somewhat nervously extended with the copy, so that, immediately upon emerging from his retreat, Bartleby might snatch it and proceed to business without the least delay."[17]

In response to the lawyer's command, Bartleby first issues what Gilles Deleuze refers to as his "queer formula": "I would prefer not to." The lawyer explains, "In this very attitude did I sit when I called to him, rapidly stating what it was I wanted him to do—namely, to examine a small paper with me. Imagine my surprise, nay, my consternation, when, without moving from his privacy, Bartleby, in a singularly mild, firm voice, replied, 'I would prefer not to.'"[18] "I would prefer not to" (and "I'd prefer not to") are among the few words Bartleby utters throughout the rest of the story, as he becomes increasingly obstinate: moving into the office and living there until the lawyer has him arrested, and ultimately dying in jail.

Melville's "Bartleby the Scrivener" has for decades inspired contemporary philosophers and literary critics, such as Gilles Deleuze, Giorgio Agamben, and Slavoj Žižek, to take up the challenges posed by the literary figure and his queer formula, "I'd prefer not to." In this "Interregnum," I am concerned with "the unaccountable Bartleby," a phrase used by the narrator of Melville's story. Naomi C. Reed explains why Bartleby is "unaccountable" from the narrator's perspective: "The lawyer's system of reasoning cannot account for him, cannot insert him into a system of economic calculation."[19] Unaccountable, Bartleby refuses to participate in capitalist circulation, which relies upon commensuration in order to ensure relations of equivalence and exchange. Within the existing systems of commensuration significant to the lawyer—that is, normative bourgeois sociality and civility as evinced (however imperfectly) by himself, Nippers, and Turkey; capitalism and the financial tools and documents that facilitate capitalist exchanges; the Law; as well as the forms of social life created and maintained through these—Bartleby remains opaque. He does so in part by relying, up to his death in prison, on his "queer phrase." Even the "one little item of rumor" that for the lawyer holds a "certain suggestive interest"—that Bartleby previously worked in "a Dead Letter Office in Washington"—can be grasped in the terms Reed provides. Reed explains:

> Bartleby's desire not to circulate extends to the sphere of interpretation, and the Dead Letter Office marks his desire to remain the "unaccountable" Bartleby, not to be brought into circuits of recognizable meaning.

The desire, as it seems with all Bartleby's desires, is an impossible one, an impossibility marked by the structure of the story itself, for we have Bartleby's story only through the meaning-making efforts of the lawyer. (The predicament, of course, is only redoubled by my own, or any, reading of the text.) This desire for illegibility is another manifestation of Bartleby's resistance to relations of equivalence, and it reminds us that we cannot easily or carelessly make Bartleby into a representative, for Bartleby is, to put it mildly, an unwilling delegate.[20]

Reed offers a way of thinking a politics of opacity by insisting on Bartleby's spectral existence in Melville's story as a "figure." The figural marks a "transformation of discourse" as well as "a means for understanding the functioning of power in given societies."[21] To embrace Bartleby as a figure, therefore, is to acknowledge the extent to which he functions to "disorder" the "proper forms of discourse."[22] By wrenching indices from their presumed referents, Bartleby opens onto a politics of opacity along the lines offered by Édouard Glissant.[23] An "unwilling delegate," Bartleby resists the injunction to represent anything else.[24]

Glissant argues it is important for marginalized groups to "insist" upon remaining opaque to the terms, languages, and logics of dominant groups.[25] Insisting upon opacity acknowledges the co-existence of systems of signification and valuation alongside, yet inaccessible to, dominant ones. Within this context, "unaccountability" marks a refusal to be bound to dominant standards of measure, recognition, and evaluation.

For Giorgio Agamben, Bartleby remains unaccountable because Melville entrusts an "experiment without truth" to him. Agamben observes that such experiments (which are conducted not only by "science but also poetry and thinking") "do not simply concern the truth or falsity of hypotheses, the occurrence or nonoccurrence of something, as in scientific experiments; rather, they call into question Being itself, before or beyond its determination as true or false. These experiments are without truth, for truth is what is at issue in them."[26] Agamben claims:

> What is at issue in Melville's story can . . . be formulated in a question of the following form: "Under what conditions can something occur

and (that is, at the same time) not occur, be true no more than not be true?" Only inside an experience that has thus retreated from all relation to truth, to the subsistence or nonsubsistence of things, does Bartleby's "I would prefer not to" acquire its full sense (or, alternatively, its nonsense).[27]

For Agamben, Melville's experiment with Bartleby concerns, in other words, "de contingentia absoluta": absolute contingency. Here, Bartleby is a figure of absolute contingency, with radical temporal implications for existing schemas of Being. Referring to Leibniz's "elements of natural right," Agamben explains that the "fourth figure, the contingent, which can be or not be and which coincides with the domain of human freedom in its opposition to necessity, has given rise to the greatest number of difficulties. If Being at all times and places preserves its potential not to be, the past itself could in some sense be called into question, and moreover, no possibility would ever pass into actuality or remain in actuality."[28]

In the face of these objections to contingency, Western philosophy has assembled a variety of principles, concepts, and other responses. These include, according to Agamben, Aristotle's principles of "an impossibility of realizing the potentiality of the past," and of "conditioned necessity, which limits the force of contingency with respect to actuality" by insisting that "all potentiality is, at the same time, potentiality for the opposite"; Leibniz's theory of "future contingents," according to which, if something happens today, it was going to happen, was true in the past, and will continue to be true in the future; and Leibniz's "best of all possible worlds," according to which God's mind contains "possibilities for all eternity."[29]

Melville conducts his experiment by "calling into question the principle of the irrevocability of the past, or rather, by contesting the retroactive unrealizability of potentiality."[30] He thus "inaugurates" the proposition of "past contingents." Here, "the necessary truth of the tautology 'Sextus-will-go-to-Rome-or-will-not-go-to-Rome'" retroactively acts on the past not to make it necessary but, rather, to return it to its potential not to be."[31] In this regard, "Bartleby calls the past into question, re-calling it—not simply to redeem what was, to make it exist again but, more precisely, to consign it once again to potentiality, to the indifferent truth of tautology. 'I would prefer not to' is the *restitutio in integrum* of possibility, which keeps possibility suspended between occurrence and nonoccurence, between the capacity to be and the capacity not to be."[32] To put this in other terms, Bartleby is a figure of "futures past."[33]

When Bartleby, a scrivener, gives up copying, he stops laboring to reproduce what was. He stops creating equivalences. Working as a legal copyist, Bartleby's job involved, in Agamben's terms, canceling "the difference between the actual world and the possible world and returning potentiality to what was."[34] Bartleby's "renunciation of copying," therefore, "is also a reference to the Law."[35] Agamben's presentation of Bartleby as a Christ figure (following Deleuze and others) embraces a Bartleby who "comes to abolish the old Law and to inaugurate a new mandate. . . . But if Bartleby is a new Messiah, he comes not, like Jesus, to redeem what was, but to save what was not."

This is "de-creation," in which "what could have not been but was becomes indistinguishable from what could have been but was not."[36] Bartleby, who renounces the Law, dies in prison, irredeemable and unaccountable. Agamben makes this point poetically, which is to say, in a search for reference:[37]

> His word is not Justice, which gives a reward or a perpetual punishment to what was, but instead Palingenesis, *apokatastasis pantōn*, in which the new creature—for the new creature is what is at issue here—reaches the indemonstrable center of its "occurrence-or-nonoccurence." . . . It is here that the creature is finally at home, saved in being irredeemable. This is why in the end, the walled courtyard is not a sad place. There is sky and there is grass. And the creature knows perfectly well where it is.[38]

Bartleby is "irredeemable" because his figuration is such that he saves what was not rather than restoring what was. That Bartleby might "save what was not" points to an understanding that the past in general exists in its entirety even as the trajectory of events affirms certain past elements, keeping them perceptible to us as past, and hides others, rendering them imperceptible or impossible. This understanding of the past as the past in general resonates with Glissant's way of thinking of history as "accumulation" (in the sense elucidated by Ian Baucom, as discussed in the introduction).[39] If, for Glissant, time "piles up," then what Bartleby brings to our attention is the extent to which that piled up or sedimented past remains as a constitutive, yet often imperceptible, component of the present. Thus, any struggle over or for the future must also attend to futures past. Because Bartleby saves what was not, he works at the level of the imperceptible; what never was cannot be redeemed, yet remains, piled up in a present that need not be, but is.

The temporality, encapsulated in the formula, "I would prefer not to," is queer; Bartleby's "queer formula" reveals the queerness in time. Bent not toward redemption but "de-creation," Bartleby is a figure who unsettles the existing social organization of things. "A new creature," Bartleby prefers to die in prison rather than resume his vocation of copying, creating equivalences, or any other mode of reproduction or reinscription through which what exists survives as such. He even stops eating, preferring not to reproduce himself.

About Bartleby's formula, "I would prefer not to," Gilles Deleuze argues:

> Without a doubt, the formula is ravaging, devastating, and leaves nothing standing in its wake. Its contagious character is immediately evident: Bartleby "ties the tongues" of others. The queer words, I would prefer, steal their way into the language of the clerks and of the attorney himself ("So you have got the word, too"). But this contamination is not the essential point; the essential point is its effect on Bartleby: from the moment he says "I would prefer not to" (collate), he is no longer able to copy either.[40]

That something is happening with "the formula" on the level of language is clear. Slavoj Žižek, for example, writes, "In his refusal of the Master's order, Bartleby does not negate the predicate; rather, he affirms a nonpredicate."[41] Deleuze points out that *I prefer not to* "stymies the speech acts that a boss uses to command, that a kind friend uses to ask questions or a man of faith to make promises."[42] The formula "excludes all alternatives and devours what it claims to conserve." It "hollows out a zone of indetermination that renders words indistinguishable, that creates a vacuum within language."[43] It is radically de-creative; "after the formula, there is nothing left to say."[44] Not unlike "the Indian" elsewhere in Deleuze's work (as elucidated and critiqued by Chickasaw scholar Jodi A. Byrd), Bartleby's formula "combats mechanisms of interpretation through an asignifying disruption that stops, alters, and redirects flow."[45]

That Bartleby is also "unaccountable" highlights that he, as Reed argues, is a figure that produces incommensurables. Bartleby refuses to produce equivalences, he is "strange," "not particular," and has nothing general about him. Radically antisocial, Bartleby does not sit in an antagonistic relationship vis-à-vis the social; rather, he prefers not to inhabit the social at all: "if Bartleby had refused, he could still be seen as a rebel or insurrectionary, and as such would still have a social role. But the formula stymies all speech acts, and at the same time, it makes Bartleby a pure outsider (*exclu*) to whom no social position can be attributed."[46] As a "pure outsider," Bartleby's "absolute vocation" is "to be a man without references, someone who appears suddenly and then disappears without any reference to himself or anything else."[47] Without references, Bartleby is "inscrutable,"[48] opaque.

Bartleby's formula operates on and through language, one of the primary ways commonalities and equivalences are established among collectives. Deleuze claims, "Bartleby has invented a new logic, a logic of preference, which is enough to undermine the presuppositions of language as a whole. . . . The formula 'disconnects' words and things, words and actions, but also speech acts and words—it even severs language from all reference."[49] From within the conceptual logic of film studies, a disciplinary formation I discuss in the following chapters, it could be said that Bartleby's formula wrenches images from their indices. Wrenching language from the logics through which it establishes equivalences, Bartleby's formula "sends language itself into flight," opening "a zone of indistinction or indiscernability in which neither words nor characters can be distinguished."[50] The "de-creation" effected by Bartleby proceeds through language and radically decenters language. The formula reveals the opacity at the heart of communication, which language seeks to ameliorate by establishing equivalences.

Unaccountable, Bartleby cannot be reconciled with existing logics. The lawyer's expression at the close of "Bartleby the Scrivener," "Ah Bartleby! Ah Humanity!," leaves the relationship between the two, "Bartleby" and "humanity," indeterminate. Deleuze claims that with his final words the lawyer "does not indicate a connection, but rather an alternative in which he has had to choose the all too human law over Bartleby."[51] Bartleby's existence demands that those logics give way to something else: Agamben's "new creature" or Deleuze's "new, unknown element . . . the mystery of a formless, nonhuman life, a *Squid*." The formula thwarts even poetics, seeking not to "emancipate language and old ways of thinking," but to undo them and reveal the radical contingency of the worlds they create.

Squidlike, Bartleby upends Western humanism's categories. He exists as "vibrant matter," insisting upon the existence (in Melville's time, in Deleuze's time, in Agamben and Žižek's time, which is to say in our time) of the (im)possibility of a renewed relationship between the living organism and the environment.[52] In Melville's time, such a renewal was unimaginable—Bartleby dies in prison.

At the end of her essay, "Venus in Two Acts," Saidiya Hartman (authors, artists, and other things will continue to cohere as such throughout this book even as our analysis strives to de-create them) turns to a work of literary speculative fiction by Octavia Butler to explain Hartman's (and our) relationship to the enslaved girls who died on the slave ship Hartman encounters in the archives. Referring to the main character from Butler's 1979 novel *Kindred*, Hartman writes, "When Dana, the protagonist of Butler's speculative fiction, travels from the twentieth century to the 1820s to encounter her enslaved foremother, Dana finds to her surprise that she is not able to rescue her kin or escape the entangled relations of violence and domination, but instead comes to accept that they have made her own existence possible."[53]

Bartleby's queer formula refuses to reproduce what is. Žižek argues that Bartleby's "refusal is not so much the refusal of a determinate content as, rather, the formal gesture of refusal as such."[54] It offers a way to grasp the challenges of opacity and gestures toward an ethics that eludes the lawyer, the Law, and everything else of significance in his time. That his queer formula also must non-violently de-create Bartleby through his death reminds us that his existence, like ours, is inextricable from the very ways of being and knowing that we must refuse in order to call forth new relations for all.[55]

"It's after the End of the World (Don't You Know That Yet?)"

Afrofuturism and Transindividuation

Finally, one opens the circle a crack, opens it all the way, lets someone in, calls someone, or else goes out oneself, launches forth. One opens the circle not on the side where the old forces of chaos press against it but in another region, one created by the circle itself. As though the circle tended on its own to open onto a future, as a function of the working forces it shelters. This time, it is in order to join with the forces of the future, cosmic forces. One launches forth, hazards an improvisation. But to improvise is to join with the World, or meld with it. One ventures from home on the thread of a tune.
—Gilles Deleuze and Feliz Guattari, *A Thousand Plateaus*

"In the Dark"

Somewhere in the middle of the 1974 film *Space Is the Place*, Sun Ra's band, The Arkestra, begins to play a tune called "It's after the End of the World." That tune launches forth with a few bars of tentative tones and sounds. Then come lyrics—a refrain sung and shouted in a voice that we recognize today as feminine, if not female, by its quality. Over and again, this voice insists, "It's after the end of the world. Don't you know that yet?"[1]

This refrain—"It's after the end of the world. Don't you know that yet?"—asserts another temporality and coordinates, which exist within, but are incommensurate with, those taken as the dominant logics of existence of a world (only one) characterized by statistical predictability, control, temporal continuity, and coherence. The feminine voice creates a "calming and stabilizing, calm and stable, center in the heart of chaos," which insists that it is "after the end of the world." This voice "jumps from chaos to the beginnings of order in chaos and is in danger of breaking apart at any moment."[2] This refrain opens a marvelous (im)possibility: "the world" does not cohere as such. If it once did, it no longer does. Already, it has ended. Whatever existence "we" can claim, wherever that can be claimed, and however it can be characterized, cannot take the continuity and stability of a world as axiomatic.

Soon after it begins, the refrain in *Space Is the Place*—"It's after the end of the world. Don't you know that yet?"—is overtaken by other sounds, another attempt to organize chaos. Perhaps the limited space organized by these sounds is not music but a wall of noise, loud yet fragile. It collapses and . . .

"At Home"

. . . leaves "us" homeless. Homelessness is our home. We carry the abyss that Édouard Glissant characterized so well. For Glissant, the Middle Passage of the transatlantic slave trade and the formation of "the new world" mark an apocalyptic catastrophe. We are forged in its wake. With specific reference to those who can be identified as Caribbean, Glissant explains, "The abyss is also a projection of and a perspective into the unknown. . . . This is why we stay with poetry . . . We know ourselves as part and as crowd, in an unknown that does not terrify. We cry our cry of poetry. Our boats are open, and we sail them for everyone."[3] At home in open boats and spaceships launching for the unknown, we hum the refrain, "It's after the end of the world. Don't you know that yet?" Homeless at home. We improvise.[4]

"Toward the World"

The soundtrack of *Space Is the Place* segues into "Under Different Stars." Here, cosmic forces are perceptible even as the earthly forces of the abyss linger and are transduced into another world, here, now, in the world some believe is (a) just one. The sound and image tracks of *Space Is the Place*, the matter on which they are recorded, and the discourses that circulate about it—in other words, all that constitutes *Space Is the*

Place—melds with that world, which is not (a) just one, opening that world all the way, to a point where we can believe in it again. And it leaves us with only a belief in this world.

Now. Where to begin?

In response to that question, Meaghan Morris starts—in the middle of the chapter in *Identity Anecdotes* entitled "Crazy Talk Is Not Enough: Deleuze and Guattari at *Muriel's Wedding*"—with the first paragraph of Gilles Deleuze and Felix Guattari's plateau "Of the Refrain," found in the middle of their book *A Thousand Plateaus*. Morris explains, "The paragraph itself can be read as a little song, a nocturnal creation myth or 'sketch' in the middle of the book; it is not a genesis story of the logos and light, but a song of germination in darkness."[5] Although, as Morris points out, "there is no special analytical virtue in emphasizing 'Of the Refrain' over any of the other plateaus in *A Thousand Plateaus*," I begin with it because doing so calls attention to the improvisational elements of any beginning, which always happens in the middle of other things, and because it makes Deleuze and Guattari's concepts of "the Refrain," "Milieus and Rhythms," "the Cosmos," and "the Unequal or the Incommensurable" available to this book as heuristics and technologies through which to encounter the space-times at the intersection of contemporary formulations of "queer" and "Black," which we can grasp, here at the beginning anyway, as schematically structuring antagonisms of our present social and ontological systems, respectively.[6]

With this metaphorical use of the musical refrain, Deleuze and Guattari offer a method of creative production that also offers insight into what, as I discuss later in this chapter, Gilbert Simondon refers to as processes of collective individuation. Deleuze and Guattari explain that the Refrain consists of three aspects which Morris describes using Deleuze and Guattari's formulation in the "Contents" section of *A Thousand Plateaus* as "in the dark, at home, toward the world." Deleuze and Guattari state: "The refrain has all three aspects, it makes them simultaneous or mixes them." One sketches an uncertain "center in the heart of chaos" in order to "organize a limited space" that can protect "the germinal forces of a task to fulfill or a deed to do." One "launches forth, hazards an improvisation." As in music, the refrain offers an anchor to which we return after any improvisation.

Alondra Nelson points out that it has become a habit to start projects about Afrofuturism with Sun Ra.[7] Later in *Queer Times, Black Futures*, I will start again elsewhere. Here, however, I sketch an uncertain center via a refrain from Sun Ra, a musician best known as an innovator of free jazz. I start with Sun Ra because he created his own cosmology, eschewing his given name and place of birth, Herman Blount, born in 1914 in Birmingham, AL, and taking the name Sun Ra, claiming to be from Saturn. I understand this to be a generative act of (re)creation that, as I have suggested in reference to his film *Space Is the Place*, posits an alternative imaginary of extant space and time, and the set of possibilities that reside therein. Although he was an eccentric jazz musician, his interest in outer space and unconventional musical expressions influenced later musical groups, such as George Clinton and Parliament Funkadelic, Digable Planets, Public Enemy, and Shabazz Palaces, among others. It also finds a filmic expression in *Space Is the Place*.

In the opening sequence of *Space Is the Place*, Sun Ra's character announces that he wants to set up a colony for Black people on another planet to "see what they can do on a planet all their own, without any white people there." About that utopian aim, he states, "Equation-wise, the first thing to do is to consider time as officially ended. We'll work on the other side of time. We'll bring them here through either isotopic teleportation, transmolecularization or better still, teleport the whole planet here through music."[8] The rest of the film involves Sun Ra's character playing a game of cards with a character called "The Overseer" to win a bet for control over the destiny of Black people, and traveling between 1943 Chicago and 1969 Oakland, California, to convince Black people to travel to that planet with him. The film ends with Sun Ra defeating "The Overseer" and setting into motion an "altered destiny."

As Sun Ra surveys the planet he discovered at the beginning of the film, he announces, "The music is different here. The vibrations are different. Not like planet earth." The idea that music might affect vibrations and energy patterns and, hence, consciousness aligns with the ideas of other avant-garde artists of the 1950s and 1960s, who used aesthetic techniques of "plastic dialogue" to articulate what was then perceived to be "a new relationship between individuals, society, and the environment."[9] Sun Ra's innovations within jazz and Big Band improvisation were part of a larger subcultural preoccupation among avant-garde artists with then-emergent metaphors of "energy, spirituality, metaphysicality, and freedom" and "new definitions of improvisation."[10] Various conceptualizations of Afrofuturism have drawn on the temporality of, or the organization of time within, Sun Ra's particular version of plastic dialogue and the politics it supports.[11]

Music offers an especially rich terrain for Afrofuturist expression because it imbricates sentient bodies with technology, such as microphones that amplify and project a singer's voice, or the tools of music production, recording, and dissemination, such as mixing boards, synthesizers, musical instruments, radio, television, the Internet, and so on. Increasingly, music and audio culture are inseparable from digital technology, as Alexander Weheliye and others have reminded us.[12] A burgeoning interest in a serious critical engagement with music and aurality has emerged at the end of the twentieth century and beginning of the twenty-first as one of the richest and most dynamic areas of intellectual cultural production today. From within African American Studies, for instance, thinkers such as Weheliye, Lindon Barrett, Daphne Brooks, Fred Moten, and Paul Gilroy, among others, have called our attention to the convergence of "Blackness" and "sound" and "music" in order to complicate the hegemony of vision in the epistemologies of race.

The timing of this reemergence of a sustained and dynamic scholarly interest in music and aurality in Black studies is significant. In *The Witch's Flight: The Cinematic, the Black Femme, and the Image of Common Sense*, for example, I begin by noting the historical coincidence of the invention and dissemination of moving image technologies with W. E. B. DuBois's prescient statement that "the problem of the twentieth century is the problem of the color line."[13] Working with and sometimes against Deleuze's writing on cinema, *The Witch's Flight* explores the ways that the ontologies and epistemologies that cinema makes perceptible and organizes—especially those informing social relations ordered along lines delineated by commonsense understandings of race, gender, and sexuality—have become imbricated with how capitalism exploits labor power, enabling it to reach into even our leisure time and make it productive for Capital.[14]

The Witch's Flight has a soundtrack that provides a way to mark both the importance of sound to "the cinematic" and how music might offer an epistemological, and, as Fred Moten's work suggests, ontological, register within the cinematic that (perhaps) allows one to sense what does not appear or resists appearing through its currently available logics. Yet, in film, the soundtrack is customarily secondary to the image track in terms of eliciting a commonly available perception of present images; as such, it is available in *The Witch's Flight* and in the cinematic more broadly as a reservoir of uncommon sensibilities and subterranean knowledges at the same time as it becomes part of the cinematic's workings, perceptible as what Deleuze refers to in his work on cinema as "sound situations" or "sound-images."

In chapter 1 of Deleuze's *Cinema 2: The Time-Image*, "Beyond the Movement-Image," Deleuze identifies Italian Neo-Realism as the mode of filmmaking through which a new cinematic image, the time-image, becomes perceptible. This image is constituted through "the purely optical and sound situation which takes the place of the faltering sensory-motor situations" after World War II.[15] The increased significance of the time-image in filmmaking after World War II marks a historical transition in which what Deleuze calls "the soul" of cinema shifted away from the regime of the movement-image, which was characterized by its reliance on sensory-motor situations. As the sensory motor image—the movement-image—collapses, a "pure optical-sound image" emerges, "any-space-whatevers" proliferate, and another regime of the image makes itself felt: that of the time-image. The time-image makes "time and thought perceptible" by making "them visible and of sound."[16] The relationship between the movement-image and the time-image is important in Deleuze's work on cinema because it allows for a range of expressions, perceptions, and possibilities within the cinematic while pointing to what Deleuze calls "an outside more distant than any exterior," or a radical Elsewhere that does not belong to the order of the cinematic, yet invests in the cinematic in order to rip it open from the inside.

The last sentence of the final chapter before the "Conclusion" of *Cinema 2* reads: "What has now become direct is a time-image for itself, with its two dissymmetric, non-totalizable sides, fatal when they touch, that of an outside more distant than any exterior, and that of an inside deeper than any interior, here where a musical speech rises and is torn away, there where the visible is covered over or buried."[17] *The Witch's Flight* ends with Deleuze at this point, with a provocation that reads like an (im)possible, perhaps fatal, promise.[18] Deleuze seems to suggest that the cinematic movement-image and the time-image, regimes that organize the hegemony of vision in modernity, orchestrating their service to money's interests among other things, come under pressure from sound and music, which Deleuze refers to at the end of *Cinema 2* as "musical speech."[19]

One of the intellectual projects that Afrofuturism, with its interest in technology, asks us to engage involves exploring what the digital regime of the image, sound, and/or perception makes available to thought. Throughout the present project, therefore, I take seriously the ways that the rise and tearing away of what Deleuze calls "a musical speech" might mark a third passage from one regime to another within the cinematic.[20] Although toward the end of *Cinema 2* Deleuze considers what he refers to as "the electronic image" in ways I will explore throughout *Queer Times, Black Futures*, the digital regime of the image is a component of what Deleuze elsewhere refers to as "societies of control." The digital regime of the image facilitates the phase of racial capitalism Jodi Melamed has called "neoliberal multiculturalism."[21] The growing significance of sound and audio culture is among the many important transformations one might trace with(in) the digital. Eccentric jazz musician Sun Ra and other avant-garde jazz artists likewise situate sound and audio culture as central to technological transformation.[22]

Sun Ra's Afrofuturist interventions in *Space Is the Place*, as well as his performances and recordings of free jazz, are best contextualized within the broader sociocultural, political, and economic context of struggles against Jim Crow segregation, and for Black Power and pan-Africanism as they were innovated and expressed in the United States throughout the 1950s, 1960s, and 1970s. In "Appropriating the Master's Tools: Sun Ra, the Black Panthers, and Black Consciousness, 1952–1973," Daniel Kreiss argues that *Space Is the Place* should be understood, at least in part, as Sun Ra's response to the performative politics of the Black Panther Party and especially their emphasis on organizing community programs as a way to undermine the authority of the United States government. In *Space Is the Place*, Sun Ra suggests that community programs and the aestheticized politics of the Black Panther Party and other Black radicals of the time go only so far in addressing the fundamental socioeconomic inequities that keep the souls of Black folk from taking flight into the cosmos. What is necessary instead, Sun Ra argues, is a fundamental rupture in the vibrations through which Black peoples' consciousness has been constituted—a vibrational rupture in consciousness capable of creating a new world in a new spatiotemporal configuration. Sun Ra further argues that sound and music can spark that rupture and offers his improvisational compositions as a means to achieve an energetic transformation. Stripping Black folks of their belief that they are Black, of their investment in the ontological coherence of Black existence, whether as positive or negative, Sun Ra reveals an underlying condition of the historical existence of Black folks.

Sun Ra's project, as "far out" as it seems, is relevant to current conversations about the persistence of forms of social and psychic death (which can also be understood as forms of social life that are opaque as such within the system of signification through which they are deemed "dead"), such as those that arise from the relations that characterize the prison-industrial complex and from contemporary geopolitics that disproportionately target Black people and people of color, diminishing our life chances and rendering us vulnerable to premature death, even as theoretical interventions into the assumed coherence of racial categories, such as acknowledgments of the social construction of race, have become more widely accepted.[23]

Articulations of the social construction of race insist that "race" is a category that has accrued meaning and material force over time due to social, cultural, economic, and historical factors rather than immutable natural or biological ones. Sun Ra advances an argument along these lines in one striking sequence from *Space Is the Place*: Sun Ra visits a group of young adults in Oakland in 1969. In his "message to the Black youth," Sun Ra refers to Black people as "myths," asserting that Black people occupy a space of nonexistence and therefore unreality in the United States and, indeed, the world.

The sequence opens with an intertitle claiming the time and place as 1967, Oakland, California. The primary setting is a pool hall/recreation center for Black youth. Young people proudly wearing Afros, tight shirts, and bellbottom pants gather there, playing pool, listening to music, singing, and talking. The singing is melodic and pleasing, and the lyrics insist "that's the way love is." Posters of Angela Davis, members of the Black Panther Party, Frederick Douglass, and others are displayed on the wall. Suddenly, a marvelous pair of gold boots materialize in the middle of the recreation hall. A jump cut frames them in the center of the screen. Quickly after that, Sun Ra's body materializes, his feet filling the boots. He says that he has a message for the Black youth of planet Earth. They ask how they can know that he is for real and "not some old hippy off of Telegraph Street." He tells them, "How do you know I'm real? I'm not real. I am just like you. You don't exist in this society. If you did, your people wouldn't be seeking equal rights. We are both myths. I do not come to you as a reality, I come to you as a myth because that's what Black people are. Myths." The Black youth of planet Earth nod their heads in agreement. Some laugh. Sun Ra explains, "I came from a dream that the Black man dreams long ago. I am actually a present sent to you by your ancestors."

The reverberations of "present" here are notable because they call attention to the way that Sun Ra's cosmology posits a continuity between the dreams of the ancestors and our present day, and it implies that Sun Ra has access to both. His statement, "I come from a dream that the Black man dreams long ago" describes that dreaming in the present tense, implying that the present coexists with "long ago" through the appearance of the myth that is Black people. That Sun Ra arrives in Oakland, California, in 1967 as a gift from the ancestors suggests that he appears to fulfill the terms of a long-ago dream, perhaps to redeem the freedom dreams of the ancestors—dreams of futures past.

Sun Ra continues his conversation with the Black youth, reminding them that white people already have been on the moon and chiding them: "I noticed none of you have been invited. How do you think you are going to exist?" A young man calls attention to the crystal ball in Sun Ra's hand as the sound and image tracks segue into a refrain: June Tyson singing, "Space Age. We are living in the Space Age." Through a dissolve from Sun Ra's crystal to June Tyson's face, the sequence's logics of space and time are suspended in her voice and image, which appear in an entirely different mise-en-scène than the recreation center where Sun Ra delivered his message to the Black youth of America. Sun Ra appears there, too, operating an audio control board, and a different geographic location, presumably still on planet Earth, is framed onscreen.

I describe this sequence to call attention to the strategies through which it sonically and visually destabilizes assumptions about the logics of material reality in order to enhance Sun Ra's proclamation, "Black people are myths." In Sun Ra's statements, we can hear echoes of earlier Afrofuturists, such as W. E. B. DuBois in his short story "The Comet," which first appeared in his 1920 collection *Darkwater: Voices from within the Veil* and was later anthologized by Sheree Thomas in *Dark Matter: A Century of Speculative Fiction from the African Diaspora*. In "The Comet," DuBois suggests, as Lisa Yaszek points out, "not only that it will take a natural disaster to eradicate racism in America, but that without such a disaster there may be no future whatsoever for black Americans."[24] In DuBois's story, a natural disaster precipitates a temporary suspension of the terms through which present reality congeals, thereby creating the conditions under which a Black man and a white woman might acknowledge a shared humanity.

Sun Ra's appeal to Black youth anticipates, in the realm of scholarly inquiry into Black existence, theories of social death such as Orlando Patterson's analysis of the conditions characteristic of "New World" slavery (and Grace Kyungwon Hong's corrective to it in her book *The Ruptures of American Capital*).[25] The assertion that Black people are not real, but myths, also resonates with Frantz Fanon's analysis of the impossibility of Black being when he writes, for instance, "The Black is not."[26] Referencing the unreality of Black people, Sun Ra's statements index the myths, beliefs, and social constructions—in short, the feats of the imagination—on which the modern world relies for its coherence. For Sun Ra, an acknowledgment of the material force of the "myths" that animate modern life opens onto the possibility that things might be organized otherwise. If the terms of modern life have been constructed as such, they also might be de-created, making another organization of things possible. Such a world exists in Sun Ra's cosmology as an impossible possibility.

In his appeal to Black youth, Sun Ra points toward the ways that whatever escapes or resists recognition, whatever escapes meaning and valuation within our commonly crafted structures of valuation and signification, exists as an impossible possibility within our shared reality (however that reality is described theoretically) and therefore threatens to unsettle, if not destroy, the common senses on which that reality relies for its coherence. Karl Marx's phrase "poetry from the future," which I discuss in more detail in the following chapter, points to just such an impossible possibility. "Poetry from the future" is a formal ("poetry," with its associated lyricism and fragmentation) and temporal ("from the future") material disruption, which functions primarily on the level of affect to resist narration and qualitative description. "Poetry from the future" is a felt presence of the unknowable, the content of which exceeds its expression and therefore points toward a different epistemological, if not ontological and empirical, regime. "Poetry from the future" indexes a surplus of meaning and valuation, unconfined to the terms through which poetry is legible today.[27] It is wealth held in escrow.

We can perceive "poetry from the future" in Sun Ra's interest in using otherworldly sounds throughout his musical oeuvre. In particular, the sounds we associate with outer space work as audible means through which to disrupt the habituated reception of music and to disturb (and redirect) the sensorium and its vibratory patterns. The title of Sun Ra's song "Music from the World Tomorrow," from the album *Angels and Demons at Play*, posits a "tomorrow" and hence a future. Yet, it does so by making of tomorrow not so much a time (as in the future), but another world ("the world tomorrow").[28] Like most of the Afrofuturism of interest to *Queer Times, Black Futures*, this song's title functions to critique the present through the production of an alternative history of its past, while making a set of claims on an (im)possible future or fashioning a cultural praxis through which to open alternative futures. This is consistent with the method Sun Ra's character announces in the beginning sequence of *Space Is the Place* when he says, "The first thing to do is to consider time to be officially ended."[29]

For Sun Ra, the official end of time is just the beginning of what Graham Lock refers to as "Blutopia."[30] Lock borrows the term "Blutopia" for the title of his book *Blutopia: Visions of the Future and Revisions of the Past in the Work of Sun Ra, Duke Ellington, and Anthony Braxton* from "Blutopia," the title of a song by Duke Ellington. Lock uses the term to refer to what he identifies as "a crossroads in the creative consciousness where visions of the future and revisions of the past become part of the same process, a 'politics of transfiguration,' in which accepted notions of language, history, the real, and the possible are thrown open to questions and found wanting." This crossroads, Lock explains, is formed when two major impulses fuse: "a utopian impulse, evident in the creation of imagined places (Promised Lands), and the impulse to remember, to bear witness, which James Baldwin relates to the particular history of slavery and its aftermath in the United States."[31] In Lock's study, these impulses, often regarded as antipathetic, point to a "Blutopia," which Lock describes, with specific reference to Ellington's song, as a "utopia tinged with the blues, an African American visionary future stained with memories."[32]

Like much of the written work produced around the beginning of the twenty-first century either explicitly formulated in terms of "Afrofuturism" or addressing concerns that have now come to be associated with Afrofuturism, Lock's book focuses on music and musicians. For practitioners and scholars of Afrofuturism, music and sound have been accorded a primary place because they are the vehicles through which, as Kodwo Eshun put it in his seminal 1998 book *More Brilliant than the Sun: Adventures in Sonic Fiction*, "postwar alienation breaks down into the 21st C alien."[33] Musicians such as Sun Ra, John Coltrane, Alice Coltrane, Duke Ellington, Eric Dolphy, and others experimented with jazz music to push it far out, into other worlds, new worlds—outer and sometimes inner space. These artists offered theorists and critics of Afrofuturism a great deal of conceptual material on which to draw.

Yet, during the 1980s and 1990s, creative energy was also expended on the production of literature, film, and video, cultural forms that open up a different set of questions from within what might still be called Afrofuturism—questions about gender, sexuality, potentiality, speculation, technology, and liberation. Insofar as writers such as Octavia E. Butler, Nalo Hopkinson, Samuel Delany, and others were innovating within science fiction and speculative fiction at that time, literature was the medium through which to forge new ideas and speculative possibilities for gendered beings, alternative sexualities, and technologically enhanced futures.

In these authors' work, Afrofuturist expression is a profound critique of those existing conditions that limit the lives of Black folks. Octavia Butler, a speculative fiction writer whose work provides another influential example of Afrofuturism, offers a space colonial vision similar to Sun Ra's in *Space Is the Place* in her 1993 novel *Parable of the Sower* and its sequel, the 1998 *Parable of the Talents*. The premise of Butler's *Parable* novels is that capitalism in the United States has progressed unchecked by government regulations to such a degree that jobs are scarce and commodities, including necessary items such as food, clothing, water, and housing, are unavailable to all but the wealthy few. Under the aegis of making America great again, politicians rely upon the perpetuation of this situation of scarcity to stay in power. Crime, addictions, and violence undergird existing modes of sociality, making it difficult to trust others, while simultaneously rendering it necessary for people to forge alliances.

The narrator and protagonist of *Parable of the Sower*, Lauren Olamina (often referred to simply as "Olamina"), has analyzed her situation, her own responses to it, and everything she could "read, hear, see, all the history" she could learn. Founded on this analysis, she has formulated Earthseed, a new religion based on a fundamental understanding that "God is change."[34] At one point in the story, while traveling across California with a small group of other people from her home (which was destroyed in an attack by people addicted to a popular drug), Olamina presents herself as a man in order to ward off those who target women for violence and exploitation. During a conversation with one of her traveling companions, a male character who will eventually become the first convert to Earthseed, Olamina states:

> God is Change, and in the end, God prevails. But there is hope in understanding the nature of God—not punishing or jealous, but infinitely malleable. There's comfort in realizing that everyone and everything yields to God. There's power in knowing that God can be focused, diverted, shaped by anyone at all. . . . God will shape us all every day of our lives. Best to understand that and return the effort: Shape God.[35]

Over the course of *Parable of the Sower*, Olamina begins to plant Earthseed communities, with the understanding that, as she puts it later in the conversation referenced above, "the Destiny of Earthseed is to take root among the stars." The ultimate aim of Earthseed is to settle other "living worlds" in "other star systems." Olamina explains, "The Destiny of Earthseed is to take root among the stars. . . . That's the ultimate Earthseed aim, and the ultimate human change short of death. It's a destiny we'd better pursue if we hope to be anything other than smooth-skinned dinosaurs—here today, gone tomorrow, our bones mixed with the bones and ashes of our cities, and so what?"[36]

In Butler's work, an engagement with Black existence (that is, the material and cultural realities and expressions indexed by the persistent presence of those we call "Black people" over time) is anchored in an understanding of its entanglements with various modes of human existence. The group with which Olamina travels is racially and ethnically heterogeneous, a characteristic of the social world of many of the characters across Butler's oeuvre. Another of her novels, *Wild Seed*, for example, is part of a trilogy that starts with two main characters, Doro and Anyanwu, who can change physical form: Doro takes over bodies, effectively killing whatever animated those bodies previously by replacing it with himself, and Anyanwu is a shape-shifter who can change her physical composition and appearance at will. *Wild Seed* begins during the transatlantic slave trade, with Doro searching for the African communities that he had been developing by selectively breeding people with special abilities. He is upset because his careful work is being undermined by slave traders, who keep raiding his carefully cultivated villages, when he chances upon Anyanwu, whose special abilities are unlike any he has seen.

An engagement with Black existence in these novels can be found in their references to the disruption caused by the world historical transformation initiated by the transatlantic slave trade; since neither Doro nor Anyanwu is bound within recognizably Black bodies, the novels generate what we might perceive as "Black existence" as a historical sensibility anchored in the ongoing transformation of the world, related but not bound to genetic or otherwise biological categories premised on the continuity of specific bloodlines. "Black existence" confounds the epistemological certainty vis-à-vis race that presently is widely assumed to be guaranteed by specific phenotypical and other perceptible cues.

For Sun Ra, a serious engagement with Black existence leads, on the one hand, to vital articulations of music and sound in the face of various forms of death and, on the other hand, to the quotidian violence that authorizes and reproduces present social relations. In both Sun Ra's *Space Is the Place* and Octavia Butler's *Parable* novels, space exploration and settlement in outer space provide an opportunity to forge new relations by radically disrupting existing relations and the logics and violences through which they are held in place. To the extent that space exploration seeks to find another place to escape a catastrophic situation on earth, it should not be surprising that it is a recurring theme of Afrofuturism.

Yet, in Sun Ra's articulation of the utopian impulse of Afrofuturism, which for him involves the colonization of another planet, the quotidian violences of settler colonialism characteristic of modernity are simply transposed—transmolecularized, teleported—elsewhere to "another place in the universe, up in the different stars." Rather than Édouard Glissant's imagined and still parenthetical "(at long last communal) land" or Octavio Paz's yearning, while "Reading John Cage," that "the U.S.A. may become just another part of the world. No more. No less," Sun Ra's solution in *Space Is the Place* to the violence and humiliation of US race relations is to give Black folks a world they can own. Sun Ra seems unconcerned about the specter of African American and Black complicity in a settler colonial project when he advocates for a spatio-temporal rupture in Black consciousness sparked by his musical vibrations and profound enough to transport Black people to another planet. Afrofuturist narratives that advocate for colonizing another planet raise (and less often consider, and/or offer, speculative strategies and solutions to) the ethico-political issues that have attended anti-Black settler colonial societies.[37]

Sun Ra's political vision in *Space Is the Place* is impossible: predicated on the (non)existence of a cheesy psychedelic planet, we might say that Sun Ra's futuristic vision is one with no future. Yet, this does not mean that its assumed complicity with the logics of settler colonialism ought to be excused. On the contrary, perceiving its impossibility ought to authorize further flights into and imaginations of the impossible that might address the complicity of Sun Ra's vision with settler colonialism. As in DuBois's "The Comet," Sun Ra's quest to send Black people to another planet is an impossible alternative to a spatiotemporal order in which there is no desirable future for Black people. From within the logics of existing possible worlds and the range of possible trajectories into the future that they currently make perceptible, a Black future looks like no future at all.

Speculation on the impossible and what Agamben calls the "impotential" characterizes those Afrofuturist cultural productions that invest in a future where "Black lives matter" because such a future radically breaks with existing timelines and historical logics so that the subterranean energies of past freedom dreams might be re-released and gain material force. For Lauren Olamina, Butler's protagonist in *The Parable of the Sower*, one of the technologies that might achieve this is poetry. The spiritual text Olamina writes, "Earthseed: The Books of the Living," consist of a series of short poems, aphorisms, and brief statements, such as:

FROM EARTHSEED: THE BOOKS OF THE LIVING

By Lauren Oya Olamina

Here we are—
Energy,
Mass,
Life,
Shaping life,
Mind,
Shaping Mind,
God,
Shaping God,
Consider—
We are born
Not with purpose,
But with potential.[38]

While Butler's speculative fiction (novels and short stories) imagines scenarios wherein the relations that animate her present might seem strange and perhaps even malleable within her own time, Olamina's poetry crystalizes insights and intuitions that can reshape the novel's speculative fictional world, thereby allowing the characters to grasp how what seems intractable might be resisted, shaped, transduced into something else entirely. Moreover, we can read Olamina's claim about "potential" as also including a claim about "im-potential," or the potential not to do something.[39]

For Sun Ra, sound and music carry a capacity to transduce the qualities of consciousness holding present relations in place into something qualitatively different. For Butler and Sun Ra, the technologies employed—sound, music, poetry—formally disrupt habitual responses and perceptions. The challenge in these speculative fictions is to create another world by spreading things and phenomena, including ideas and modes of embodiment and living, which are not recuperated into the familiar ones undergirding property, ownership, dispossession, white supremacy, and misogyny, as well as their attendant modes of propriety.[40]

When we sit with avant-garde music, expressed most deliberately in free jazz, as a means through which to transform consciousness, when "we stay with poetry" as a collective, formal disruption, something else with a capacity for movement opens up.[41] Perhaps what Afrofuturism offers to thinking, with its yearning for another world, another planet that operates according to the space-time of Black liberation, is a way to enter into relation with an autochthonous space of and for Black existence. Such a world is not premised on dispossession, ownership, property, and exploitation. As I will suggest in the "Intercession: The De-American Bartleby," this mode of relation can be conceptualized as a creative, eccentric way of sinking deeply into the space held open in music and engaging with what is always there already.

Drawing our attention toward sound, affect, music, and silence, Afrofuturist sonic culture, like Herman Melville's character Bartleby, brings language to its outside. At its most compelling, Afrofuturist music is a nonlanguage; it "evokes the future without predicting it."[42] Such Afrofuturism musically invokes a "new world" that does not appear as expansion, immigration, and nations—indeed, it does not appear as such; it is presently impossible. Yet, the sonic, including the poetic, Afrofuturisms of interest here are generative. They posit autopoiētic and autogenetic transindividual being, stubbornly insisting on a capacity for self-creation within the languages they constantly push to their outsides even as they remain tethered to the collective projects through which they emerge. These Afrofuturisms' investments are not in the future, or even *a* future, but Now—a now that Afrofuturism constantly destroys through its insistent discordance with it, unleashing presents with pasts that never were and will be.

That theories of autopoiēsis, autogenesis, and the transindividual currently are being taken up and extended from within the traditions of Western philosophy points to the impasse at which the Western "human" presently finds himself. The relevance of these theories to analyses of Afrofuturism and vice versa (as argued above) lies in their offering alternative conceptualizations of being, which are consistent with those that have been formulated from an engagement with the range of phenomena and other data associated with Black existence in the West. In other words, theories of autopoiēsis and autogenesis have been generated through a sustained intellectual, theoretical engagement with Black existence and ways of thinking about being that are consistent with those coming to the fore in Continental philosophy to address a set of crises faced by the Western human. We might say, then, along with James A. Snead, that the Western human is heading toward where the Black already is.[43] Theories of ontogenesis and autopoiēsis articulate how the order of being that we can perceive through analyses of Black cultural productions makes other ways of being available in a more generalized and dispersed manner than those that previously animated Western Being's white supremacist epistemologies and ontologies.

Gilbert Simondon's theories are of particular interest here because they systematically attempt to rethink the relationship between the individual and the collective within Western philosophy traditions with a particular emphasis on technics. Insofar as Black existence has challenged Western theories of "Being" to contend with what they exclude (in order to cohere "Being" as such), Simondon's challenges to those theories from within their logics are salutary. Concepts like Simondon's have been generated from within Western philosophy in a variety of Black diasporic thought, traditions, and practices in order to critique Western civilization and the assertions, assumptions, and habits of mind that have sustained and enabled it over time. The affinities between Simondon's work and that of Black Caribbean intellectuals such as Édouard Glissant and Sylvia Wynter remind us that those thinkers for whom Black existence has been a generative site of inquiry and experimentation have already challenged Western conceptions of Being from within organic formations of intellectual and artistic practice as well as offered viable alternatives, many of which resonate with those I discuss below.

Here, however, I stay with Simondon in order to take, along with Muriel Combes, "but one" of the pathways "within Simondon's philosophy," which runs "from preindividual to transindividual by way of a renewal of the philosophy of relation."[44] Combes notes in *Gilbert Simondon and the Philosophy of the Transindividual* that "it is possible to read all of Simondon's work as a call for a transmutation in how we approach being."[45] The constitution of "Being" in Western thought has been one of the modes through which "the Negro," "the Black," "the African," as well as "the Oriental" and "the Native" and "the Primitive" have been excised from the sphere of the properly human. In this book, I engage with Simondon's transmutation of the Western philosophy of "Being," and put it in conversation with theories offered by Glissant, in order to suggest how we might think ontology, psychosociality, and collectivity in ways that do not rehabilitate a dying human but instead usher, peacefully, I hope, another being into the world of the Black radical imagination. To the extent that Black Studies has identified Western theories of ontology as part of the architecture that upholds and perpetuates white supremacy and anti-Black racism, philosophical attempts to transmute how Western philosophy approaches being can have significant implications for Black Studies, as well as, perhaps, offer ways to explode Western being such that what it violently disavows, yet still carries at its core—that is, what we now perceive as "Blackness"—might be unleashed.

Sylvia Wynter's significant intervention into Western philosophy offers a complementary framework for narrating how the present structure has been assembled and points toward other modes of existence beyond what we currently perceive as possibilities.[46] Technology and autopoiēsis are of concern in certain of Wynter's work, and she has written about aesthetics and film.[47] Here, Simondon's theories help to flesh out this book's larger concerns with cinema and media in relationship to the Afrofuturist themes of "imagination, technology, the future, and liberation."[48] Simondon's theory focuses specifically on the implications stemming from relations between living beings and technology, with an emphasis on transduction. Additionally, Simondon's work, which influenced Deleuze, complements my analysis of the digital regime of the image and societies of control by offering a way to conceptualize their preindividual and transindividual dimensions.

Combes argues that Simondon's thought challenges two main tendencies for conceptualizing being in the Western philosophical tradition: atomism and hylomorphism. Atomism "posits the atom as primary substantial reality that . . . deviates from its trajectory and enters into assemblies with other atoms to form an individual," whereas hylomorphism "makes the individual the result of an encounter between form and matter that are always already individuated."[49] According to

Combes, Simondon's work navigates these two poles through which Western Being has been conceptualized by distinguishing being-as-such from being-as-individual. Combes explains:

> A philosophy that truly wishes to address individuation must separate what tradition has always conflated, to *distinguish being as such from being as individual*. In such a perspective, being as such is necessarily understood in terms of the gap separating it from individuated being. And by the same token, we can no longer remain content to confirm the "givenness" of being, but would have to specify what properly character- izes "being as such," which is not only its being but also is not being one. In Simondon's thought, being as being is not one, because it precedes any individual. This is why he calls it *preindividual*.[50]

Rather than search for a principle of individuation, Simondon focuses on it as a process. The individual becomes "merely the result of an operation of individuation."[51] Simondon advances a novel concept of transduction to envision "the mode of relation obtaining between thought and being" anew. Combes quotes Simondon's first definition of transduction as "the operation whereby a domain undergoes informa- tion": "By transduction, we mean a physical, biological, mental, or social operation, through which an activity propagates from point to point within a domain, while grounding this propagation in the structura- tion of the domain, which is operated from place to place: each region of the constituted structure serves as a principle of constitution for the next region."[52] Transduction thus expresses the processual sense of indi- viduation and "holds for any domain, and the determination of domains (matter, life, mind, society) relies on diverse regimes of individuation (physical, biological, psychic, collective)."[53]

Simondon's concept of the "transindividual," connected to that of ontogenesis, challenges existing understandings of "Being" and offers a way to conceptualize "being" in relation to a collective. Thinking "being" through Simondon's theory of the "transindividual," and alongside Glis- sant's "poetics of Relation," offers a way to conceptualize Black existence and indeed existence itself, as a transindividual relation. If, following Sun Ra, we can entertain a formulation of Black people as "myths," the understanding that ontology is an expression of a process involving transindividual relation helps to elucidate the dimensions of Black existence that resist incorporation into an Enlightenment conceptualization of "Being" and its attendant formulations of "the human." As Combes puts it, "Simondon's approach entails a substitution of ontogenesis for traditional ontology, grasping the genesis of individuals within the operation of individuation as it is unfolding."[54] For those whose individuation must pass through the collective enterprises currently organized through identity categories, "ontogenesis" offers a conceptual framework for thinking collective existence, which posits what Simondon calls "an aperion," a "real preindividual potential," that tethers any collective category to a potential to be otherwise, including refusal and/or not to be as such. About this aspect of Simondon's philosophy, Combes explains:

> Properly speaking, we would have to say that being is more-than-one, which is to say it "can be taken as more-than-unity and more-than-identity." . . . In such enigmatic expressions as "more-than-unity" and "more-than-identity," we see coming to light the idea whereby being is constitutively, immediately, a power of mutation. In fact, the non-self-identity of being is not simply a passage from one identity to another through the negation of the prior identity. Rather, because being contains potential, and because all that is exists within a reserve of becoming, the non-self-identity of being should be called more-than-identity. In this sense, being is in excess over itself. . . . Before all individuation, being can be understood as a system containing potential energy. Although this energy becomes active within the system, it is called potential because it requires a transformation of the system in order to be structured, that is, to be actualized in accordance with structures. Preindividual being, and in a general way, any system in a metastable state, harbors potentials that are incompatible because they belong to heterogeneous dimensions of being.[55]

Combes points out that, for Simondon, being can be understood as a system containing incompatible potentials within the reservoir of being, which may become active following a "transformation of the system." If being is "constitutively, immediately, a power of mutation," containing "potential energy" that is actualized in accordance with structures, such as, for example, structural racism or heteropatriarchy, then it follows that changing the structures of the system through which Being presently coheres might call forth new, currently incompatible potentials. In other words, systemic transformations might actualize other dimensions of being, presently harbored as potential within preindividual being. The dimensions of being through which white existence has historically cohered, and through which white supremacy continues to reassert itself globally, might not be actualized in a transformed system. Abolishing the systemic structures through which white existence reproduces itself might create conditions under which it becomes possible to be otherwise. Along the lines of how Audre Lorde and Franklin Rosemont conceptualize the power of poetry to carry dimensions of the unknown and the impossible into present reality, the Afrofuturist strategies I have discussed in this chapter so far—music, sound, and speculative fiction—can carry other dimensions of being into existing structures.[56] Simondon's formulation allows us to consider the role that forms of mediation like Sun Ra's free jazz and Octavia Butler's speculative fiction play in structuring present systems and selecting from the incompatible, heterogeneous potentials harbored within preindividual being and activating them within existing structures.

If being is "a power of mutation," and if the concept of "preindividual being" allows for heterogeneous, incompatible potentials, then the constitutive construction of "the Human" leaves energies as inactive potentials within "the Human's" governing structures. Although we might say with Fanon that it will require a "great leap" to break the system and actualize other structures, Simondon's theory of ontogenesis, transindividuation, transduction, and technics offers a way to conceptualize Western being as more-than-identity and to challenge the existing structures of signification through which the mattering of certain collective beings matters more than others.

The current shifts within Western philosophy to notions of ontogenesis, autopoiēsis, and "sympoiesis" (a term Donna Haraway introduces to mean "making-with"), as well as to a variety of "new materialisms," signal, among other changes, a set of transformations in how racialization and engendering might be conceptualized.[57] In ways I will discuss in chapter 3, neoliberal multicultural formulations and deployments of "race" made available an understanding of "race" as technē, or, in other words, as a mode of revealing—a tool that might be put to use.[58] As technē, "race" transduces potential energy within existing structures with an abiding capacity to organize collective being otherwise. It is "vestibular" to modern Western Being.[59] Reframed as a technology, race is a form of revealing, but only one potential activated from the reservoir of heterogeneous, incompatible, elements constitutive of preindividual being. Insofar as it is imbricated with truth claims concerning perceptible biological markers, with the logics that animate a global division of labor and capitalist exploitation, and insofar as it intercuts with those vectors that determine gender and nationality, race is a particularly stubborn vestibular entrance into existing social reality and the collective beings who constitute it.

Presently working within a system that is structured by and through "race," yet aware of the reservoir of potential energy available within preindividual being, we . . . improvise.

"It's after the End of the World. Don't You Know That Yet?"

At the beginning of this chapter, and in the spirit of improvisation, I offered the poetic formulation of the sonic refrain found in the middle of the film *Space Is the Place*—"It's after the End of the World. Don't you know that yet?"—because it makes perceptible a logic of futures and futurity that stymies conventional organization of time and space in which the present precedes that future for which it is destined to become the past. Today, this spatiotemporal organization is held in place by the processural capacities of race—that is, "racialization"—and gender—or "gendering" and "engendering"—along with other modes through which identity might be organized at various phases of collective individuation, such as, for example, class, sexual orientation, nationality, ability. Throughout the present project, I build upon the ways that this organization of time and space has been criticized, complicated, and reformulated by others. I do so by focusing on how conceptualizations of "race" and non-normative expressions of gender and sexuality make perceptible alternative organizations of space and time that do not conform to the "empty homogeneous time" that animates conventional conceptualizations and commonsense understandings of futures, futurity, and speculation, and the range of sociopolitical and economic possibilities those formulations support.

At the same time, the poetic formulation that opens this first chapter of *Queer Times, Black Futures* illustrates how Sun Ra's *Space Is the Place* invokes a set of spatiotemporal logics consistent with those animating Black existence in a world that is not (a) just one. The refrain "It's after the end of the world" anchors a present that is, as Joy James puts it, "the henceforward."[60] James references Frantz Fanon's statement in *The Wretched of the Earth* that "henceforward, the interests of one will be the interests of all, for in concrete fact *everyone* will be discovered by the troops, *everyone* will be massacred—or *everyone* will be saved."[61] For James, "The moment of *henceforward* is the moment of the transformation of the native intellectual, the "organic intellectual," into a revolutionary."[62]

Here, the concept of "henceforward" is a temporal anchor for the creation of what James describes as "the new being," who, through struggle and an internalization of the Other, also becomes "individual and collective, in overt and covert rebellion, alive because everyone has now become mechanized in its rebellion, with the spiritual force of freedom driving it—biological, mechanical, divine."[63] While James refers to this new creature as a "cyborg" in order to differentiate it from struggles attached to "the human," I embrace it here as a presently unintelligible assemblage of technology, flesh, imagination, and spirit. Consistent with the thoroughgoing critique of "the human" that is part of James's revolutionary project, James attributes the pronoun "it" to the new creature, explaining, "For when the 'one' solitary merges with others to become the revolutionary, he or she is no longer a conventional human. As . . . one/mass unified against the divine, mechanical, and biological terror of the colonizer, as its own biological, mechanical, and divine formation, a human being as a conventional being no longer exists (at least momentarily)."[64]

In James's reading of Fanon, decolonization is an apocalyptic event of complete disorder effected by violence; the colonial world is held in place by violence, and violence will be a force of decolonization. In the meantime, "henceforward" stands as a revolutionary moment that must always be renewed. James writes (noting the religious resonances of Fanon's choice of the word "saved" in *The Wretched of the Earth*): "Part of the puzzle or challenge of being saved is how to stay alive and stay saved; that is, it is not a onetime achievement or acquisition but an ongoing struggle. The revolution that must come the rebellion that precedes it and await the rebellion that will come means that *henceforward* is a war without end, movement without end. *Henceforward* is the name for the struggle that must always begin again."[65] The syntax of James's sentence here evokes the avalanche of experiences and the stalled temporality characteristic of "henceforward," a never-ending struggle to stay alive while also fighting for and through the ethics and vision of decolonization.

Advancing an argument that decolonization has not (yet) been achieved is not the same as arguing that nothing changes, that battles are not won along the way, and that things do not get better and worse and better and worse and worse and the same. It acknowledges that chattel slavery has ended and that African countries have achieved their independence. At the same time, it announces that we remain in the thick of things, on still-colonized land, in the midst of a long-haul effort toward liberation for all, in "the henceforward."[66]

Saidiya Hartman has referred to this as "the afterlife of slavery" and "the afterlife of property" as a way to formulate a present still suspended in ongoing violences of white supremacy and the socioeconomic logics of racial capital put into motion by the transatlantic slave trade and the colonization of Africa, Asia, and the Americas.[67] Other scholars have turned to Freudian formulations of melancholia to conceptualize the structure of feeling in which a traumatic past (colonization, settler colonialism, enslavement) continually pervades our present. The temporality that Sun Ra's refrain "It's after the end of the world. Don't you know that yet?" invokes is consistent with these more recent formulations. But rather than linger there, after the end of the world, in the still fresh and powerful traumatic past though which "the world" ended, Sun Ra asserts that we must consider time as officially ended and should head up to another planet "under different stars."

Where to begin without a past? Because life goes on. Life is going on. How to begin anew after the end of time, when catastrophe is what lingers as time and *future* is what remains of temporality?

The refrain—"It's after the end of the world. Don't you know that yet?"—and Sun Ra's suggestion, in the wake of the end of the world, that we consider time officially ended might be thought in conjunction with Glissant's concept of "the Abyss," mentioned earlier. In an interview with Manthia Diawara, Glissant explains that Black people in the European's "New World" carry the Abyss inside of us because of the circumstances through which that "New World" was created. Glissant's notion of the Abyss is central to his theory of the temporality of the Caribbean. As John E. Drabinsky points out, for Glissant, the Middle Passage marked a radical rupture that has implications for the ancestors of the Africans who survived it. The trauma of the Middle Passage—the bodies of those newly enslaved thrown overboard to die an anonymous death at the bottom of the sea and then lost forever so that only their shackles remain, the continuity of languages and cultures and familial lines disrupted, the horror of living with the violences of subjection to white supremacy and in relation to its settler colonial project, and all of the other everyday micro-terrors that we do not or no longer imagine today, or that we have habituated ourselves to accept—severs roots and pasts and histories. Even "loss itself is stolen in the Middle Passage."[68] Drabinski explains:

> For Glissant, the Caribbean is futurity precisely because of the abyssal effect and affect of loss. Impossible history is not the loss of what was. It is, rather, what it means to begin without even the memory of having once possessed. The Middle Passage is just this much violence, and yet life goes on. At the shoreline, then on the plantation (which Glissant calls "one of the wombs of the world" in *Poetics of Relation*), the future is a kind of facticity, not a project. The name *Caribbean* is itself inseparable from the openness of what is to come. The future, insofar as it can be taken up, offers less than nothing as wreckage within which a movement to the future can take root.[69]

When the future "offers less than nothing as wreckage within which a movement to the future can take root," a nomadic and multiple subjectivity emerges from the material conditions indexed by the name "Caribbean." But, as Drabinski states, "This is to say, nomadic is not the qualifier of subjectivity as the result of a critique of metaphysics, nor does it respond to various epistemological paradoxes" (as it does for Deleuze and Guattari's nomad). Drabinski continues: "Glissant's nomad has another materiality and therefore another genesis."[70] To put this in Simondon's framework, Glissant's nomad emerges through different structures of transindividuation than Deleuze and Guattari's nomad.

"Abyss" names Glissant's formulation of the conditions of possibility for "Caribbean" as futurity, for "what it means to begin without even the memory of once having possessed."[71] This resonates with Sun Ra's admonition that we consider "time as officially ended" and points to the bifurcations and forks in temporality that have come to characterize Western modernity. We might say, then, using Fred Moten's terms, "Blackness" is another name for Black history, which is to say, "now." In his book *In the Break: The Aesthetics of the Black Radical Tradition*, Moten puts it this way:

> One of the implications of blackness is that those manifestations of the future in the degraded present that C. L. R. James described can never be understood as simply illusory. The knowledge of the future in the present is bound up with something Marx could only subjunctively imagine: the commodity who speaks.[72]

As "new materialisms," including theories of "vibrant matter" and "thing power," "object-oriented ontologies," and other ways to rework and rethink spatiotemporal relations and their sociopolitical force and implications etch pathways through Euro-American knowledge production, I continue to take seriously James Snead's proposition that, within the spatiotemporal logics of our shared modernity, "the Black" is always there already. I return to Snead's proposition in chapter 3, where I consider what it has to do with a historical affiliation between race and technology. Here, however, I note that the transatlantic slave trade and the conceptions of the world that supported it pressed living beings into objects hundreds of years ago, and the epistemological and ontological legacies of that world historical transmutation are with us still today. The cultures, politics, and theories, among other elements, produced by those whose existence is objecthood and thingness offer stunning correctives and open onto remarkable possibilities in the newest theoretical turns. Opening ways to connect formulations of time and space that are generated out of a sustained engagement with those contexts in which living objects and breathing things exist might advance an ethics through which to anchor the just world stirring beneath our feet. We can listen for the refrains of those living objects and breathing things, rehearsed, improvised, even those we perceive as just noise. Here and now. In these Black futures.

"It's after the end of the world. Don't you know that yet?"

2

Yet Still

Queer Temporality, Black Political Possibilities, and Poetry from the Future (of Speculative Pasts)

As an epigraph to the conclusion to *Black Skin, White Masks*, Frantz Fanon uses the well-known observation made by Karl Marx in *The Eighteenth Brumaire of Louis Bonaparte* that, as Fanon gives it (according to the translation by Richard Philcox),

> the social revolution cannot draw its poetry from the past, but only from the future. It cannot begin with itself before it has stripped itself of all its superstitions concerning the past. Earlier revolutions relied on memories out of world history in order to drug themselves against their own content. In order to find their own content the revolutions of the nineteenth century have had to let the dead bury their dead. Before, the expression exceeded the content; now, the content exceeds the expression.[1]

Fanon's choice of this oft-cited quotation substantiates his book's concluding claim that the psychopathologies of colonialism are a problem of time. As an epigraph, Marx's formulation of the organization of time within the proletarian movement of the nineteenth century underscores Fanon's own aim both to explode the temporality of the colonial mode of representation of otherness and to reveal a temporality that raises the possibility of the impossible within colonial reality: Black liberation. Elsewhere, I have explored what Fanon's emphasis on the temporality of the Black and Blackness means for studies of the Black image in cinema.[2] Here, I return to the temporality Fanon reveals in order to follow another relevant line of flight from it—specifically, that which opens through his citation of Karl Marx's notion of "poetry from the future" and what thinking that formulation at the conjunction of what we know today as "race," "gender," and "sexuality" might offer Cultural Studies and Queer Theory now.

For, if "poetry from the future" can effect a radical break with the past, a break in which "Black liberation" still might be located—a rupture from within history that also breaks from history—then four very different films, *Looking for Langston* (directed by Isaac Julien, 1989), *The Watermelon Woman* (directed by Cheryl Dunye, 1996), *Brother to Brother* (directed by Rodney Evans, 2005), and *The Aggressives* (directed by Daniel Peddle, 2005), offer ways to think such a presently impossible possibility from within our historical conjuncture (for we cannot think outside it). Throughout this book, my attempt to articulate something that exceeds its expression inevitably also produces a surplus, one that cannot be seen or understood, but is nevertheless present as affect.

I use the term "affect" in its sense of that which is felt as a present sensation in or on a sentient body, a valence of the term adapted from the work of Gilles Deleuze.[3] In his books on cinema, Deleuze relies upon Henri Bergson's definition of "affect" as "a kind of motor tendency on a sensible nerve."[4] In Deleuze's Bergsonian formulation, affect marks a body's seemingly unproductive effort to respond to stimulation. Most commonly, we talk about affect as a feeling or an emotion, but it is important to think about affect also as the embodied mental activity required to make sense of the world.[5] In order to highlight the active dimensions of affect, which require an expenditure of time and effort, I use "affectivity," following Marcia Landy, to mark "a form of labor expended in the consumption of cinematic images, in the enterprise of voluntarily offering up our lives as free contributions to capitalist power."[6] I further expand it to define a form of labor through which sentient bodies work to constitute themselves as such by interacting with other phenomena.[7] In my formulation, insofar as affectivity accesses our individual past experiences and the forms of common sense we have forged over time (even when it breaks the sensory-motor link that chains us to the past), it has both subjective and collective elements to it.

This concept of affect and affectivity is important to this project because it underscores the extent to which our efforts in the face of that which moves us are bound to the ethico-political context of our times and available to Capital and its normative structures of command, as well as to the related yet distinct operations we know as racism, settler colonialism, homophobia, misogyny, transphobia, and ableism, among others. At the same time, it points toward the ways that whatever escapes recognition, whatever escapes meaning and valuation, exists as an impossible possibility within our shared reality, however one theoretically describes that reality, and therefore threatens to unsettle, if not destroy, the common senses on which that reality relies for its coherence. Marx's phrase "poetry from the future" marks just such an impossible possibility. It is a formal ("poetry," with its associated lyricism, fragmentation, and logics) and temporal ("from the future") disruption, which functions primarily on the level of affect to resist narration and qualitative description. It is a felt presence of the unknowable, the content of which exceeds its expression and therefore points toward a different epistemological, if not ontological and empirical, regime.

Throughout this book, I seek to remain aware of what escapes my attempts to contain it in the material on which I am working, yet can nonetheless be felt and perceived even though—or especially if—it remains unrecognizable or unintelligible to current common senses. Attempts to contain it include processes of recognition, narrative and/or other formal devices of texts, and the current logics and categories of cultural criticism, among other things. We can think of what escapes these operations as the content that exceeds its expression, through which poetry from the future might be perceived, yet not recognized. The danger in tarrying with the surplus is that we fall into a habitual reception of sensory experiences and information, reifying the collective narratives of the past and celebrating their expressions, drugging ourselves to the present content of that which moves us. "Poetry from the future" interrupts the habitual formation of bodies, and it serves as an index of a time to come when what today exists potently, even if not (yet) effectively, but escapes us, will find its time.

Poetry's capacity to disrupt habitual ways of knowing and understanding the world has been remarked upon by many others. Taking his lead from Aimé Césaire, Robin D. G. Kelley, for instance, explains that

> progressive social movements do not simply produce statistics and narratives of oppression; rather, the best ones do what great poetry always does: transport us to another place, compel us to re-live horrors and, more importantly, enable us to imagine a new society. We must remem-

ber that the conditions and the very existence of social movements enable participants to imagine something different, to realize that things need not always be this way. It is that imagination, that effort to see the future in the present, that I shall call "poetry" or "poetic knowledge."[8]

In Kelley's formulation, "poetry" or "poetic knowledge" has a temporal dimension: anchored in a "now," it strives toward the future of a different present, a future presently accessible as a kind of yearning within a shared imagination. It does not provide a blueprint; it is prophecy undergirded with belief and tenacity. The role of the imagination is central here because it animates the production of "poetic knowledge" (which may be constituted by and accessed through any and all of the senses, or simply through a kind of intuition), giving it a form and content through which it might accrue a material force.

Kelley turns to poetry, which he calls, following Césaire, "a revolt: a scream in the night, an emancipation of language and old ways of thinking," in order to describe a characteristic of "Black radical imagination."[9] For Kelley, the "freedom dreams" that animated prior movements that aimed to change the world by eradicating racism, colonialism, sexism, homophobia, imperialism, and capitalist exploitation provide records of those movements' vital contributions to a collective radical imagination, on which today's activists, artists, intellectuals, and visionaries might draw for insight. The role of poetic knowledge in this radical imagination is to disrupt the transparency and authority of present perceptions, to "take us to another place, envision a different way of seeing, perhaps a different way of feeling."[10]

While Kelley wants to advance a utopian project based on the belief he inherited from his mother that "the map to a new world is in the imagination, in what we see in our third eyes rather than in the desolation that surrounds us," my interest in poetic knowledge lies in how it might spark whatever viable kindling might be found in "the desolation that surrounds us" to light a fire here in this now. My turn to poetry, therefore, is less about bringing about a utopian future and mapping another world, and more about the access poetry provides to a notion of futurity as both a promise and a wish, at the same time as poetry unsettles the assuredness that there is a future as such.

I am interested in poetic formulations such as "we are the ones we have been waiting for," which collapse the distance between this present and a future, challenge the confidence with which narratives of reproductive futurity are advanced, introduce risk and uncertainty into present speculations about futures, and urge those of us still here now to action without guarantees.[11] I use the word "poetry" to mark a perceptual or "preceptual" event that communicates most profoundly when it works affectively to open existing languages to subterranean significations or to create new languages altogether; "poetics" marks the ensemble of such events, their theorization, their duration, and the terrains they forge in their becoming.[12] Here, the poetry and poetics of particular interest reveal queer temporalities. The queer times that animate them and that they in turn orchestrate have made them especially powerful to anti-racist, anti-colonial, de-colonial, post-colonial, and pro-Black activists, artists, and theorists, whose oeuvres have sought to reveal and redress the quotidian violence that undergirded and continues to inform the existing material relations, whose roots are in European colonial enterprises in Asia and in Africa, including the enslavement and forced migration of Africans. In such queer times, the poetics of those activists, artists, and theorists can ignite existing yearnings to imagine, and moreover to enact, another world here now in this one.

Invocations of "the future" are common in political discourses that assume that today's actions and decisions will continue to be felt tomorrow and will have implications for future generations of people somehow related to those of us presently making the decisions. Most political discourses posit one singular future as the temporal horizon of possibility toward which our actions today tend. Yet, for reasons explained in the introduction, I insist on using the term "futures," with all of its economic valences intact, in order to underscore that even the imagination might be rendered complicit with Capital. (Capital in fact increasingly relies upon it, even as the imagination might be a force in capitalism's undoing.) Still, the temporal logics undergirding this project are consistent with political praxes that insist upon presently impossible possibilities issued from collectively forged radical imaginations such as "liberation" or the coexistence of "another world" within the presently perceptible one. Such praxes rely upon a temporality consistent with that described by Deleuze as "cinematic," for instance, or by Fanon as the temporality operative in Marx's invocation of "poetry from the future."[13]

Though different in their particulars, these theories share an interest in advancing an understanding of time and of the collectively achieved organization of time, or temporality, in which the presently irrational and unpredictable, or what is presently unrecognizable or assimilable only as "alien" or as simply a "thing," might disrupt common habits of apprehension and perception to clear a path for something else. For several of the thinkers I focus on here, that "something else" is a radical rupture within the quotidian, one that harbors presently impossible possibilities, such as Black and/or queer liberation and radically transformed, newly imagined, egalitarian, socioeconomic relations. A similar set of assumptions about temporality are perceptible in recent theories of queer temporality, such as Elizabeth Freeman's, Jose Muñoz's, and Lee Edelman's, among others.[14]

Muñoz has argued convincingly that queerness can be understood as "a structuring and educated mode of desiring that allows us to see and feel beyond the quagmire of the present."[15] It is a historically specific, collectively produced, shared sense that insists upon an immanent "potentiality or concrete possibility for another world."[16] "Not yet here," "queerness" for Muñoz marks a utopian project (in the sense of "utopia" elaborated by Ernst Bloch) that might activate what is "no longer conscious" in the past in the interest of moving toward a "not yet here." Muñoz understands queerness as a "horizon," which allows it to be perceived as "a modality of ecstatic time" in which the "temporal stranglehold" of straight time "is interrupted or stepped out of."[17] Significantly, understanding "queerness" as a temporal mode yet to be achieved means that "doing, performing, engaging the performative as force of and for futurity is queerness's bent and ideally the way to queerness."[18] A temporal mode "always in the horizon," "queerness" also spatializes, even if only through the imagination of or the desire for it. Queerness produces horizons and, as Sara Ahmed points out in her study of queer phenomenology, other spatial orientations.[19]

Freeman's important work on queer temporality in the book *Time Binds: Queer Temporalities, Queer Histories* calls attention to the imbrication of "queerness" with capitalism. Freeman writes that for the artists of interest to her project, "the point is to identify 'queerness' as the site of all the chance elements that capital inadvertently produces, as well as the site of capital's potential recapture and incorporation of chance."[20] Again, theories of queer temporality have spatial implications as well; the way that Freeman spatializes queerness (even if only in the imagination of the critic and artist) by identifying it as a "site" of Capital's production of "chance elements" that Capital may in turn recapture serves as a reminder of this. It also underscores how queer spaces and indeed "queerness" as a material practice call attention to the instability of existing relations, the (im)possibility of a rupture in any moment whatever. Bound to chance, queerness has a capacity to proliferate unpredictable connections and encounters between seemingly random, exhausted, or useless things.

Like Muñoz's "queer utopian hermeneutic," which would "be epistemologically and ontologically humble in that it would not claim the epistemological certitude of queerness that we simply 'know' but, instead, strain to activate the no-longer-conscious and to extend a glance toward that which is forward-dawning, anticipatory illuminations of the not-yet-conscious," Freeman's interest is in works that "collect and remobilize archaic or futuristic debris as signs that things have been and could be otherwise."[21] The queer projects Freeman analyzes retroactively activate and deploy the excess or surplus that Capital variably, yet consistently, produces and casts aside as useless, nonproductive, or dead: "The queerness of these artists consists in mining the present for signs of undetonated energy from past revolutions."[22] In Freeman's queer temporality, new life might be breathed in any moment whatever into that which has been pronounced dead, reinvigorating it, and, like a specter or, perhaps, a witch in flight, setting it to work unpredictably.[23]

Freeman and Muñoz write against the celebration of negativity and negation characteristic of, as Muñoz refers to it, the "antirelational approach" in Queer Studies, theorized perhaps most influentially by Leo Bersani in his book *Homos*.[24] Muñoz argues that "although the antirelational approach assisted in dismantling an anticritical understanding of queer community, it nonetheless quickly replaced the romance of community with the romance of singularity and negativity."[25] Freeman repudiates what she refers to as the model of Queer Theory that posited that "truly queer queers would dissolve forms, disintegrate identities, level taxonomies, scorn the social, and even repudiate politics altogether."[26]

For Freeman, this strain of Queer Theory operates along the lines of the paranoid criticism described by Eve Sedgwick, wherein critics or readers know in advance the outcome of their reading or criticism, and read only for signs of what they already know to be the case. Against paranoid criticism, Freeman claims that she believes the point now is "to be interested in the tail end of things, willing to be bathed in the fading light of whatever has been declared useless." She explains, "For while queer antiformalism appeals to me on an intellectual level, I find myself emotionally compelled by the not-quite-queer-enough longing for form that turns us backward to prior moments, forward to embarrassing utopias, sideways to forms of being and belonging that seem, on the face of it, completely banal."[27]

I share both Muñoz's and Freeman's visions of alternatives to the antirelational approach in Queer Theory; still, I want to retain something of an investment in the labor of the negative, but without reifying a dialectic in which there is negation and negation of the negation. Referring to the capacity of "queer" to function as a structuring antagonism within the social as "antirelational" misses the ways "queer" is a product of social relation, a condition of possibility for sociality as we know it. It is a mode of relationality that generates surprising, pleasurable excess within the social precisely because it is structurally antagonistic to the properly social. At the same time, it also appears as what must be banished from the social; therefore, those perceived to inhabit "queer" suffer the brunt of the violence that maintains normative relations. Rather than simply a mode of negativity with the capacity to destroy, "queer" exists as a generative force that works unpredictably (and therefore sometimes as simple negation, but even then always restlessly) within the social, shaking loose surplus and investing it in creative modes of sociality that may not be recognized as such. Rather than a term in a dialectic, "queer" can be understood as a force coursing through the veins of modernity and its socioeconomic logics. It lives in the temporal logics of modernity and the social relations and spatial configurations those logics orchestrate. Queerness is endogenous to time. My version of "queer" resonates with that of Freeman and Muñoz. It also is not inconsistent, however, with the utopian association of "queer" in the work of the negative characteristic of antiformalism and antirelationality in some Queer Theory.

Edelman's claims regarding the "sinthomosexual" within the reproductive processes organized by a society's libidinal economy, for example, are structurally analogous to Fanon's assertion in *The Wretched of
the Earth* that, according to the logics of the colonial order, the Black is
"the corrosive element."[28] That is, for Edelman, the queer (or, more accu-
rately, the sinthomosexual) is the figure currently capable of unraveling
the libidinal economy of signification (as read through Jacques Lacan)
through which a historically specific dominant socius reproduces itself.
In Fanon's analysis, which takes the colony as its purview, the figure with
the capacity to explode the Manichean ontology of colonialism is the
native in the colony: "the Black" within the colony's Manichean logics.
Although by no means exhaustive of the range of theoretical stances on
the temporality of the radical change that might liberate oppressed and
exploited groups, these two theories mark the shared historical interest
of both queer and Black liberation projects in thinking a radical rupture
from within the extant theoretical structures informing the temporalities of Black existence and homosexuality and queerness. In identifying
a figure of radical alterity, and therefore potent danger to the existing
structures of signification and the inequities and violence they rationalize, both the antirelational mode of Queer Theory and anticolonial
theories that target for destruction and rebirth the ontological construction of "the Human" in Western thought and civilization share a utopian
vision that the world as we know it can be absolutely destroyed through
the mobilization of an agent produced within it. Edelman advocates for
an ironic embrace of that figure and a rejection of politics tout court
because any politics would drag that figure back into the structures of
signification he (Edelman's sinthomosexual) threatens to destroy. Fanon
advocates for a revolutionary, cleansing violence, a radical violence
through which the existing structures would be destroyed and a new
man would be born.

Much of the debate about *No Future* involved a critique of Edelman's
analysis for hinging on a figure with the characteristics and privileges
that accrue to those things we recognize as middle- and upper-class
white gay men. Calling for "no future," it has been argued, might inform
a (non)politics only for those for whom the future is given, even if un-
desirably so. The rest, those for whom the future remains to be won in
each moment and who labor within the hellish temporal cycle Fanon

describes, continue to dream "freedom dreams" of a better day ahead, remaining open to the disruptions that poetry from the future might make in the symbolic order of the past/present.

Fanon, for his part, has been criticized for his construction of a putatively male, decidedly masculine, agent of revolutionary struggle, and for valorizing a mode of struggle driven by heterosexuality. While both Edelman and Fanon construct "problematic" figures to embody the (im)possibility of rupture that serves as the very condition of possibility for a current spatiotemporal order and the socioeconomic relations it maintains, they differ in their assessment of the political implications of their analyses and hence in their visions for the aftermath of the destruction. The tension between the hermeneutics of recognizing one's alterity within the structures that guarantee futurity and the determination of a politics in the face of such a recognition is of concern here. This concern is with the terms of reconciliation and evaluation of the here and now, the meanwhile of theorizing and imagining otherwise. Addressing such a concern in the meanwhile, the break, or the interval, without the security of a place and time currently recognizable as a habitable future, let alone a utopian one, is a challenge of our time.[29]

The rest of this chapter thinks at the nexus where any distinction between Black politics, feminist politics, and queer politics collapses, with particular attention to forging a set of connections through the temporalities thought to inform each. "Futures" are at stake here, and they hinge on looking and on the labor "poetry" and its affects might perform. By way of three Black queer films—*Looking for Langston, The Watermelon Woman,* and *Brother to Brother*—this chapter considers what Daniel Peddle's documentary *The Aggressives* offers to a project that thinks the temporal structures of Blackness and queerness in conjunction with one another and, hence, understands that the politics thought to be proper to each are inseparable from those of the other.

Looking, Desire, and History

Isaac Julien's 1989 film, *Looking for Langston*, Cheryl Dunye's 1996 film, *The Watermelon Woman*, and Rodney Evans's 2005 film, *Brother to Brother*, are motivated by a desire to look to the past for recognizable signs that might authorize the existence of particular collective sociopolitical formations in the present. *Looking for Langston* presents itself as a meditation on Langston Hughes (1902–1967) and the Harlem Renaissance. It features the poetry of Essex Hemphill (1957–1995) and Richard Bruce Nugent (1906–1987) and is dedicated to the memory of James Baldwin (1927–1987). Invoking these figures at its opening, the film rehearses a subterranean history of a gay identity perceptible from within the dominant history of Black cultural production, and presents that history as the frame in which Langston Hughes might appear as a historical persona who both frustrates and fulfills a Black diasporic desire for a historical ground of a contemporary Black gay identity.

Like *Looking for Langston, Brother to Brother* searches for and locates a Black gay male past as a component of a present production of Black gay desire and identity. *Brother to Brother* also employs the Harlem Renaissance in the service of a contemporary production of Black gay male identity and survival. There, Bruce Nugent is foregrounded in a long overdue creative assessment of his contributions to the artistic sensibilities of the writers of the Harlem Renaissance, especially Langston Hughes, Zora Neale Hurston, and Wallace Thurman. Different in style from *Looking for Langston, Brother to Brother* looks to the past to provide a cultural context for its efforts to valorize present Black gay desire and cultural production. By insisting on the presence of a queer Harlem Renaissance in a world still recognizable to us today, *Brother to Brother* makes visible the queer desire that haunts Black creativity and cultural politics.

Explicitly constructing an imagined past, even as it plays with the conventions of documentary realism, *The Watermelon Woman* posits a fictionalized past as a condition of possibility for the film's construction and valorization of a Black lesbian identity in the film's present. Although they evince the concern in different ways and with varying degrees of nuance and complications, each of these films is fundamentally concerned with questions arising from the production of a past calibrated to meet current demands for a cogent, viable, and recognizable Black queer existence in the present.

Like *Looking for Langston* and *Brother to Brother*, Daniel Peddle's 2005 documentary *The Aggressives* asks us to consider, albeit indirectly, the temporality of a present sense of political possibility. Each film's temporal framework hinges on the film's production and deployment of a politics of visibility aimed at making its queer subjects intelligible from within different systems of valuation. Some of the differences in the ways *Looking for Langston, The Watermelon Woman, Brother to Brother*, and *The Aggressives* work in relationship to time can be attributed to the filmmakers' formal choices, including the differences in genre: *Looking for Langston* is an experimental film that presents a temporality organized affectively via "desire"; *The Watermelon Woman*, a "mockumentary," playfully deploys documentary realist conventions to generate a desire for a past it constructs to serve present needs; *Brother to Brother* is a work of dramatic fiction that seeks to provide a queer history of the present; and *The Aggressives* strives to be a conventional documentary, yet organizes time idiosyncratically. The differences between them are instructive because they point to two impulses in contemporary thought about temporality that Queer Theory has posed as mutually exclusive, with one understood as less capable of supporting a politics than the other.

The Watermelon Woman and *Brother to Brother* represent an impulse to put the past in the service of a contemporary production of queer visibility that might support a present and future lived expression of same-sex desire. *Brother to Brother* searches confidently for gay identity across time and from within a familiar historical narrative of Black cultural production. While *The Watermelon Woman* also insists upon the significance of the past in sustaining present appearances, it embraces the task of producing that past as fiction, thereby complicating both the extent to which a "true" past connected to the present is necessary as well as common assumptions about the work of historiography and the versions of the past it gleans.[30] "History" is offered in *The Watermelon Woman* as the existence of a past that can be narrated as a necessary anchor for presently viable appearances of an existing identity category, namely, "Black lesbian filmmaker." The film calls attention to the interested and partial nature of that history by functioning as the vehicle for the production and dissemination of a history: in fabricating a fictionalized history in the film-within-the-film for Cheryl, the character in the film played by the film's actual filmmaker Cheryl Dunye, *The Watermelon Woman* anchors itself within film history as the first feature film by a Black lesbian filmmaker. Even as it teases present desires for a viable past to anchor existing modes of identification, in its insistence on the past as "history," *The Watermelon Woman* complicates, but does not depart from, a linear temporality.

The Aggressives, on the other hand, organizes time idiosyncratically and, in so doing, reveals and must contend with the cutting edge of visibility, a border between the visible and the invisible that is sharp as a razor and as difficult to rest on. In this regard, *The Aggressives* illuminates a view of history as, in words from *Looking for Langston*, "the smiler with the knife."[31] This metaphor, like poetry, functions affectively, calling forth an image of history as, say, a responsible film editor, leaving to decay on the cutting room floor everything that does not serve to "further the action," or a kindly killer, jovially excoriating those who cannot serve that killer's needs and interests and leaving the silent corpses in unmarked graves. The metaphor underscores history's brutality and holds it in tension with history's natural, inevitable, alluring appearance.[32] This is not to say that the metaphor has no meaning except to establish equivalences; rather, it makes perceptible an affective dimension of historical processes without firmly restricting the range of meanings it calls forth in the mental image it conjures.

Brother to Brother and *The Aggressives* represent divergent impulses vis-à-vis the narration of the past. History as "the smiler with the knife" is evidenced in the latter; in the former, it is history as the past in service of the present. Both impulses can be seen in *Looking for Langston*, though history as the "smiler with the knife" is stronger. With the emergency siren sounding at the beginning and the end, *Looking for Langston* indicates that its meditation on the past is a response to present pressing concerns. We can understand this film's turn to the past as a version of what Walter Benjamin referred to in his *Theses on the Philosophy of History* as seizing "hold of a memory as it flashes up in a moment of danger."[33] Rather than assuming an accessible gay identity that is coherent and recognizable over time, Isaac Julien's emphasis on "looking" produces a queer Harlem Renaissance as a present desire in a moment of danger. It might be said that the queer Harlem Renaissance finds its fulfillment in and draws its poetry from the historical conjuncture in which Isaac Julien frames the images that constitute *Looking for Langston*.

According to Julien, the choice to focus on Langston Hughes, a figure who is central to the Harlem Renaissance and whose sexuality has been a troubling question for historians, was animated by "a very genuine search for desire" that ultimately renders *Looking for Langston* "more about looking [than it is about Langston]. . . . [It] is about Black gay desire; it's an imaginary search for a Black gay identity." In a chapter that focuses on *Looking for Langston* and another film of relevance to the present discussion, *BD Women* (directed by Inge Blackman / Campbell X, 1994), Grace Kyungwon Hong characterizes "queer reproduction" as a process based not on "the real" but rather on a creative seeking that generates the past one seeks. Hong muses, "Perhaps that is all that we are now and will ever be: the fragments and figments of someone's imagination, of someone's desire for us to exist, much like *Looking for Langston* . . . dreams something in the 'past' into existence."[34]

Situated in an imaginary space of shifting and interlocking temporalities, *Looking for Langston* works to retrieve an image of the past (such a retrieval is a creative operation of desire) and make it recognizable as a present concern. Like Benjamin's historical materialist, the film seeks to retrieve the image of Langston Hughes from the weight of traditional depictions and narratives that rely on keeping Hughes's probable homosexuality invisible. Searching for black gay desire, *Looking for Langston* produces it in the Harlem Renaissance by calling attention to moments when something queer might appear, such as the publication of the short-lived journal *Fire!*, which included Bruce Nugent's *Smoke, Lilies, and Jade*, quoted in the film, and the queer songs by Blues woman Bessie Smith. The act of looking for Langston produces a Langston Hughes and a queer Harlem Renaissance and makes them available for further transductions of value and future commodification, such as *Brother to Brother*. Working to seize from "the true picture of the past" (in which we only ever recognize what interests us) an "image which flashes up at the instant when it can be recognized and is never seen again," the temporality that animates the search, which can be characterized in Benjamin's terms in the ways I just referenced, participates in making these elements of the Harlem Renaissance available for future use, and hence in dragging a queer Harlem Renaissance out of shadows and innuendos, behind the back winks and reluctant nods, and into the footnotes and speculations of the official history of Black cultural production.[35] It makes the Harlem Renaissance queer now and in so doing participates in a Black diasporic temporal accumulation in which we might now perceive queer Black desire among the animating logics of Black culture.

Looking for Langston, the film, is a type of looking after Langston Hughes in two senses. The first is sequential and aligns with a temporality in which the past is put in the service of the present. It is a type of "making visible" in the present what had been hidden through the struggle for hegemony in the past. Consistent with this first sense of looking after Langston Hughes, *Looking for Langston* attempts to provide a poetic account of Hughes's own time by relying on found footage and audio recordings of Hughes, in order to look at his time *after* Hughes himself could be said to have looked at and made his mark on it. The second way that *Looking for Langston* "looks after" Langston Hughes is colloquially and affectively; it generates Hughes's purported homosexuality and makes it recognizable in a time when it might be useful, thereby protecting or sheltering a homosexual desire it attributes to Hughes by making it meaningful for and within a collectivity that presently needs it and therefore affectionately "looks after," or cares for, it.

Making a queer Harlem Renaissance available in these two different, but related ways, *Looking for Langston*, in the time of its initial release, was part of a broader deployment from within queer cultural production of a queer historiography that relied on various techniques for making visible that which had been "hidden from history," to invoke the title of an anthology of lesbian and gay history published in the same year as *Looking for Langston* appeared. Importantly, unlike the historical scholarship that characterizes the anthology *Hidden from History*, the queer historiography of *Looking for Langston* is not invested in a production or assertion of a historical truth that might become a ground for the redemption of Hughes's homosexuality. Rather, the creative work that *Looking for Langston* does vis-à-vis Hughes's homosexuality is an affective labor that puts Hughes's homosexuality to use and valorizes it, even if only from within a besieged group, rather than somehow redeeming it. The sirens that begin and end the film underscore how the temporality of "looking after" Langston, as it is organized affectively, is unfaithful to any dream of ultimate redemption because they call attention to the violence underpinning the very terrain of looking. The sirens sound to signal a raid of the queer gathering. When the thugs and police arrive, there is nothing to see; they find no one there, and the angel floating above them, smiling and laughing, is imperceptible to them.

Like the interested desire that animates *Looking for Langston*, my interest below in the documentary *The Aggressives* is more about looking and the temporality of "making visible" than it is about the construction of the character "M—," the documentary subject who focuses my analysis. Yet, unlike Julien's film, this is less a search than a circumvention. For I may not be the only one looking for M—, and, in large part because of this, my (admittedly problematic) interests here have more to do with keeping M— present, but absent, than with locating M— in time or space.[36]

The Aggressives

The Aggressives is a documentary made by a male artist and filmmaker named Daniel Peddle. It follows several "aggressives," who identify as female and/or as women and present themselves as masculine. The complexity of this mode of self-identification in relationship to gender is highlighted by M—'s claim at the beginning of the film that M— lives life as a man, but that doesn't change the fact that M— is a woman. *The Aggressives* was an important intervention into contemporary discourse about the politics and lives of lesbian, gay, bisexual, and transgendered people, precisely because it refused to be located easily within the terms that currently animate the mainstream of that discourse and its manifold movements. Instead of "lesbian," or "gay woman," "ftm," or "genderqueer," the film offers us "aggressives," a term through which complex senses of belonging, self-creation, and self-expression related to "lesbian" "dyke," "butch," "man," "woman," and "trans*" are negotiated but are excessive vis-à-vis each of those categories. In their adoption of a language of sex and gender expression forged, at least in part, within the sociocultural spaces carved out by people of color, the aggressives participate in making genderqueer and trans* discourses more responsive to the particularities of their present experiences of gender and sexuality, which are marked by their race and class.

To the extent that, as Octavia explains in the film, "aggressive" is a formation with currency both inside and outside of prison, the designation of one as "aggressive" or "AG" is part of a broader convergence of Black popular culture with prison culture and therefore cannot be divorced from other discourses of contemporary Black existence in the United States and of class and Black masculinity as it is informed by the prison industry. Because of this, *The Aggressives* also paves avenues of common interest between maturing queer movements and dynamic, urgent prison abolitionist movements. Peddle's film is part of a larger fascination with and fear of Black sexual deviance, Black poverty, and Black masculinity at the same time as it contributes to and complicates energetic emergent US-based trans* and genderqueer movements, whose current interests antagonistically enmesh them with regulatory state regimes of identification, recognition, and valorization.[37]

Seeking to be a conventional documentary, while framing unconventional subjects, *The Aggressives* mediates its subjects' expressions of what it means to be an aggressive and its viewers' access to the social and cultural milieu the aggressives themselves create. The aggressives' organizations of social life are enabled by creative engagements with common sense. These engagements are part of what circumscribes *The Aggressives* indelibly as belonging to our time. What the aggressives articulate in the film (sometimes in spite of the film's formal constraints) as the common sense that conditions their belonging to the category "aggressives" are a set of possibilities for a range of existing expressions and politics variously perceptible at the time of filming as "transgender," "transsexual," and "genderqueer."[38] Via this articulation, the aggressives challenge existing gender discourses to become more responsible to aggressive common senses and their attendant forms of social life, which describe and navigate racialized and nonbourgeois experiences of gender expression.

Aggressive Time

The Aggressives challenges us to make sense of the world of the aggressives, a world to which it seems to provide unfettered access, yet provides few of the usual markers documentaries employ to assist their viewers in doing so. For instance, *The Aggressives* requires us as viewers to work to locate the subjects in time and space, often giving us only what the subjects themselves say about their time, location, and the passage of time captured in the film. The film was shot over a five-year span, between 1999 and 2004, but Peddle does not give us specific dates, times, or locations. He gives us the first names of the people he is interviewing and occasionally their surnames, and we know that he is present during the interviews because they react to him and his prompts. But our anchoring in space and time as viewers of this documentary remains tenuous and dependent upon the information we can glean from the interviews. There are some establishing shots (of the jail in which Octavia is incarcerated, for instance, or of street signs), but in general *The Aggressives* does little to enforce a "natural" spatiotemporal structure that anchors the action in space, like specific neighborhoods, for example, or in exact years, months, or days. While it is worthwhile to be critical of this aspect of the film because it elicits an anthropological gaze on the film's subjects and generalizes them as exotic others whose natural habitat is any urban jungle, the unintended consequence of this aesthetic choice is of interest here: it provides a highly subjective and culturally dependent sense of the subjects' time by relying upon their own references as markers of their location in space and the passage of time.

From Tiffany, for example, we learn that one of the days we see Tiffany is Tiffany's birthday. Tiffany wants someone to come uptown to join Tiffany in bed and then leave. Octavia tells us that Octavia was eighteen at the time of Peddle's first interview, which was five years ago. Several of the aggressives reference the rap song "Still Not a Player" by Big Punisher, aka Big Pun (in the radio edit of that song Big Pun repeats the phrase, "I'm not a player, I just crush a lot"), which was popular during 1998–2000, as are many popular cultural references in the film, especially musical ones.[39] Such references situate *The Aggressives'* subjects in time, as time can be said to be marked by hip-hop cultural trends and products and the libidinal investments and pleasures therein, including the misogyny and masculine privilege carried in the catchy lyrics to "Still Not a Player." That song situates "the aggressives" in a time measured by the life-span of a popular cultural commodity, a sort of market time that also corresponds to and seeks to organize the demographic the aggressives themselves might be said to inhabit—young, urban, and Black. The repetition of the song through the aggressives' references to it throughout the film underscores the complicated relationship between their aggressive masculinity and controversial popular versions of hip-hop masculinity.

Aggressive time is organized in part by patterns of consumption and other social and communicative practices that require participants in that subculture to spend time on them. By the end of the documentary, a couple of the aggressives have become distant from the subcultural activities in which they so enthusiastically participated when they were younger. Octavia, for instance, the aggressive who also does time in jail, does not have the time at the end of the film to participate in the aggressive subcultural life, a fact that reveals that, as with any category, the construction of "aggressives" as a category indexes a dynamic investment of time and labor rather than a stable and unchanging essence. Foregrounding "aggressive" as an index of an organization of time, rather than of a discrete and identifiable group, helps to explain the difficulties its subjects pose for the film's conventional, linear documentary narrative form. Prison time, the market time of popular cultural commodities, subcultural time and queer life cycles, and the temporalities of radical alterity as described, albeit differently, by Fanon and Edelman, among others, cannot be made to conform to the linear, narrative documentary time the film seeks to impose upon them at the end of the film.[40] Under irreconcilable pressure from the forced imposition of conventional documentary time, many things escape that imposition, becoming invisible and/or unrecognizable within the film's stylistic and narrative framework. One of them is M—.

The Unequal Calculuses of Visibility Distribution

As told in the film, the storyline for M— involves M— joining the military to earn money to attend college. The film provides images and interviews while M— is in the military. In the film's postscript, which is designed to provide narrative closure, the viewer learns that "during the US Invasion of Iraq, 'M—' abruptly left the Army. Her current whereabouts are unknown."

Given that M—'s disappearance from the film's mise-en-scène is a form of resistance and survival, what are the ethical implications of looking for M—, and to what extent are they imbricated in a thinking through of Black queer temporality and political possibility? M—'s disappearance from the film's mise-en-scène is M—'s refusal to remain bound to its visual economy. It is a political act that undoes the film's pretense of omniscient linear narration, narrative closure, and spatiotemporal continuity; it also opens a space of Black queer and trans* desire that arises simultaneously from M—'s resistance to M—'s working-class immobility (a resistance that rationalized M—'s enlistment in the Army), as well as from M—'s efforts toward self-valorization via mechanisms outside of the nation-state and its military, which, as M— puts it, do not "care" about M— anyway. While the military and its police might *look for* M—, or attempt to recognize M— in a specific space, they will not *look after* M— in either sense of that phrase discussed above. Although each deploys different logics of visibility vis-à-vis sexuality, the military's and police's looking for M— subsequent to M—'s disappearance is primarily spatial; they might seek to recognize M— according to their hegemonic common senses in order to locate where M— physically is now.

The collective histories that have enabled M—'s appearance to date and the future beings desiring M— into existence today are what must be excoriated from the social body with and through M—'s captivity and conscription (in whatever form of service to the State) in order for the current hegemony to be maintained.[41] This is accomplished through a variety of wars, both in the United States and beyond its borders. In M—'s case, by "abruptly disappearing" and thereby refusing to become a conscript of war, M— might live. Yet, doing so also makes M— a target of those wars and renders M—invisible and, therefore, unprotected and vulnerable.

If disappearing enables M— to live, dragging M— into my sight here implicates my own work in the very processes and situations I seek to illuminate and challenge. In order to disappear, M— also becomes invisible within the regime of the image that renders "the aggressives" visible throughout the film. The fact that M— must disappear from the film's narrative highlights the ways that a critical apparatus predicated upon making visible hidden images, sociocultural formations, ideas, concepts, and other things, always drags what interests it onto the terrain of power and the struggles through which that power is contested and/or (re)produced. On this terrain, the benefits of visibility are unevenly distributed.

In the colonial world of which Fanon writes, for example, the hypervisibility of Blacks and the organizations of space that rationalize their hypervisibility are crucial techniques through which colonial power and white supremacy were maintained.[42] Insofar as colonial logics can be said to undergird present socioeconomic relations, Black people can become visible only through those logics, so danger, if not death, attends every Black's appearance.[43] Yet, precisely because what is visible is caught in the struggle for hegemony, the violence that maintains existing power relations, and their attendant processes of valorization, one cannot not want the relative security promised by visibility.

Specifically, in relationship to the present discussion of *The Aggressives*, an earlier film, *Paris Is Burning*, a documentary made in 1990 to which *The Aggressives* is often compared, should provide an important caution. As Jack Halberstam explains, five of the subjects of that documentary were dead within five years of the film's release, whereas the film's documentarian, Jennie Livingston, became a filmmaker, and the pop star Madonna made a fortune by appropriating vogueing, the dance style innovated and displayed by the subjects in Livingston's film.[44] The point in bringing *Paris Is Burning* into this conversation is not to place blame on Jennie Livingston for the disappearance, death, or continuing poverty of her documentary subjects. Instead, I issue this caution because it underscores the complicity of critical endeavors with this unequal calculus of visibility distribution. At the same time, it calls forth the insistent need to attend to the ghosts, specters, and absences within what appears and to interrogate what is achieved through those appearances. If my own critical work might contribute to fashioning a politics capable of redressing the very inequalities and injustices it illuminates, rather than simply furthering my career by feeding the academy's contradictory need for knowledge about and sometimes by queers and trans* people of color, the first question that must be asked of M— is not *where* is M—, but *when* M— might *be*.

Fear of a Black Future

At the end of the film, it might be said that M— is out of time (and unlocatable) after the watershed moment that the official narrative of the US nation, adopted here by the film, marks with "September 11, 2001 and the subsequent invasion of Iraq." M—'s disappearance must prompt us to ask not the policing question attuned to the temporal and spatial logics of surveillance and control (*Where is M— today?*), but, rather, in this case, the political question of *when* M—'s visibility will enable M—'s survival by providing the protection that the realm of the visible affords those whose existence is valued, those we want to look for so we can look out for, and look after, them.

A "looking" for M— that begins by asking *"where* is M— now?" inevitably operates by harnessing the temporal structures and epistemological enterprises of policing and surveillance inherent in any framing of questions of representation and visibility. Because of this, asking where M— is now is complicit with the needs of the prison and military industrial complexes, the industries that proliferate the very spaces (prisons and barracks) that already violently and antagonistically structure the time of The Aggressives and, indeed, are central to the constitution of the category and some of the logics of "aggressives" itself. Rather, a "looking" for M— that asks *when* M— might be, even as M— haunts us now, invests in an interpretive project that, while circumscribed by the exigencies of the present, is nonetheless creative. It seeks to think in a moment of crisis while remaining open and vulnerable to the (im)possibility of a rupture now. It is predicated on recognizing the ways the film seeks to enforce a straight time but fails because its own subjects disturb that time by repeatedly indexing by their very existence the violences that guarantee it.

In the temporality the film seeks to impose on the aggressives, there is no known future for M—, yet M— persists in it, haunting the film's attempt at narrative closure and pointing toward another organization of time implicit in, yet antagonistic to, it. As Grace Hong reminds us through her suggestion (mentioned previously) that "perhaps that is all that we are now and will ever be: the fragments and figments of someone's imagination, of someone's desire for us to exist," a queer futurity is animated by a future desire that is only *perceptible* ("perhaps")—not *recognizable*—now. The temporal structures M— haunts are those characterized not only by a reproductive futurity wherein what is reproduced is what exists, but also by the related but distinct orders of colonial temporality: what Fanon refers to as the Black's temporal cage, with all of Fanon's formulation's resonances with the present configuration of the prison-industrial complex intact. That the straight time of reproductive futurity and, yes, still, colonial temporality is achieved at the expense of M—, several years of Octavia's life, and the subjects of Paris Is Burning, among others, should alert us to the ways that Edelman's No Future dissembles a fear of a black future—a future radically incommensurate with and therefore unthinkable within the particular structures of Lacanian psychoanalysis that Edelman presents as universal, but that a psychiatrist such as Fanon reveals are particular and historical. In other words, from within the order of the Symbolic as presented by Edelman, as from within the colonial order of temporality described by Fanon, among others, a queer/Black future looks like no future at all.

Understood in this way, then, looking for M— entails reading the historical index of *The Aggressives* while acknowledging that something always exceeds such a reading; it is precisely this excess, which we cannot name or know, that divorces our looking from all efforts to redeem it, whether in the name of a morality or law that would send M— to prison or to war, or in the form of a political project that asserts its authority as an urgent imperative in which we must participate. Here, without redemption and indifferent to its call, undisciplined and vulnerable, firmly rooted in our time, looking for M— might touch the erotic as power within us and, bringing us in touch with that power, insist that we not look away.[45]

Sakia Gunn, the person to whom *The Aggressives* is dedicated, was murdered on a street corner in Newark, New Jersey, in May of 2003. Accounts of the incident describe Gunn as either a Black lesbian or as transgendered, signaling that Gunn was masculine in appearance. The night of Gunn's murder, as Gunn and three friends were returning home from a night out in Greenwich Village, they were approached by two men who began flirting with those in the group with more feminine appearances. When Gunn intervened, asserting that they were lesbians, one of the men stabbed Gunn in the chest. At age fifteen, Sakia Gunn was out of time. But, we still look for Sakia Gunn in order to look after Sakia Gunn. Out of time, Sakia Gunn has become a figure of our time, one we invoke as a way of making palpably present the objectionable distance between, for instance, the legality of gay marriage won in the United States by national lesbian and gay political organizations and an innovative, radical politics that looks after and therefore looks out for the lives of Black folks and queer and trans* youth of color. As a figure, Sakia Gunn has been used to point to the present complexity of what José Muñoz describes as "the sensuous intersectionalities that mark our experience," and serves as an example of the modes of existence that racist, misogynist, transphobic, and homophobic violences today cut off at the root. By inciting academics and activists to "call on a utopian political imagination that will enable us to glimpse another time and place: a 'not-yet' where queer youths of color actually get to grow up," Muñoz also prompts us to ask the question we are formulating here: When might Sakia Gunn be?[46] The question is inevitably a spatiotemporal one.

That *The Aggressives* is offered "in memory of Sakia Gunn" reminds us that its subjects live, strive, labor, and love within the terms of a world whose regulatory regimes are guaranteed through a generalized, dispersed violence and reinforced via the persistent threat of physical violence directed at those whom such regulatory regimes do not work to valorize. A quotidian violence is the ground on which the spatio-temporal structures of the film rests—the violence that maintains the disjointed urban spaces in which the aggressives live, that secures the fact and characterizes the culture of Octavia's jail and M—'s barracks. Violence also underpins the labor required of aggressive and/or female and/or Black masculinity and the political economy that secures Black masculine unemployment, rising rates of incarceration, feminicide, and so on. An intolerable, yet quotidian violence, to which many of us have learned to numb ourselves out of habit, this violence marks *The Aggressives* as belonging to our time. This violence is an index of the imposition of straight times and the constraints they place on Black and queer and trans* possibility and existence. Such violence is all we can find today when we look for M—. Looking for M— from within the terms and categories of conventional, national, straight times, M—'s future looks to us like no future at all.

Undisciplined and vulnerable, firmly rooted in our time, might we nevertheless feel, even without recognition, the rhythms of the poetry from a future in which M— might be? Might we allow those rhythms to move us to repel the quotidian violence through which we currently are defined, without demanding of the future from which they come that it redeem our movements now or then? Might we look after M— now, without waiting for the future in which M— might be to issue our present cries?

Within the dynamic project that is "aggressives," there exists a remarkable capacity for self-crafting and becoming that might be part of a queer trans-liberatory project that eschews narrow notions of identity and predictable logics of identification and recognition to forge unpredictable alliances and connections, collecting other others in its movements.[47] "Aggressives" is an autopoiētic project collectively crafted through imaginations that borrow, steal, and create from the available common senses of gender roles and presentations, accessible experiences of embodiment and gender, and the matter given to each "aggressive" as a body. It carries a capacity to affect the organization of things, what Fred Moten has referred to as the "political."[48] As a social and cultural phenomenon, "aggressives" is attuned to the popular rhythms of cultural production and consumption, imbricated therefore in the cycles and logics that characterize neoliberal capitalism, and inseparable from the times and places of the construction of "aggressives" as such. Yet, not still, yearning toward a different organization of things, incommensurable with the logics and violences of straight times operating today, moving now.

The Sonic Bartleby

The Digital Regime of the Image and Musical Speech

> "Bartleby," said I, gently calling to him behind his screen.
>
> No reply.
>
> "Bartleby," said I, in a still gentler tone, "come here; I am not going to ask you to do anything you would prefer not to do—I simply wish to speak to you."
>
> Upon this he noiselessly slid into view.
>
> "Will you tell me, Bartleby, where you were born?"
>
> "I would prefer not to."
>
> "Will you tell me anything about yourself?"
>
> "I would prefer not to."
>
> —Herman Melville, "Bartleby the Scrivener"

Bartleby is often referred to as "silent," "noiseless," and, at one point in the short story, the lawyer assumes that Bartleby can no longer see well enough to perform his duties as law copyist, or scrivener. During this time, the lawyer assumes that Bartleby can hear, but not see. In the excerpt above, Bartleby slides "noiselessly . . . into view," a description that suggests a being that can sever its body's movement from the noises that would presumably accompany it. Bartleby offers a sense of the visual without the audio. At the end of the story, Bartleby, by now "the silent man," dies in a prison yard characterized by its silence; "The yard was entirely quiet," observes the lawyer. "It was not accessible to the common prisoners. The surrounding walls, of amazing thickness, kept off all sounds behind them."[1]

The tensions throughout the short story between silence and speech and sound and vision are instructive. Bartleby wrenches apart not only word and meaning, but sound from vision as well. Epistemologically, Bartleby and his queer formula short-circuit systems of equivalences and thus stymie existing modes of knowledge production; materially, they confound the perceptual apparatuses of the lawyer, the other scriveners, and the lawyer's visiting friends. As we have seen in the Interregnum, the first time he recalls hearing Bartleby utter his queer formula, the lawyer says he was sitting at his desk with his head bent over an original document and his arm outstretched, with a copy of the original in hand to deliver to Bartleby immediately upon Bartleby's arrival. The lawyer continues:

> In this very attitude did I sit when I called to him, rapidly stating what it was I wanted him to do—namely, to examine a small paper with me. Imagine my surprise, nay, my consternation, when, without moving from his privacy, Bartleby, in a singularly mild, firm voice, replied, "I would prefer not to." I sat awhile in perfect silence, rallying my stunned faculties. Immediately it occurred to me that my ears had deceived me, or Bartleby had entirely misunderstood my meaning. I repeated my request in the clearest tone I could assume; but in quite as clear a one came the previous reply, "I would prefer not to."[2]

The unaccountable, inscrutable Bartleby, with his queer preferences, incapacitates those who perceive him—Bartleby's formula stuns the lawyer's faculties. Bartleby's own body is often depicted in immobile, still, or restful poses; he is "pale, unmoving" or "silently sitting." Often sitting behind the "high green folding screen" that the lawyer erected upon Bartleby's arrival to conjoin "privacy and secrecy," Bartleby is not visible to the lawyer (nor is the lawyer visible to Bartleby), but they can hear each other. In this context, it is significant to note about a quotation already given in the Interregnum that when Bartleby first appears at the lawyer's office in response to the advertisement for a scrivener, the lawyer describes Bartleby as "a motionless young man": "In answer to my advertisement, a motionless young man one morning stood upon my office threshold, the door being open, for it was summer. I can see that figure now—pallidly neat, pitiably respectable, incurably forlorn! It was Bartleby."[3]

Bartleby is in the habit of standing for long periods "looking out, at his pale window behind the screen, upon the dead brick wall." The lawyer refers to such sessions as Bartleby's "dead-wall reveries."[4] The first wall is familiar from the Interregnum. It is one of the two views from the lawyer's office: "In that direction, my windows commanded an unobstructed view of a lofty brick wall, black by age and everlasting shade; which wall required no spy-glass to bring out its lurking beauties, but, for the benefit of all near-sighted spectators, was pushed up to within ten feet of my window panes."[5] Another is the aforementioned wall against which Bartleby dies in the Tombs: "Strangely huddled at the base of the wall, his knees drawn up, and lying on his side, his head touching the cold stones, I saw the wasted Bartleby."[6]

Described by the lawyer as "cadaverous" and "spectral" even while alive, Bartleby is of this world, but also situated at a border with another, one perhaps always imperceptible just beyond the Wall. Bartleby dies in the Tombs, huddled against the "dead-wall," curled up in the utterly silent courtyard, his eyes open, yet unseeing. Characterized by silence and immobility throughout Melville's "story of Wall Street," Bartleby's existence is a sort of death in life that is associated at several points with dead-walls.

Bartleby, as I discussed in the "Interregnum," provokes a confrontation with opacity, incommensurability, (un)accountability, radical contingency, and the impossible from within the logics of Western philosophy. Relations between sound and vision are part of this confrontation. Here, in this interlude between chapters of *Queer Times, Black Futures*, I situate the sonic and visual concepts offered in Melville's "Bartleby the Scrivener" in relation to those offered by cinematic practices and processes. I consider existing theoretical engagements with Bartleby, sound, and language, and particularly focus on Gilles Deleuze's work on cinema and his essay on Melville's character, Bartleby. In what follows, I trace through and out of Deleuze's reading of "Bartleby" a trajectory offered by Deleuze's references in his essay to music, film, and literature. That line of flight carries us through the rest of this book.

In his essay on "Bartleby," Deleuze highlights the significance of sound and silence, and motion and stillness, to the understanding the story offers of the promises and failures of American pragmatism. Deleuze's engagement with "Bartleby" offers a way into a discussion of the cinematic, including sound and music. At the end of Deleuze's two-volume study of cinema, he reminds his readers that "a theory of cinema is not 'about' cinema, but about the concepts that cinema gives rise to and which are themselves related to other concepts corresponding to other practices."[7] For Deleuze, then, cinema is a practice that produces corresponding concepts. Because philosophy, for Deleuze, is the creation of concepts, a philosophical, theoretical engagement with cinema places concepts seen to belong to cinematic practices into relation with those attributed to other practices. The concepts created through cinema, in other words, are related to those created through painting, literature, science, law, and so on.

According to Deleuze, sound and movement mark the limits to which Bartleby's queer formula pushes language and signification. Unlike another of Melville's characters, Billy Budd, who stutters in a way that, as Deleuze writes, "denatures language but also gives rise to the musical and celestial Beyond of language as a whole," Bartleby "makes do with a seemingly normal, brief Formula, at best a localized tick that crops up in certain circumstances. And yet the result and the effect are the same: to carve out a kind of foreign language within language, to make the whole confront silence, to make it topple into silence."[8]

That Bartleby brings "all of language . . . to the limit of silence and music" is part of what, in Deleuze's assessment, makes Bartleby "an Original." Deleuze explains:

> Each original is a powerful, solitary Figure that exceeds any explicable form: It projects flamboyant traits of expression that mark the stubbornness of a thought without image, a question without response, an extreme and nonrational logic. Figures of life and knowledge, they know something inexpressible, live something unfathomable. They have nothing general about them, and are not particular—they escape knowledge, defy psychology.[9]

For Deleuze, originals are inseparable from the world in which they "exert their effect," but they "are not subject to the influence of their milieu." Flamboyant, perhaps even flaming, an original "throws a livid white light on his surroundings."[10] An Original, in this case Bartleby, reveals a sensibility about empirical reality that exceeds explicable forms and escapes the concretizing common operations of knowledge. As Slavoj Žižek claims, "The difficulty of imagining the New is the difficulty of imagining Bartleby in power."[11] Bartleby, in Giorgio Agamben's terms is, "a scribe who does not simply cease writing, but 'prefers not to.' He is an 'extreme image,' one that 'writes nothing but its potentiality to not-write.'"[12] To the extent that the imagination remains bound to language and to existing concepts (such as those invoked by the signifier "power"), "imagining Bartleby in power" is an unsettling thought experiment that upends the roles customarily played by sound, vision, and other senses in knowledge production.

Engagements with music, sound, and aurality have emerged among the most dynamic areas of intellectual cultural production today. Working with Deleuze's writing on cinema, and taking my cue from other scholars in cinema and media studies, I have elsewhere argued that, at the beginning of the twentieth century, film participated in training the sensory-motor apparatuses of some living organisms, such that they could participate in a reality that itself can be characterized as "cinematic." "Cinematic reality" involves a synergistic relationship between those living organisms and the technologies, economies, and social relations they participate in producing, reproducing, and shaping. Neither cinematic reality nor film precedes or causes the other. Yet, both are constituent elements of historically, and perhaps geographically, specific, embodied encounters and the knowledges they produce.

Deleuze organizes his two-volume study of cinema around the elucidation of two kinds of cinematic images: the movement-image and the time-image. According to Deleuze's schema, from the mid-1910s through World War II, film auteurs innovated what he calls the "movement-image." It is characterized by, as its name suggests, experiments with motion and change over time that allow for continuity and action. These are the types of images that preponderate prior to World War II. That war, however, helped usher in a watershed moment in cinema, which contributed to "the crisis of action-image." About this crisis, Deleuze writes:

Nevertheless, the crisis which has shaken the action-image has depended on many factors which only had their full effect after the war, some of which were social, economic, political, moral, and others more internal to art, to literature and to the cinema in particular. We might mention, in no particular order, the war and its consequences, the unsteadiness of the "American Dream" in all its aspects, the new consciousness of minorities, the rise and inflation of images both in the external world and in people's minds, the influence on the cinema of the new modes of narrative with which literature had experimented, the crisis of Hollywood and its old genres. . . . The soul of cinema demands increasing thought, even if thought begins by undoing the system of actions, perceptions, and affections on which cinema had fed up to that point. We hardly believe any longer that a global situation can give rise to an action which is capable of modifying it—no more than we believe that an action can force a situation to disclose itself, even partially.[13]

A crisis of belief and imagination fueled the transformations Deleuze identifies within the "soul of cinema." Among the "factors" that lead to this crisis are, as stated above, "the unsteadiness of the 'American Dream' in all its aspects" and "the new consciousness of minorities," with the latter playing a significant part in the former in the United States, while also joining forces with others lodging similar struggles throughout the world.[14] On an aesthetic level, the changing state of "sound-images" is one of the hallmarks of the crisis and transformation within the cinematic.

In chapter 1 of *Cinema 2: The Time-Image*, "Beyond the Movement-Image," Deleuze presents Italian neorealism as the mode of filmmaking in which a new cinematic image, the time-image, becomes perceptible. This image is constituted through "the purely optical and sound situation which takes the place of the faltering sensory-motor situations."[15] The ability to continue movement through established habits based on specific sensory inputs falters in the face of the psychic and material destruction wrought by the bombs, artillery, and loss of life and limbs that attended World War II. At the same time, oppressed and exploited groups' challenges to the rationality and stability of the American

Dream and settler colonialism in India and Africa called into question existing authorities and how those have been justified and maintained. For Deleuze, World War II is a transformative moment in cinema's ability to sustain rational movements, such as those that animate linear, progressive, action-driven narratives (organized through stylistic conventions like continuity editing), because the modes of perception World War II made available to (largely Euro-American) filmmakers no longer naively valorize rational movements. After World War II's nuclear bombs, eugenicist holocausts, fascistic white supremacism, and the attending rape and destruction wrought on the planet and its humans, even Europeans and Americans had to admit that Reason no longer reigned (if it ever did).

The increased significance of the time-image in filmmaking after World War II marks a historical transition in which what Deleuze calls "the soul" of cinema shifts from the regime of the movement-image to that of the time-image. As the sensory motor image—the movement-image—collapses in the aftermath of World War II, a "pure optical-sound image" emerges, "any-space-whatevers" proliferate, and another regime of the image makes itself felt: that of the cinematic time-image. The time-image makes "time and thought perceptible" by making "them visible and of sound."[16]

As we have seen in chapter 1, the last sentence of the final chapter before the conclusion of *Cinema 2* reads: "What has now become direct is a time-image for itself, with its two dissymetric, non-totalizable sides, fatal when they touch, that of an outside more distant than any exterior, and that of an inside deeper than any interior, here where a musical speech rises and is torn away, there where the visible is covered over or buried."[17] The relationship between the movement-image and the time-image allows for a range of expressions, perceptions, and possibilities within the cinematic, and it organizes Deleuze's account of cinematic thought. The achievement of a time-image points to "an outside more distant than any exterior," or "a radical Elsewhere," that does not belong to the order to the cinematic, yet invests in it in order to rip it open from the inside. Deleuze suggests that the cinematic movement-image and the time-image, regimes organizing the hegemony of vision in modernity, come under pressure from an amalgamation of sound and music: what he calls here "musical speech." The rise and tearing away of "a musical speech" marks (perhaps) one more passage from one regime to another.

Thinking "poetry" as "musical speech" is felicitous for those of us exploring the continuities and discontinuities of today's digital media and its cultures with the media cultures that precede it. Although Deleuze does not engage with digital media, his discussions of electronic media and of television offer insights into how to extend his method of examining cinema as "a new practice of images and signs" to digital media.[18] Over the next two chapters, I submit that certain Afrofuturist cultural productions ask us to engage the digital regime of the image, sound, and/or perception and what it makes available to thought. The growing significance of sound and audio culture is among the many important transformations one might trace with(in) the digital.

Something remains "cinematic" within the digital regime: the proliferation of irrational cuts and the autonomy of sound-images from the general economy of images, which are primary characteristics of the digital regime of the image, mark such continuities with the filmic regime. Yet, the characteristics of the digital regime also indicate that the balance of relations orchestrated by images is shifting. For Deleuze, specific linkages on irrational cuts are one of the first consequences of the appearance of the time-image. Here, time no longer ensures a general system of commensurability. A relation is established between incommensurable images, but not in a way makes them commensurate. They can still be opaque, yet in relation. The regime of the image, built on a widespread belief in the image's relationship to a reality it was purported to represent, crumbles; "the interval is set free, the interstice becomes irreducible and stands on its own," thereby initiating the reign of "incommensurables or irrational cuts." Yet, this does not imply an absence of relation; rather, it suggests only the emergence of "incommensurability" as a new relation.[19] As I argue in the following chapters, the proposition of "incommensurability" as a new relation can help reframe conceptualizations of race and the ontologies of the human in the face of the sociopolitical and economic transformations characteristic of the digital regime of the image in contemporary societies of control. If, in the time-image, "representation" no longer pretends to animate audio-visual images and opacity replaces equivalences, digital media amplifies these relations.

Cinema 2: The Time-Image was first published in French in 1985, at a time when television was a dominant medium and computation and digital media were beginning to make widespread impacts on social, political, and cultural life. Deleuze speculates that characteristics of what he refers to as "the new image" (that is, the "electronic image") point to "certain effects whose relation to the cinematographic image remains to be determined."[20] Deleuze asserts: "The new images no longer have any outside (out-of-field), any more than they are internalized in a whole; rather, they have a right side and a reverse, reversible and non-superimposable, like a power to turn back on themselves. They are the object of a perpetual reorganization, in which a new image can arise from any point whatever of the preceding image."[21] The assertion that electronic images lack an out-of-field has a political valence akin to the transformation that Deleuze describes in his essay "Postscript on Control Societies."[22] As we have seen, Deleuze argues that the disciplinary societies detailed by Michel Foucault are giving way to "control societies," whose technologies of control are digital and electronic. Control societies work with and through undulations and transformations like those Deleuze attributes to the electronic image: "controls are a modulation, like a self-deforming cast that will continuously change from one moment to the other, or like a sieve whose mesh will transmute from point to point."[23]

Digital film and media sit in relationship to this transformation in ways that Deleuze only points toward at the end of *Cinema 2*. In addition to producing images that "are the object of a perpetual reorganization," many works produced on digital media, including those on digital video, such as HD Video or Digibeta tape, can be characterized by an autonomy of sound. According to Deleuze, this autonomy of sound "increasingly lends" sound "the state of image": "the two images, sound and visual enter into complex relations with neither subordination nor commensurability, and reach a common limit in so far as each reaches its own limit."[24] The electronic image, in other words, facilitates a set of relations between the sonic and the visual, not to establish a hierarchy between them or render them commensurate, but to push them toward their limits. Like Bartleby's ability to "noiselessly" slide into view, today's digital media wrench sound from vision, amplifying the incommensurate as both an opportunity for further modulations of control and a challenge to them.

3

Black Cinema and Questions Concerning Film/Media/Technology

There is a sense in which my generation, those not born that far from 1968—but not far enough for it to have a past in which we had any meaningful political agency—received most of our understandings of the politics of identity and race as a digital signal, as an upload, if you like, of an always-already marked set of structured absences: Fanon, The Panthers, Black Power and so on. So there is a sense in which the founding regime, the narrative regime that overdetermined everything we did, came to us as a set of digital simulacra; as traces of moments forever fixed as virtual references, but always deferred and always already there as a signal, a noise, a kind of utopian possibility. And if you look at most of the films we did, either Black Audio or Smoking Dogs, you get the sense that they are marked by this sense of the utopian as a digital referent.

Many of the films we made seem to me defined by that impossible gesture, a desire to cease and entrap the ghost, to try and reconcile history and the traits of this digital referent, to reconcile the facsimile and the real, history and myth. These seem to me to be profound digitopic yearnings for those of us who did not live certain, shall we say, suturing moments as "real moments." They seem to me to also hold out the promise—which is why we like them so much—of a life that can be located outside the tyranny of time.
—John Akomfrah, "Digitopia and the Spectres of Diaspora"

On "Digitopia" and the Digital Regime of the Image

Questions concerning technology have informed studies of Black film and media for a long time. Indeed, as John Akomfrah points out in the above epigraph, that anti-Black racism inheres in the film apparatus has concerned film and media scholars and makers seeking to craft theories, analyses, films, and videos that reveal another organization of things within the cinematic in order to transform existing race relations. More recent scholarship, such as Alice Maurice's 2013 book *The Cinema and Its Shadow: Race and Technology in Early Cinema*, has enriched our understanding of how the production of recognizable racial difference has been central to technological innovations in film since the silent era. My 2007 book *The Witch's Flight* begins by noting the "historical coincidence" of the invention of film with W. E. B. Du Bois's prescient statement that "the problem of the twentieth century is the problem of the color line," and works to conceptualize what undergirds and authorizes the ways those problems become perceptible as such.[1]

Although "Digitopia and the Spectres of Diaspora," the short essay from which the epigraph from Akomfrah above has been excerpted, should not be taken as an authoritative statement about the general relationship of Black filmmakers to digital technologies, it does articulate some of the most salient issues and questions raised from within the history of Black film and media about transitions to digital media. I engage it throughout this chapter alongside one of Akomfrah's films, *The Last Angel of History* (1996), and a shorter work produced more recently, Arthur Jafa's film *Love Is the Message, the Message Is Death* (2016). These films anchor my analysis of the digital regime of the image in relationship to this book's larger concerns with queer temporality, futurity, and speculation, as well as the scope, pitfalls, and possibilities that become perceptible through a sustained attention to Black existence over time. In the process, this chapter seeks to contribute not only to current scholarship in Black Studies and Queer Theory, but also to the rich theoretical work in Cinema and Media Studies on the transformations underway in film technology.

As one example of the imbrication of Black film with questions of technology, Akomfrah notes that none of the major film stocks were manufactured with a technical ability to bring out the richness and variety in black skin tones. None of the film stock produced by Fuji (whose primary hue was blue), Kodak (whose primary hue was red), or Agfa (which privileged brown) particularly appealed to cinematographers filming subjects with dark skin tones. Referencing this debate about the biases inherent in film technologies, which major Black filmmakers, including Senegalese director Ousmane Sembene, took part in, Akomfrah recounts a by-now legendary tale: "Throughout the 1980s, . . . Julie Dash and Arthur Jafa talked about a 'return to Technicolor,' about going to China (then the only place where using the three-dye processing technique of Technicolor was still a possibility) to retrieve an archaic technique, but also, in a digital, default-redefining attempt, to re-inscribe the black figure in the photochemical matrix—to revisit cinema's analogue history with a new (digital) promise."[2]

This tale about film stock and the heroic efforts of Black filmmakers like Arthur Jafa and Julie Dash (whose collaboration on the 1991 film *Daughters of the Dust* stands as an exquisite cinematic achievement) serves as one reminder of the way that the 1980s and 1990s remain exceptionally rich and vibrant times for innovative Black filmmaking and scholarship. It is worth recalling that the filmmakers from the Black Audio Film Collective (of which Akomfrah was a member), like the LA Rebellion (the film movement from which Julie Dash hails), innovated within the existing conventions of the media with which they worked. Their films and statements arrive for us today as what Akomfrah would call "digital signals," which underscore the dynamic possibilities of culture in Black politics since the 1960s and of formal innovation.

The film and media produced by Black diasporic artists and scholars in the 1980s and 1990s were cultural products of a phase of racial capitalism described by Jodi Melamed as "liberal multiculturalism." Melamed identifies three phases of racial capitalism that have unfolded since the global dynamics of World War II and the advent of the Cold War pressured the United States to recalibrate its overtly white supremacist modes of governance and officially adopt an anti-racist stance, while "making the inequalities that global capitalism generated appear necessary, natural, or fair." The "three successively prominent versions of official antiracism" Melamed offers are: "racial liberalism (mid-1940s to 1960s), liberal multiculturalism (1980s to 1990s), and neoliberal multiculturalism (2000s)."[3] Melamed explains that "liberal multiculturalism" (the phase of interest in the present chapter) is a "means of counting and managing" the deployment of culture by the "robustly materialist anti-racisms of the 1960s and 1970s new social movements, including revolutionary nationalisms (Black Power, the American Indian Movement, Chicano nationalism), the third-world Left, the Asian American civil rights movement, black lesbian feminism, and women-of-color feminism" by "turning it into aesthetics, identity, recognition, and representation."[4]

Liberal multiculturalist discourse and practice sought to defuse those movements' materialist praxes by integrating into the official narrative of the US State a textual, aesthetic engagement with the stories about and cultures of the groups most adversely affected by existing social and economic relations. Struggles around filmic, literary, sonic, and other cultural representations were politicized long before the period Melamed identifies as "liberal multiculturalism"; however, Melamed's analysis (which focuses primarily on literature) identifies how the logics of liberal multiculturalism defanged the materialist dimensions of the cultural practices animating the struggles of the 1950s, 1960s, and 1970s and incorporated them into the workings of racial capitalism.

During the liberal multiculturalist period, many debates about cinematic cultural practices operated within binary terms, such as whether films were complicit with or resistant to commodity culture, or whether they positively or negatively represented a certain group. Melamed's focus is on how the "official or state-recognized liberal anti-racisms that emerged after World War II . . . have strongly shaped and determined the limits of social possibility in the United States and within fields of U.S. global intervention."[5] I find Melamed's analysis and periodization helpful in thinking about Black British and Black American film in the context of the transition to digital media technology because, even though the specific logics of racialization differ in the United States and Great Britain, both aim to project state logics of liberal anti-racism during the time period under consideration here. In response, the Black British and Black American intellectuals and cultural producers considered here sought to elucidate the ways racism continues to shape national discourses, policies, and social and economic relations in each country.[6]

Akomfrah's formulation of "digitopia" offers a way to work within, but against, liberal multiculturalist cultural politics. For him, the history of debate, analysis, experimentation, and failure within analogue media forms, such as film and analogue video, raises the possibility that those forms might support anti-racist and/or Black media practices and points toward what he calls a "digitopic desire" or a "digitopic yearning" that haunts analogue media praxis.[7] Akomfrah argues that such a "digitopia," perceptible throughout film history, anticipates today's digital media technologies without being fulfilled by them. He offers three different "conceptual tyrannies that set the discursive boundaries" for his interest in the digital. First, Black filmmakers' debates, disruptions, and innovations in the face of the inherent biases of available film stock is an element of the "conceptual tyranny" he calls "the image of self obsession" (which can be understood as an investment in representational politics). Second is a "tyranny of propriety" that centered on rhythm and posited that "to be truly great, black art needed to" be like Black music (indicating an investment in authenticity). The third is "the postcolonial screen debate," which included political investments in culture, the image, and its relationship to history, such as those of Third Cinema and the decolonization projects of people like Amilcar Cabral and Léopold Senghor (this might also fall under the rubric of the "politics of aesthetics," but Akomfrah's classification offers a helpful historical marker). According to Akomfrah, there is a sense in which "all critiques of the cinematic apparatus are by default and implication a utopian call for the post-chemical, the digital which is to come."[8]

For Akomfrah, digital film technologies solve many of the problems identified in the scholarship about and artistic production of Black cinema, which are informed by these three paradigms (or "tyrannies"): an investment in representational politics and their adjudication, an investment in authenticity, and an assessment of the politics of aesthetics. Regarding the first "tyranny"—that of representation: because a digital film involves much less capital than a celluloid film and is less cumbersome than videotape, its accessibility makes possible a wider range of representations. In regard to the second—the investment in making Black film more like Black music: since digital filmmakers can take more footage for less cost, and more easily access a wide variety of editing and post-production tools, they can experiment more with making Black art closer to Black music. Finally, regarding what Akomfrah calls "the postcolonial screen debate": digital cinema has the potential to revolutionize the mode of production of images, and thereby fulfill a dream of Third Cinema, by making it possible for anyone with an iPhone and editing software to make a film.

I am less invested in "the digital" as marking a change from one type of recording technology to another, and more interested in what thinking with and against "the digital" opens and/or forecloses vis-à-vis the cinematic. This is because I understand "the cinematic" as involving not only the audiovisual technologies through which the cinematic continues to be produced and maintained as our commonly perceived reality, but also the sociopolitical and cultural processes through which we perceive what appears in any present thing. Debates about the disappearance of cinema's indexical qualities (which seemingly were secured through the logics of analogue media technologies) are of interest here because they point to the emergent logics of the digital regime of the image as they might be perceived in the technologies of media production. Yet, these recent debates within film theory largely overlook how, throughout the history of cinema, as Alice Maurice has recently explained, film technologies have been imbricated with racial epistemologies. As I have argued elsewhere, the history of the debates about Black images attests to the fact that the production of those images refutes the logics of "profilmic reality" on which predominant theories of film's indexical nature have relied.[9]

In Black film production, elements of the cinematic are intensified in the digital regime of the image.[10] As Akomfrah points out, attending to what the digital makes more widely perceptible within the cinematic might simultaneously allow for new assessments of analogue media along different historical, theoretical, and analytical lines than those cinema and media scholars have pursued to date. These could include paying more sustained attention to the transformation from disciplinary societies to societies of control, as I do in the next chapter. At the same time, predilections of the analogue regime of the image continue in the digital.[11]

The propositions with which Akomfrah ends his essay suggest how attending to the logics of the digital in film and media studies might support the production of alternate histories of cinema and a renewed attention to the imbrication of cinema and power. He writes:

BLACK CINEMA | 123

Once you begin to work with the immediate retrievals that the digital allows, you can begin to construct all sorts of new histories. When one brings diaspora and cinema together, it seems to me that one can come up with a completely new sense not simply of what is cinema but how one might define it. It makes it perfectly possible not to start with Méliès but with Jeremy Bentham's panopticon, made so famous by Michel Foucault; it would be a definition of cinema which would start with how cinema from the 1890s was somehow implicated in a kind of biopolitics, with colonial film; you could look at its Eugenic moment by looking at all the cinematic travelogues in which the black body was not simply the object of fascination but also a certain squeamish disquiet; *The Birth of a Nation* would thus make complete sense in this genealogy.[12]

While Akomfrah's proposed genealogy of film takes flight from attending to the "immediate retrievals the digital allows," focusing on questions raised by a perceptible Black existence within the cinematic means not only that another legitimate history of cinema can be written, but also that relationships between Black existence and technology emerge as central considerations no matter at what point in the history of the cinematic one focuses.

Akomfrah reads the preoccupation with the technologies of media-making within the history of Black film praxis as a yearning for today's digital technologies. As I argue throughout the present chapter, digital media technologies, like the analogue ones to which they are related, raise a series of issues about the ongoing centrality of technology, technics, and technē to Black existence. Rather than fulfilling a promise made and broken by celluloid and other analogue media technologies, digital media intensifies cinematic elements by making them more broadly perceptible. In other words, it is most fruitful to engage with the emergence of new media technologies as part of the transformations occurring within the cinematic, rather than as a break from the cinematic.[13] By conceptualizing new media within the dynamics and logics of the cinematic, we may find that insights generated about and through earlier media can inform engagements with today's new media and vice versa. As I mentioned previously, the emergence of new media technologies within cinematic reality can also be understood as part of a broader shift, perceptible in many other arenas in addition to cinema and media, from disciplinary societies to "societies of control" (as Gilles Deleuze refers to them) and the regimes of the image through which societies of control maintain and reproduce themselves.

"The Data Thief," Algorithmic Editing, and the Database of Human History

Akomfrah's 1995 documentary film *The Last Angel of History* illustrates many of the points he makes in "Digitopia and the Spectres of Diaspora," his 2007 keynote. *The Last Angel of History* is one of many films that Akomfrah shot on Digibeta tape in the 1990s. The film focuses on the sonic aspects of Afrofuturism, especially music, and the geographical, industrial, political, and philosophical logics that have informed their production. It also frames a discussion of literary production, particularly the queer work of Octavia Butler and Samuel Delany (though it does not engage with their queerness per se), as well as issues concerning space exploration, including the significance of the first Black astronaut in outer space and the fictional character from *Star Trek*, Lieutenant Uhura (as portrayed by Nichelle Nichols). I engage *The Last Angel of History* here to flesh out Akomfrah's concept of "digitopia," as well as to highlight how the film itself might be situated at a crossroads between formulations of "Black futures" and their relationships to technē in the transition from liberal multiculturalist logics of governance within control societies to neoliberal multicultural ones.

The Last Angel of History provides a glimpse into the cultural formation known as Afrofuturism as it was articulated in the late 1980s and early 1990s. In addition to giving filmic expression to Afrofuturism as a dynamic cultural formation currently experiencing revitalization and transformations, *The Last Angel of History* itself is a creative Afrofuturist enactment insofar as it relates Black existence to technology through cinema. Coming to us today as a digital signal, *The Last Angel of History* exists as, among other things, an audiovisual index of the power relations in its time and as an aesthetic artifact (displayed, for example, in galleries and projected on computer screens via the recently released DVD distributed by Icarus Films).

While *The Last Angel of History* centers issues of Black existence, Black culture, and science and technology, the film's formal characteristics as well as the specific contexts of its production and circulation tap into the aesthetics and logics of computational, database-driven media. For example, a sequence at the beginning of the film experiments with what might be called "algorithmic" editing styles, through which any image can be inserted into or combined with another. As I discuss in greater detail later in this chapter, a character from the film, the "data thief," animates the processes through which images from the database of "human history" can be cut, selected, and framed according to an algorithm that celebrates the intersection of Black history and technē. We can see the computation and database logics in the "data thief's" access to the range of images, histories, and narratives about the past. In this regard, the "data thief" is a character through which *The Last Angel of History* layers associations between audiovisual images from disparate times and geographical locations to reveal a commonality between filmmaking and computation. If, as D. Fox Harrell points out, "computers can improvisationally and dynamically combine media elements in new ways, at the same time as responding to user interaction," then within the world of *The Last Angel of History* the data thief might be understood as an expression of a human/computer interface from the film's future, who responds to the film's present by offering novel combinations of digital archival images.[14] In a quick succession of images, including sounds, the data thief invokes a present that, to reference the text from which Akomfrah takes the title of the film (Walter Benjamin's "*Theses on the Philosophy of History*"), "comprises the entire history of mankind in an enormous abridgment."[15]

Referring specifically to the computer's ability to combine elements in new ways, Harrell explains: "This process always involves both human interpretation of meaning and the limited types of formal symbol manipulation possible on a computer. . . . Such meaning construction processes also underlie many uses of the computer for expressive purposes."[16] With this in mind, it might be said that *The Last Angel of History* offers a cinematic meditation on the extent to which what Wendy Hui Kyong Chun refers to as "programmed visions" shape in advance the futures imagined through the Afrofuturism of the documentary's day.[17] While the range of possibilities for formal symbolic manipulation, as well as the digital archive of "human history," are limited to what has been programmed into them, the combinations cut, selected, and framed by the data thief in response to present concerns may still involve elements of surprise. For, there is more in any present image than we commonly perceive, and any act of perception involves a creative element.[18] The past appears with every present, harboring dimensions of itself that might challenge what already has been perceived about it.

Referencing Benjamin's influential essay "Theses on the Philosophy of History" in its title, *The Last Angel of History* presents the data thief as a figure from the future who haunts the documentary's present. An angel of history, he "would like to stay, awaken the dead and make whole what has been smashed."[19] As the *last* angel of history, he animates a temporality in which the past in general exists as a reservoir of potential presents, futures lying in wait, now. The film's present is his distant past, and he arrives to redeem it. In "Theses on the Philosophy of History," Benjamin states:

> The past carries with it a temporal index by which it is referred to redemption. There is a secret agreement between past generations and the present one. Our coming was expected on earth. Like every generation that preceded us, we have been endowed with a weak messianic power, a power to which the past has a claim. That claim cannot be settled cheaply.[20]

The data thief haunts the present from the future. He is a messianic figure whose coming is expected in that present—who is, in Benjamin's words, "man enough to blast open the continuum of history."[21] Indeed, *The Last Angel of History* is celebratory of and optimistic about the possibilities that reside at the intersections of techno-culture and Black masculinity. The *last* angel of history's ability to stay and awaken the dead hinges on his understanding the techno-culture of the film's day and the cultural commodities put into circulation within that culture, which evidence the progress that propelled him back in time. Eschewing the dynamic, progressive gender politics articulated elsewhere in the Afrofuturist cultural productions and scholarship of the 1990s, this last angel of history weathers the storm of progress, redeeming the techno-culture of the 1980s and 1990s as progressive.[22]

The opening seconds of the film posit an any-space-whatever, characterized by buildings partially submerged in water and a digitally washed-out color palette, and offer bars from the recording of the song "Me and the Devil," as sung by legendary Bluesman Robert Johnson. After a few seconds, a narrator's voice, one of the sounds he emits, becomes audible along with Johnson's singing. Then, from some elsewhere, the narrator's body suddenly appears on the side of the frame via a jump cut, revealing a different segment of the any-space-whatever from the film's opening. *The Last Angel of History* thus begins with a marvelous diasporic audio-visual portrayal of a crossroads—a song legendary in Black diasporic history, an any-space-whatever, and a story-teller, pulled into the frame via a jump cut, who ties together the film's seemingly disjointed spatio-temporal organization by naming it "the crossroads" of the deep South.

In a subtle British English accent, the storyteller relates the story of Robert Johnson, who "sold his soul to the devil at the crossroads of the deep South" in exchange for a "secret of a Black technology, a Black secret technology that we know to be now as the Blues." The story-teller and various spaces of the crossroads are framed from different perspectives through a series of jump cuts as he further conveys that "the Blues begat Jazz. The Blues begat Soul. The Blues begat Hip-Hop. The Blues begat R&B." Disjointed images rapidly fill the frame as the music fades and machine-like, whirling sounds become perceptible.

On "Race as Technology": Technē and Black Existence

The concept of the Blues as a Black secret technology foregrounds the historical role of sound and music in Black culture and places the film's engagement with technology in the realm of technē. It calls attention to the intimate relationships between the history of Black existence and questions concerning technology, and how Black music historically has functioned as a mode through which to "bring forth" alternative possibilities and conceptions of the world. Technē as "bringing forth" refers to what is perhaps the most well-known statement about modern technology among students and scholars of film and media studies, written by one of the most controversial and influential philosophers of the twentieth century, Martin Heidegger. In "The Question Concerning Technology," Heidegger begins by explaining that the essay will involve "questioning concerning technology," because, as he puts it, "questioning builds a way" of thinking.[23] Heidegger is interested in part in how "technology" endures.[24] Introducing a "questioning concerning technology" that "opens our human existence to the essence of technology," Heidegger addresses a set of questions raised by modern technologies, arguing, somewhat famously, that "the essence of technology is by no means anything technological."[25]

Heidegger uses the concept technē to bring questioning concerning technology into the terrain of truth, rendering technology a form of revealing akin to art. Calling attention to the relationship between technē and poiēsis in the work of Plato, Heidegger claims:

> It is of utmost importance that we think bringing-forth in its full scope and at the same time in the sense in which the Greeks thought it. Not only handcraft manufacture, not only artistic and poetical bringing into appearance and concrete imagery, is a bringing-forth, poiēsis. Physis also, the arising of something from out of itself, is a bringing-forth, poiēsis. Physis is, indeed poiēsis in the highest sense. For what presences by means of physis has the bursting open belonging to bringing-forth, e.g., the bursting of a blossom into bloom, in itself (en heauto ī). In contrast, what is brought forth by the artisan or the artist, e.g., the silver chalice, has the bursting open belonging to bringing-forth not in itself, but in another (en allo ī), in the craftsman or artist.[26]

Positing technology in relationship to poiēsis, Heidegger explains how technology is like poetry, and both are technē. Heidegger explains (pointing out that the word "technology" stems from tecknikon in Greek), "Technikon means that which belongs to technē. We must observe two things with respect to the meaning of this word. One is that technē is the name not only for the activities and skills of the craftsman, but also for the arts of the mind and the fine arts. Technē belongs to bringing-forth, to poiēsis; it is something poietic."[27] For Heidegger, philosophy, or "the arts of the mind," as well as the fine arts, are ways of "bringing forth" or "presencing." Reintroducing technē's etymological relationship to poiēsis (and to physis), Heidegger ontologically and epistemologically reframes technology. He writes, "The question concerning technology is the question concerning the constellation in which revealing and concealing, in which the coming to presence of truth, comes to pass."[28]

Heidegger cites German poet Friedrich Hölderlin as exemplary of the temporality of such modes of bringing forth. For Hölderlin, as for Hegel and Heidegger, that temporality relies upon a coherent past, present, and future in which art and philosophy work from the rootedness of their own time; yet, as Angelica Nuzzo explains, poets in their specific activity come to their time "always too late."[29] "Poetry comes 'too late,'" Nuzzo explains, "because it comes after all practical solutions to the contradictions of the historical present have been attempted (and have often failed). It is precisely this late-coming that allows poetry to present a poetic or indeed poiētic solution; however, this solution lives in the different 'element' provided by aesthetic intuition and imagination."[30] Based on her reading of Hegel, and of Heidegger's philosophy of poetry and the fine arts, Nuzzo poses what she calls a "renewal" of the question she understands them to have been asking: namely, "What are poets for in destitute times?" For today's destitute times, Nuzzo follows Heidegger's thought, which, in her reading, posits history as "the history of metaphysics from Parmenides to Nietzsche with its oblivion and concealment of Being and its event . . . a history that is fundamentally linked to the question regarding the essence of technology, the danger produced by the obliteration of this question, and the possibility of a salvation met perhaps precisely with and in the most radical danger; but is also linked to the rise of political totalitarianism in the first half of the twentieth century."[31]

Indeed, Heidegger's work can be situated within a longer history of racism that is foundational to German idealism; the link between Heidegger's *Dasein* or "Being," his questioning concerning technology, and the rise of political totalitarianism, especially in the form of Nazism, cannot be easily dismissed as mere coincidence. The publication of Heidegger's *Black Notebooks* in 2014 feeds an ongoing debate about the centrality and inextricability of Nazism and anti-Semitism to Heidegger's thinking throughout his oeuvre. Christian Fuchs, for example, has argued that the *Black Notebooks* make it clear that Heidegger's philosophical contribution to Western thought disseminates anti-Semitism into the mainstream of Western philosophy, which has implications for film and media studies because of how influential Heidegger's writing about technology has been in those fields.[32]

As James A. Snead, Ronald A. T. Judy, and many others have demonstrated, Kant's and Hegel's ontologies of Being rely upon a conceptualization of "the African" as the "Other" on which Being relies for it ontological coherence over time.[33] The staggering implications of the revelation that Heidegger's work brings forth the racist anti-Semitism that has informed German idealist philosophy is indeed cause to pause and consider how to, as Jürgen Habermas put it, "think with Heidegger against Heidegger," or find another way to address the racism of German idealist philosophy.[34] Such critical reflections, however, must not leave German idealism's anti-Blackness intact by focusing solely on the anti-Semitism in Heidegger's Nazism. Rather, the ongoing revelations about and critical assessments of Heidegger's Nazism might anchor a more thoroughgoing assessment of German idealism's racism. Many scholars, activists, artists, and other intellectuals have already contributed to anti-racist engagements that significantly recalibrated and intervened into the authority of German idealist philosophy. It is precisely the inextricability of Heidegger's questioning concerning technology from his anti-Semitism and from German idealism's anti-Black and other forms of racism that might trouble easy assessments of "the coming to presence of truth" that constitutes technē's ontological and epistemological underpinnings.[35]

Through its description of the Blues as "a Black secret technology," its interest in electronic music and spaceships, and its presentation of the data thief's affinity for "technogadgets" and audiovisual archives, The Last Angel of History explores a set of relationships between Black people, Black culture, technology, and technē. A documentary released seven years after The Last Angel of History, Afro@Digital (directed by Balufu Bakupa-Kanyinda, 2003), features an interview with Akomfrah in which he articulates deep connections between the logics of the digital and those of early African tools. In both cases, one of the important interventions involves debunking the myth that Africans are pre-technological. As Alexander G. Weheliye and others have argued, a consideration of sound technologies plays an important role in the embrace of technology and technē by those who were actively forming the first wave of Afrofuturist cultural and intellectual production during the 1980s and 1990s.[36]

In this chapter and the next, I push these insights further by engaging with recent scholarship, some of which draws on Heidegger, which formulates "race as technology" to argue that attending to Black existence as it is perceptible within the digital regime of the image opens onto a different formulation of "being" than Heidegger's, and at the same time reveals historical imbrications of Black existence, technology, technē, and speculation. *The Last Angel of History* was produced in the midst of transformations that characterize societies of discipline shifting to those of control. The film therefore does not fully appreciate the ways that the Afrofuturism it celebrates also offers itself up for capture by mechanisms of control. The film's version of Afrofuturism does so through its insistence on Black representation as a way to redeem Euro-American technoculture, and through its moments of complicity with a mode of speculation and futurity that, as Kodwo Eshun points out and as I discuss in more detail in the introduction to this book, also animates corporate futures scenarios as profit-maximizing enterprises.[37] Still, Akomfrah's articulation of "digitopia" subsequent to his creative work in the 1990s might be understood retrospectively as a predecessor of a notion of "race as technology" along the lines offered in Beth Coleman's foundational essay, "Race as Technology."

In that essay, Coleman argues for an understanding of race as prosthesis, algorithm, genomic data, and tool.[38] She offers a way of thinking with(in) racial difference that posits "race" as technē. She writes:

> In extending the function of technē to race, I create a collision of value systems. In this formulation, race exists as if it were on par with a hammer or a mechanical instrument; denaturing it from its historical roots, race can then be freely engaged as a productive tool. For the moment, let us call "race as technology" a disruptive technology that changes the terms of engagement with an all-too-familiar system of representation and power.[39]

The proposition that race can be engaged as a productive tool responds to what, in another context, Herman Gray identifies as "a 'waning' in what a cultural politics of representation can yield."[40] Although, as I discuss below, Coleman's specific formulation of "race as technology" emerges in the post–civil rights era in the United States (in the context of a conservative revanchist effort to reverse any material consequences of formal racial equality), its broader historical context is what I have presented in earlier chapters, following Deleuze, as a transition to societies of control facilitated in part by the emergence of a "digital regime of the image" within the cinematic. To invoke a different, but related, analysis, "race as technology" also can be understood as a response to what Melamed calls "neoliberal multiculturalism."[41]

The confluence of neoliberal multiculturalism as a mode of governance with a virulent anti-Black racism that maintains the socioeconomic relations based in white supremacy indicates that analytics that rely upon "race," "representation," "difference," "recognition," and "power" must be recalibrated. Gray diagnoses the situation when he writes:

> Today "the recognition of social difference" allies with a conception of the modernist subject and practices of government where the free market reigns and self-governance provides for collective and individual needs of the population. The object of recognition is the self-crafting entrepreneurial subject whose racial difference is the source of brand value celebrated and marketed as diversity; a subject whose very visibility and recognition at the level of representation affirms a freedom realized by applying a market calculus to social relations. This alliance of social, technological, and cultural fields constitutes a new racial regime—the shift from race to difference—and the recognition and visibility on which it depends is a form of power. This newly realized social visibility and cultural recognition is a form of power that regulates and manages through appeals to identifications with styles of life tied to identities based on difference.[42]

Gray's assertion that an "alliance of social, technological, and cultural fields constitutes a new racial regime" today might also be understood as a shift not only from "race to difference," as Gray describes it, but also within the valuation and deployment of racial differences themselves. If, for example, "Black," "white," and other racial designations have indexed biological difference in ways that historically anchored power hierarchies (keeping in mind that there always were exceptions that themselves authorized the rule), today their correlation to socioeconomic power hierarchies is underwritten by the renewed significance of those differences as themselves generative of Capital and the modes of governance through which capital accumulates. Furthermore, recall Lawrence Grossberg's argument (discussed in the introduction), that "what is frequently dismissed as branding and niche-marketing signals a radical restructuring of value beyond our capacity to measure it. The result is, apparently, a situation of the increasing sense of the unpredictability of value itself."[43] Taken together, Gray's diagnosis of a "new racial regime" and Grossberg's assertion that the very things constitutive of this new regime signal "a radical restructuring of value beyond our capacity to measure it" indicate that "race as technology" is becoming available at the same time that transformations in the realm of representation are affecting our ability to narrate, assess, and intervene in how certain matter comes to matter more than other matter.

The understanding of "mattering" here can be grasped in the context of work by Karen Barad, who, trained as a physicist, brings insights of quantum physics to bear on the philosophical issues of consequence in the humanities today, and vice versa. For her, "matter" can be understood "as a dynamic and shifting entanglement of relations, rather than as a property of things."[44] In much the same way that my earlier work's formulation of "cinematic reality," adapted from Deleuze's work on cinema, insists that material relations are imbricated with, and therefore inseparable from, those technologies that have been assumed to "represent" or "mediate" reality, Barad's influential theory of agential realism "rejects the notion of a correspondence relation between words and things and offers in its stead a causal explanation of how discursive practices are related to material phenomena."[45] According to Barad, "Matter is neither fixed and given nor the mere end result of different processes. Matter is produced and productive, generated and generative. Matter is agentive, not a fixed essence or property of things. Mattering is differentiating, and which differences come to matter, matter in the iterative production of different differences."[46]

An ontological understanding that situates "apparatuses" as part of the material world is key to Barad's account of how certain phenomena come to matter epistemologically, and therefore also socially, politically, culturally, and ethically. In Barad's terms, "apparatuses are specific material reconfigurings of the world that do not merely emerge in time but iteratively reconfigure spacetime matter as part of the ongoing dynamism of becoming."[47] In a universe in which "matter's dynamism is generative not merely in the sense of bringing new things into the world but in the sense of bringing forth new worlds, of engaging in an ongoing reconfiguring of the world," apparatuses are "boundary-making practices."[48] If, in Barad's terms, matter's dynamism carries a sense of "bringing forth new worlds" and "apparatuses are the material conditions of possibility and impossibility of mattering; they enact what matters and what is excluded from mattering,"[49] then, in our terms here, techně is a mode of bringing forth within a reality whose boundaries are (still) being adjudicated through the cinematic apparatus and the conditions of possibility and impossibility it brings forth.[50]

By thinking the disparate theories of Heidegger's techně, Barad's agential realism (based on quantum physics—that is, *physis*), Simondon's theory of the transindividual (discussed in chapter 1), and a delineation of cinema as an "apparatus" (in Barad's terms and keeping intact the term's meaning in classical film theory) together, there emerges a way to engage matter as dynamic, creative, and, to invoke Barad's terms, agential, and material relations as themselves open and processual within a temporality whose future is open. For Barad, matter's dynamism is such that "particular possibilities for (intra-)acting exist at every moment, and these changing possibilities entail an ethical obligation to intra-act responsibly in the world's becoming, to contest and rework what matters and what is excluded from mattering."[51] Theories of affect and affectivity that conceptualize "the cinematic" can be understood in Barad's terms as acknowledging that a kind of agency is dispersed throughout matter; the cutting and framing particular to the cinematic apparatus (through which what I have called "cinematic reality" becomes commonly perceptible) is thus "intra-active." What matter comes to matter and how it matters is a dynamic intra-action within matter.

If neoliberal multiculturalism involves, in Gray's words, a "waning in what a cultural politics of representation can yield," then a formulation of "race as technology" might offer another way to grasp the centrality of race as part of "the material conditions of possibility and impossibility of mattering" within cinematic reality, as well as how we might recalibrate

what matters and what is excluded from mattering vis-à-vis race. A formulation of "race as technology" offers a way to conceptualize the possibilities for materialist anti-racist praxis that still inhere in the cinematic.
Similar to Heidegger's technē, however, "race as technology" is also
forged in a crucible of violence and carries that context with it. "Race
as technology" becomes perceptible to Coleman, for example, through
then-Senator Barack Obama's 2008 "More Perfect Union" speech, which
exemplified the consolidation of neoliberal multiculturalism's hegemony
and successfully severed the material conditions organized by race from
the power of modes of official racial representation and recognition to
effectively redress them. Coleman formulated "race as technology" to
describe Obama's neoliberal multicultural severing of race from material conditions, which, in Melamed's words, seemed to "have fatally limited the horizon of social possibility for overcoming racism to U.S.-led
global capitalism."[52] As we shall see, in Coleman's analysis, the figure of
"the Black" threatens to evade control. It raises a series of questions and
provocations to the ontological and epistemological authority of the logics of neoliberal multiculturalism.

Highlighting the extent to which thinking "race as technology" itself
involves a reconsideration of temporality, aesthetics, and subjectivity,
Coleman turns to James Snead's essay "Repetition as a Figure of Black
Culture" at the end of her own. In that essay, Snead engages with the
temporality of Hegel's construction of Being, primarily as it is offered in
Phenomenology of Spirit as a teleological progression through different
phases in what might be understood as a history of German consciousness.[53] For Coleman, Snead's essay calls attention to the emergence of a
"mobile agent, whose lightness enables his or her being not to be mired
entirely in traditional historical constructions."[54] As race becomes recognizable as a "tool" or a "prosthesis," "the mobile agent" who emerges
within this conjuncture has, Coleman suggests, a capacity to evade "traditional historical constructions," however fleetingly and precariously.
Indeed, Coleman is interested in the ways that constructions of "race"
have been historically mobilized to achieve certain ends in various relationships to power.[55] Taking Obama's 2008 speech "A More Perfect
Union" as a point of departure, Coleman states her interest in moving
"race away from the biological and genetic systems that have historically dominated its definition toward questions of technological agency.

Technological agency speaks to the ways by which external devices help us navigate the terrain in which we live."[56]

While Coleman is careful to acknowledge that race has been used as a tool of subjection, she is also interested in explaining that a different organization of power vis-à-vis race becomes perceptible in how Obama wields "race." She writes: "Working essentially against the ocular 'proof' of race, Obama, in his Philadelphia address, presented a particularly American oratory that brands race as the familial (as a characteristic of the 'American family') and as a tool he would enlist toward societal change."[57] In other words, Coleman turns to a formulation of "race as technology" to describe the transformations Grossberg notes, and that Gray and Melamed understand to be part of neoliberalism, and sees in those transformations a set of possibilities for recalibrating "race."

Several recent studies have centered on the complex ways Black culture sits within these transformations.[58] In Snead's essay, originally published in 1981, "Black culture" is a spatial as well as a temporal proposition. It has been constructed in conjunction with a geopolitical interest in differentiating the "Occident" from both the "Orient" and "the African." That Coleman's provocative "postscript" brings Snead's essay into a conversation about "race as technology" calls attention to how the formulation of "race as technology" has spatiotemporal and aesthetic implications, as well as carrying significance for potentially reconceptualizing contemporary subjectivity.

The Last Angel of History seeks to excavate such potential through its engagement with Black culture as technē. As I have elucidated, the data thief figure structures a messianic time, through which the documentary argues for the redemptive capacity of technologies (the Blues, electronic music hardware, spaceships, and so on) vis-à-vis Black Atlantic culture. The data thief figure works with the archive of Black diasporic history as a "digital referent." In this context, Akomfrah's claims about the salience of 1968 and the 1960s in general as digital signals point to the presence of another organization of things within the cinematic. For Akomfrah, as stated in the epigraph at the beginning of the chapter, they seem to "hold out the promise of a life that can be located outside the tyranny of time."[59] He clarifies that the films from the late 1980s and 1990s to which he refers "seem to be charged by this desire to realign what one could thematize as the relation between character, location, and temporality," thereby holding out "the possibility that there might be something outside the pre-givens of time." Because of this, Akomfrah describes them as "profoundly digitopic gestures, which carry with them both the promise and the impasse of the digital."[60]

Though in his brief remarks Akomfrah does not elaborate on these points (indeed, he offers them with the caveat "there is another dimension to digitopia that I don't have time to develop here but would like to touch on briefly"), the spatiotemporal logics of "digitopia" make "the utopian" immanent to "the digital," rather than positing a utopian "no place" or a "non-place" that can transcend the present messy and sticky organization of things. Thereby conforming to the usual logics of utopian thought and praxis, "digitopia" understands the work of the digital to involve an unmooring of spatiotemporal logics (which has been described in film studies in various ways, including the proposition of wrenching the index from its referent), which, in turn, opens a possibility that there is no outside to the digital image. It might be said that there is no inside to it either; within the logics of the digital, remaining distinctions between "outside" and "inside" collapse. Lingering logics of the image tethered to analogue media are reworked with(in) the digital regime of the image. And vice versa, if only in retrospect. As with Deleuze's "new image," digital images "are the object of a perpetual reorganization."[61] Like ideology, but of a different order, they seem to constitute no outside for themselves; they include everything within their purview, and, at the same time, they are nothing but outside.[62] They create their own blind spots, and constantly seek to incorporate those within their logics. As I discuss in the following chapter, Coleman's shadowy figure, "the Black," lies there in wait. Yet, not still, yearning toward a different organization of things, incommensurable with the logics and violences of straight times operating today, moving now.

If *The Last Angel of History* portends neoliberal multiculturalism by seeking to redeem the Euro-American technoculture of the 1980s and 1990s from the logics that would deny its potential political force, the film to which I now turn is a more recent example of what can be understood as a database film, characterized by an algorithmic editing style. It was produced in the mid-2010s, during the phase of racial capitalism that Melamed characterizes as "neoliberal multiculturalism," a mode of governance that severs the material conditions organized by race from the power of official racial representation and recognition to effectively redress them. As I have argued throughout this chapter with recourse to Gray's recent scholarship, the confluence of neoliberal multiculturalism as a mode of governance with a virulent anti-Black racism that maintains the socioeconomic relations based in white supremacy indicates that analytics that rely on "race," "representation," "difference," "recognition," and "power" must be recalibrated. Accordingly, the algorithms in the film I discuss below, Arthur Jafa's seven-minute and thirty-three second film *Love Is the Message, the Message Is Death* (2016), are not driven by redemption, but by what Édouard Glissant has theorized as a "poetics of Relation."

Jafa is the same Arthur Jafa who Akomfrah recalls went to China with Julie Dash in the 1980s in search of Technicolor film stock that would redeem the figure of the Black within the photochemical matrix. While Jafa's cinematography is well known for bringing out and revealing the beauty of the rich textures and skin tones of Black actors in *Daughters of the Dust* (1991) and Spike Lee's film *Crooklyn* (1994), he has been experimenting in his more recent work with ways to counter, or at least complicate, the politics of respectability—or "uplift," as Allyson Nadia Field has characterized it with reference to an earlier period of Black film production—by allowing his spectators to sit with the strangeness or alien-ness of Black people and Black culture alongside those aspects that could more easily be conscripted into respectability or uplift.[63] Jafa's recent work is preoccupied with what in Black American existence has not been made to work in the interest of narratives of national or racial progress. In *Love Is the Message*, Jafa's editing choices suggest that it is precisely these aspects of Black American vernacular culture that harbor a type of wealth that might be felt, if not yet understood, within and through the technologically mediated culture of the late 2010s.

In *Love Is the Message*, Jafa, like the data thief in *The Last Angel of History*, establishes a set of relations between various images and sequences found in the digital archives of human history. Yet, unlike the data thief's editing logic, which achieves a rapid-fire assault on the senses, Jafa's editing algorithm is an audiovisual improvisation within the rhythms, yearnings, tempos, and lyrics of Kanye West's song "Ultralight Beam" from the 2016 album *Life of Pablo*. Jafa's *Love Is the Message, the Message Is Death* is a masterful montage of moving images and sonic expression. Among the primary elements of Jafa's editing algorithm are sets of affinities between kinds of movement, particularly those innovated and/or expressed through bodies of Black folk. Through his editing, he also creates visual and sonic matches between seemingly disparate selections of audiovisual phenomena to create associations and disjunctions between and questions about those phenomena. I use "editing algorithm" to characterize what film studies usually consider to be editing—that is, a film's style or logic of connection that motivates a cut from one shot to another. I call Jafa's editing "algorithmic" to underscore that the aesthetic logic in *Love Is the Message* is enabled by and comments on the digital image's relationship to computation, databases, and commensuration. The operative definition of "algorithm" here is the second one found in the *Oxford English Dictionary*: "a procedure or set of rules used in calculation and problem-solving; (in later use spec.) a precisely defined set of mathematical or logical operations for the performance of a particular task."[64]

One of the tasks of *Love Is the Message* involves working out a cinematic "poetics of Relation" through which one might grasp what Édouard Glissant refers to as "the threatened beauty of the world."[65] Jafa's montage inserts opacity into images of Black bodies in motion in a variety of settings, activities, time periods, and geographic locations. It establishes sets of relations that connect and associate those images, but do not render them equivalent. *Love Is the Message* begins with news footage that went viral in 2013 via YouTube.[66] As Kanye West's song quietly begins in the background, we hear and see Charles Ramsey state, "And she says 'call 9–11. My name is Amanda Berry.' . . . I knew something was wrong when a little pretty white girl ran into a Black man's arms. Something is wrong here. Dead giveaway. Dead giveaway." Ramsey's words carry across Jafa's cut from the news footage of Ramsey to a small basketball arena where the game's audience dances, waving their hands in the air, synchronized. As West's song drowns out other sounds on the soundtrack, the audience and players seem to move along with it—most are recognizable as Black people. As the camera pans the entire court, the players on the court wave their arms and bounce in time with the audience.

The lyrics to "Ultralight Beam" are foregrounded as a voice sings— "I'm tryin' to keep my faith / but I keep lookin' for more"—and Jafa's carefully orchestrated montage of images offer commentary on West's song, its rhythms, melodies, and music, while the music offers its own commentary on the images. A moving image in black and white, a Black woman walking in a robe down an institutional hallway followed by people in uniforms, is followed by a cut to black and white footage of Black men and women, nicely dressed and holding hands, smiling as they move playfully down the street, presumably during a protest march during the civil rights struggles, and then a cut to a young Black boy being carried on someone's shoulders. The boy faces the camera, clapping, smiling, and wearing a big pin with illegible writing on his shirt. The person carrying him holds a hat up in the air as they walk from the right side of the screen to the left. Bayard Rustin, smartly dressed and confident, with rolled up sheets of paper in his hand, moves fluidly toward the right side of the screen, around people who probably are on a speaker's platform. The next cut is to color footage of a dance competition; a Black man dances with impressive elasticity toward the right side of the screen while other Black men cheer. The resolution of this color footage is crisper than the images from the 1960s, and the branding on the image alerts us to the fact that it circulated sometime after the World Wide Web was invented. A quick cut to smartphone footage shows a police officer positioned outdoors, on the right side of the screen. His gun is pointed at a Black man running away from him, to the left side of the screen, so his back faces the officer when the officer shoots him. This is cell phone video of Officer Michael Slager shooting Walter Scott. We see one shot, and then Walter Scott falls. We know from the trial that concluded in 2017 that Slager shot Walter Scott eight times and that this image shows the last minutes of Walter Scott's life. "We're on an ultralight beam. We're on an ultralight beam. This is a God dream. This is a God dream. This is everything." The film continues, creating clusters of association and juxtaposition by matching movement or establishing visual and/or sonic resonances between things. The editing algorithm generates a palpable Whole that cannot be represented or contained.

Many of the images Jafa uses are likely familiar to viewers. They consist of historical footage of famous people or events, sequences from films that have been significant to the history of African American cinema, such as D. W. Griffith's *Birth of a Nation* (1915) and Charles Burnett's *Killer of Sheep* (1978), or digital videos that have gone viral in recent years. There are images of explosions on a planet and other footage of outer space. Some of them, like the color video of the man dancing referenced above, may not be widely familiar, but carry brands or other identifying markers. The color video of the man dancing is branded with "Dance or Go Home," a phone number, and "www.dcole74.com." Some are high-definition footage of sporting events carrying "NBC" or another network's logo. Others are prominently marked: "Getty Images." Some seem to be selfie videos—a young man sings into a camera "I've been dreaming"; a woman is framed in medium close-up on the right side of the screen in what is likely the driver's seat of a car; a toddler dances in the space between the front and backseat of a car; a man's voice can be heard while the face of a very young boy takes up the entire frame. The man tells him, "This is how the police do you," and the boy is instructed to put his hands up against the wall, facing the wall. The boy does as he is told, placing his hands against the wall, and turning around to look into the camera. He is crying.

Sometimes, the soundtrack works associatively—for example, when Minister Louis Farrakhan mentions Mr. Wallace, the film cuts to Christopher George Latore Wallace, aka The Notorious BIG. We get to hear him rap once again. At times, the film coalesces around certain themes to create cinematic ideas, like a visual exploration of Greg Tate's likening of Black existence in the United States to an alien abduction story in the early days of Afrofuturism, and its recent refutation in Martine Syms's "Mundane Afrofuturist Manifesto." This sequence begins when the diegetic sound of a video of Martine Syms reading a line from "The Mundane Afrofuturist Manifesto" disrupts West's song. Staring directly at the camera framed in the center of the screen with a yellow background, Syms says, "The mundane Afrofuturists recognize that we are not aliens," and the statement sparks a montage around the idea that "we are not aliens," which calls its certainty into question through a quick series of visual matches between a blockbuster film alien attacking a city and images of amazing physical feats by Black athletes and expressions by Black performers.[67] Throughout, the film interrogates the continuing resonance of early cinema, particularly *The Birth of a Nation*, and the efforts by filmmakers and others to redress those early images and representations. The mix of images of such wildly different resolution and provenance, such as Getty archival footage, cell-phone video, C-Span footage, and clips from high-definition professional sports broadcasts, calls attention to the status of the digital image and the problems and possibilities of the archive of Black culture.

The temporality that emerges in *Love Is the Message* is not that of redemption, but of radical contingency. The film's temporal mode draws on elements of improvisation (and therefore fulfills a longstanding desire stated by Jafa, Akomfrah, and other Black filmmakers to make Black film more like Black music), but also features sequences characterized by repetition and stasis.[68] By calling attention to scale, *Love Is the Message* returns at various times to an image, an affect, or an idea of what could have not been, but was, or what could have been, but was not.[69]

Love Is the Message is a companion film to Jafa's 2014 film, *Dreams Are Colder than Death*. Indeed, there are references to and images from *Dreams* in *Love Is the Message*, and both films include shots of outer space that raise questions of scale and the (im)possibility of commensuration in the face of Black expressive culture, Black bodies, the vulnerability and pleasures of Black flesh, and the temporal sedimentations that comprise Black existence. Although there are no talking heads in *Dreams*, there are notable intellectuals, artists, and performers who offer insights and commentaries about Blackness that help to direct attention to what might be significant in that film's images, even if any authoritative meaning or reading of that film remains a dynamic operation between the film's audience or spectators and the openness of the cinematic images the film selects, cuts, and frames.

In *Love Is the Message*, however, there is no commentary besides the interplay between the sounds and the images that constitute the short film. There are many ways one can read or interpret *Love Is the Message*, and various anchors through which one may give the film this or that meaning and assign significance to the images it assembles from the digital archives of Black history and culture. Yet, as a cinematic experience, *Love Is the Message* does not invite meaning so much as it makes Black existence resonate within a media ecology in which the accumulated meanings ascribed to and on Black flesh continue to render Black bodies fungible, hypervisible, and legible in ways that reproduce existing power relations. The film is one response to the modes of governance characteristic of neoliberal multiculturalism: it mines the digital archives to assemble a "feel of life" and relies heavily on intertextual references that are likely available to some viewers and not others.[70] It pokes holes in clichéd images, including historical events and people, as it traffics in those clichés. It frustrates attempts to offer an authoritative "reading." By radically decontextualizing certain familiar images of Black people and arranging them in a different affective constellation, *Love Is the Message* interrupts its spectators' habitual reception of these images. With his editing algorithm, Jafa "strives to know the totality of the world yet already knows he will never accomplish this and knows that is precisely where the threatened beauty of the world resides."[71]

Calling attention to scale by, for example, associating images of monumental historical significance, such as those of Martin Luther King Jr., with those that are not easily assimilated into national narratives of Black uplift, respectability, and progress, or, as mentioned previously, by turning at times to a cosmic perspective, *Love Is the Message* gestures to a core of existence and creativity that animates Black existence, a kind of incalculable spiritual core. Jafa's algorithmic editing introduces opacity into the calculations that govern Black life in the early twenty-first century.[72] When high resolution, color, C-Span footage of President Barack Obama singing "Amazing Grace" at an address to an African Methodist Episcopal Church congregation appears in the film, it is sandwiched between shots of D. W. Griffith's paranoid rendering of Reconstruction in *The Birth of a Nation*. The association between these two cinematic and televisual ideas prompts, without resolution, reflection on how Obama's resonant performance of Black racial belonging might function as part of an ongoing calibration of power and white supremacy vis-à-vis race. Similar to Beth Coleman's use of Obama's "More Perfect Union" speech in her essay "Race as Technology," the editing algorithm here uses Obama's performance of "Amazing Grace" at the Black church to raise questions about how race can function in societies of control as a tool for severing the material conditions organized by race from the capacity of modes of official representation and recognition to effectively redress them. The men behind Obama on the stage begin laughing, clapping, and/or standing from their seats as they recognize that the President of the United States of America is standing before them singing "Amazing Grace" with what might be heard as Black vocal inflections. Their enthusiastic, joyful, surprised response underscores the element of surprise and (im)possibility that attended Barack Obama's two terms in office and complicates an easy "reading" of Jafa's association of this event with Griffith's *The Birth of a Nation.*

While Beth Coleman claims that Obama's 2008 address in Philadelphia offers a way to grasp how "race" works as a "prosthesis" in neoliberal multicultural societies of control, *Love Is the Message* reattaches racial difference to a historical accretion of sensible matters, allowing its spectators to re-member the material relations that undergird Black existence and sense the possibilities it harbors. As technē, *Love Is the Message, the Message Is Death* presences a feel of life, making a "poetics of Relation" resonate within and through technologies of control, especially audiovisual technologies. It brings forth a conceptualization of Black American existence over time that includes those who continue to be excluded from the promises and protections of full citizenship in the United States of America.

Rather than pointing to a set of utopian promises for media-making that today's digital media technologies have emerged to fulfill (however unevenly), the renewed focus on questions concerning technology in film and media studies and other related fields suggests that sustained engagements with race and cultural politics can contribute to ongoing efforts to reassess material ontologies of being and the socioeconomic and geopolitical relations they animate in societies of control, precisely because questions of Black existence have long been imbricated with those concerning technology, poiēsis, speculation, and refusal.

4

"Corporate Cannibal"

Risk, Errantry, and Imagination in the Age of Catastrophe

I couldn't sell out, but I created the space for others to be able to make it, without the pressure of being a pioneer. They can play the pioneer without taking the actual risk. Because to take the risk means to never soften enough that you can become truly successful. It means saying no to things that might give you success . . . but not necessarily. I am to this day a radical about not going with the flow. I decided after disco that I would not follow the formula, that I would create something else. If I had followed the crowd, by now I would be as rich as people think I am.
—Grace Jones as told to Paul Morley, *I'll Never Write My Memoirs*

This costume is just a part of the nakedness 'cause how long am I really gonna have it on if someone starts throwing money? If someone likes how I look with this costume on and they want me to take it off and they're throwing the money, I'm gonna have to take it off. So, really I just feel like the nakedness is the uniform. The costume is just the accessary to it, kinda like a bracelet or some earrings."
—Portia Jordan, in *Dreams Are Colder than Death*

A black woman's body was never hers alone.
—Fannie Lou Hamer, as conveyed in Chana Kai Lee, *For Freedom's Sake: The Life of Fannie Lou Hamer*

"Pull Up to the Bumper, Baby"

Let's start with Grace Jones. Grace Jones has been an active and controversial fashion model and performer since the late 1960s. She is perhaps best known for the music she recorded during the 1970s and 1980s, and for her association with the Studio 54 disco scene in New York City, but her performances and likeness have been disseminated across media—including on phonographs, cassette tapes, compact discs, mp3s, and other digital audio formats, on celluloid, television, digital video, and in print. Her career is remarkable, not least for her ability to modulate her star image and celebrity to adapt to and address changing circumstances, trends, languages, and locations by forging new paradigms within and without them. She is an Original.

Jones's innovative performances have been met with varying degrees of commercial success, and, as her epigraph to this chapter attests, she claims not to be driven by its pursuit. An audacious singer with ten studio albums to her name, a gay icon celebrated and fetishized for her black skin and androgynous appearance, she is controversial for several reasons, many of which stem from her collaborations with various white men, most infamously, with Jean-Paul Goude. Many of those collaborations feature an erotic aestheticizing and fetishization of her dark skin. Her performances often highlight the masculine elements of her appearance and personality, and she displays a penchant for masculine clothing. Goude's photograph of her naked in a cage with a piece of raw meat and a sign that reads "Do not feed the animal" still circulates and has influenced other performers. She performed in a "one-man show." She's nurtured an androgynous public persona, inviting confusion about her gender and sexuality in a manner similar to that of other musicians during the 1980s, such as Boy George and Annie Lenox.

Throughout her career, Grace Jones has been embraced as an iconoclastic celebrity and criticized as an unwitting dupe of white European or American men. Her performances often blur the lines between man, woman, and machine, and play with the racial dimensions of distinctions between the human and the animal. Francesca T. Royster asserts about Grace Jones: "She is so fantastic at becoming an object—animal, machine, space invader, multiplying robot, hurricane—that we might not hear her also explaining what it's like to be an object."[1] Jones's performances often explore dimensions of the objectification and fetishization of black skin.

In this chapter, I discuss the music video for Grace Jones's song "Corporate Cannibal," a digital video that draws on the mutability of Jones's star image and is most precisely characterized by "modulation," a term with significance in computation, economics, and culture. My consideration of the cultural commodity "Corporate Cannibal" extends the insights about "race and/as technology" in the previous chapter toward a more sustained consideration of finance capital, computation, race, and gender. I take a cue from an aspect of James A. Snead's essay "Repetition as a Figure in Black Culture" that often is overlooked: his interest in the way repetition functions in economic discourse.

In the first paragraph of that essay, Snead asserts about culture in general: "Transformation is culture's response to its own apprehension of repetition."[2] Snead argues that cultures differ as to whether they tend "to admit or cover up the repeating constituents within them."[3] Schematically speaking, Black culture tends to admit elements of repetition, while European culture strives to cover them up. Each is animated by particular logics regarding how it deals with repetition in terms of "coverage, both in the comforting sense of 'insurance' against accidental and sudden rupturing of a complicated and precious fabric," and in the "less favorable sense of a 'cover-up,' or a hiding of otherwise unpleasant facts from the senses."[4] Snead turns to "insurance" as a metaphor, since culture, like financial futures, builds into its logics a particular stance toward the future: "Like all insurance, this type of coverage does not prevent accidents but promises to be able to provide the means to outlive them."[5] One strand of Snead's argument about the differences between Black and European cultures vis-à-vis repetition focuses on the ontological differences that European Enlightenment humanism (specifically as articulated by Hegel) posited between European culture and Black culture; another turns to economic discourse to differentiate between the two paradigms. Snead argues: "The discourse used of capital in European economic parlance reveals a more general insight about how this culture differs from black culture in its handling of repetition. In black culture, repetition means that the thing circulates (exactly in the manner of any flow, including capital flows) there in an equilibrium. In European culture, repetition must be seen to be not just circulation and flow but accumulation and growth."[6]

The song and video for "Corporate Cannibal" provide an opportunity to engage with both of these trajectories of Snead's argument. My consideration of them here weaves in an acknowledgment of the ontological problems that Black existence raises for European Enlightenment thought with an argument about the economic risks that Black existence poses to capitalist structures of command, even as Black culture has become one of the motors for economic growth.

"I'm a Man-Eating Machine"

My interest in the music video for "Corporate Cannibal" lies in how it makes perceptible an association between Grace Jones's celebrity persona, the allure of her dark skin (which is inseparable from her performances of non-normative genders and the fluctuations of capitalist structures of command characteristic of societies of control and the modulations that characterize them), and her long association with technology. Take one striking example: a 1985 advertisement directed by Goude for the French automobile company Citroën. In that commercial, a massive, automated likeness of Jones's head, sporting a masculine high-top fade haircut, rises out of the desert. The head turns to the side as the mouth slowly opens on a metal hinge. A Citroën CX comes speeding out of the mouth. It becomes clear that Jones is driving the vehicle. Her hands on the steering wheel, she turns toward the camera and opens her mouth to boldly sing "Yeah" three times. The car drives back into the mouth of the massive Grace Jones head. The mouth closes as the head swivels back to face the camera directly. The eyes are made out of a shiny metal. A hand, proportionate to the head, comes up to cover the mouth as if to indicate that it burped after consuming the car. The eyes close and the head sinks back into the desert. This commercial is just one striking example of the manner in which Grace Jones and technology have been associated with each other throughout Jones's career. As in the Citroën car commercial, which was produced specifically for a French market, that association is calibrated for a marketplace that can reward the racially inflected, gender-fucking, artistic risks Jones and her collaborators take with her star image.

In 2008, Jones released *Hurricane*, her first album of new material since 1989. Jones worked with director and engineer Nick Hooker to produce the music video for "Corporate Cannibal," which is the third track on the album. On the album version, the song begins with a segue from the previous track, entitled "Williams Blood," which references Jones's family background and touches on her experience growing up in Jamaica as part of a strict Pentecostal family. The lyrics to "Williams Blood" begin "You can't save me / You can't save a wretch like me." The song includes references to Jones's maternal grandfather, John "Dan" Williams, who was a musician in a dance band in Kingston, Jamaica, during the 1940s. As Jones explains in the first chapter of her memoir, *I'll Never Write My Memoirs*: "There is music in our family that goes back a long time, but the religious element turned their back on music as any kind of pleasing show business or fun."[7] On "Williams Blood," Jones sings:

> Why don't you be a Jones like your Sister and your brother Noel
> When are you gonna be a Jones your just like your Dad
> God bless his soul.

Her assertion throughout the song—"I've got the Williams blood in me"—is affirmed in her memoirs where she writes: "The idea of there being an extroverted, displaced entertainer in the family who made records and got up to wonderful no-good in after-dark exotic nightclubs was much too sleazy a distraction from the all-important church. I, though, must have inherited his rhythmical wanderlust through the blood. His banished energy was transmitted through me."[8]

"Williams Blood" ends with Grace Jones singing:

> Amazing Grace
> how sweet the sound
> that saved a wretch like me.

She sings it straight, as it might sound in many Black churches, but another voice, a distorting echo, not mechanical-sounding but otherworldly, sings it out of time. A listener might consider how the sonic composition plays with the meanings associated with the "Grace" of

Grace Jones and the grace of God referenced in the well-known gospel song that ends "Williams Blood." Then, before the next song, "Corporate Cannibal," begins, a man with a charismatic Black preacher's inflections says: "Praise God . . . come on put your hands together for . . . the Jones clan. Amen. I don't want to say much more but Grace Jones is in the house." Clapping can be heard as the music begins to swell. Then, over the music, Grace Jones says, in a booming, technologically enhanced voice: "Pleased to meet you / Pleased to have you on my plate."

Positioned between two autobiographical songs, "Williams Blood" and "I'm Crying (Mother's Tears)," "Corporate Cannibal" might be read as continuing the commentary on Grace Jones's life. Reading the lyrics to "Corporate Cannibal" allegorically suggests a narrative that spans the first three tracks: the iconoclastic Grace Jones leaves a Pentecostal Christian household in Jamaica and becomes imbricated within the system of corporate cannibalism. Read in this way, it is impossible to differentiate the celebrity "Grace Jones" from the modes of exploitation encapsulated by the song, or to disentangle Jones's complex performances of race, gender, nation, and sexuality from capitalism's capacity to bring everything into its realm of control.

The lyrics to "Corporate Cannibal," Grace Jones's star persona, and the digital effects achieved by Nick Hooker combine to make the video a remarkable work of digital art. With the modulations of the image driven by the song's rhythm, the video for "Corporate Cannibal" menacingly stitches a meditation on digital media aesthetics and Grace Jones's body to the narrative conveyed in the song's lyric—about Capital's ability to capture and devour whatever it encounters, taking it into its body, which in the video also is Grace Jones's electronic, morphing body. According to the lyrics, Jones, a corporate cannibal, is a self-proclaimed "man . . . eating machine." The pause after "man" underscores Jones's insistence on playing with the image of herself as a "man" at certain moments in her career ("I'm a man"). Then, "eating machine" calls to mind a fear of being consumed by a mysterious femininity or an opaque darkness, like "the Dark Continent" itself ("a man-eating machine"). Although these dangers of Black race and non-normative genders resonate throughout, the music video most explicitly dramatizes Capital's generative ability to animate objects and forms, incorporating them into a rhythmic body-machine of desires and appetites.

Steven Shaviro presents Hooker's video as exemplary of what he calls "post-cinematic affect." He describes the video's artistic production process as follows:

> Nick Hooker's video for Grace Jones's "Corporate Cannibal" is in black and white. Or, more precisely, it is just in black. The only images that appear on the screen are those of Jones's face and upper body. These images were captured by two video cameras, in a single take. The director recalls that, at the time of the shoot, Jones had just spent several months in Jamaica; as a result her skin "was intensely black, like dark, dark black." There is no background to contrast with the black of Jones's figure, or with what Hooker calls "the raw glow of her skin." . . . The video was actually shot in colour, with a white wall for background; but in postproduction the director "desaturated the footage . . . and brought up the contrast which made the white wall fall away entirely and consequently enhanced the blackness of her skin." . . . As a result of this treatment, there is literally nothing in the video aside from Jones's skin, her features and her silhouette. Behind her, there is only an empty blankness; it is this absence of any image whatsoever that we see as white.[9]

Hooker relies upon the digital capture and manipulation of Jones's performance and of her dark skin in order to render an image that shifts and mutates on screen. It is clear that Hooker's artistic sensibility, like that of several other men before him, such as, famously, Jean-Paul Goude's, was captivated by what he perceived as the exoticism of Jones's black skin. The video asks us to sit with the potential boundarylessness of Grace Jones's digital image, which at times in the video bleeds out of and perhaps beyond the screen (which is indistinguishable here from the frame), and thus always seems to threaten to overwhelm the white nothingness that surrounds it. The video asks us to consider the allure and danger of Jones's digital image, its power and vulnerability. Although Jones's voice is a sonic driver of the composition, her skin is, as Shaviro explains, the significant visual element. It indexes not only what Shaviro calls the "allure" of Jones's celebrity but also its imbrication with a racialized economy of desire. In that regard, Jones's performance is not unlike Portia Jordan's, the Magic City dancer featured in Arthur Jafa's film *Dreams Are Colder than Death*, quoted in the second epigraph to this chapter. Both Jones and Jordan work with the value of the erotic allure of their nakedness and the risks and rewards therein.

In *Dreams*, Portia Jordan says the clothes she wears while she is working at Magic City in Atlanta, Georgia, are "just a part of the nakedness"; "nakedness" is her work uniform. This keen insight calls our attention to the convergence between skin, flesh, property, and profit. It resonates with insights generated by Nina Simone's version of the song "Ain't Got No / I've Got Life," released in 1968. About that song, Daphne Brooks explains: "In her cover versions of music from the 1967 countercultural musical *Hair*, Simone yokes together two of that show's signature numbers, 'Ain't Got No' and 'I Got Life' to build a new Black anthem—one that can stand alongside her self-authored protest songs from that decade ('Mississippi Goddam,' 'Four Women')."[10] In the second half of 'Ain't Got No / I've Got Life,' after listing in the first half of it all that she ain't got, Simone asks: "What have I got nobody can take away?" With this question, she seeks the fundamental tools for liberation. She sings: "Got my hair, Got my head, Got my brains, Got my ears." She adds: "I've got my boobs. . . . I've got my sex. . . . ," and so on. What she's got are the fundamental elements over which Black feminists continue to struggle—our minds, our bodies, our souls, and our brains—our life energy. She's got the raw material for the production of what Fred Moten, quoting Karl Marx, explains is "wealth." As discussed in the introduction, Marx muses in *The Grundrisse*: "What is wealth other than the universality of individual needs, capacities, pleasures, productive forces, etc., created through universal exchange?" He asks whether it is "the absolute working-out" of "creative potentialities, with no presupposition other than the previous historic development, which makes this totality of development, i.e., the development of all human powers as such the end in itself, not as measured on a predetermined yardstick."[11] She got stewardship over what we all in various ways hold in common.

As if offering an accounting of her assets, in "Ain't Got No / I've Got Life," Simone stridently catalogues what she's got, singing each entry as a confident chant to a persistent rhythm. Her joyful assertion at the end of the song—"I've got life"—re-sounds after the song ends. With these lyrics, Simone narrates her discovery (which is also a recovery) of fundamental political tools. The very elements through which we materialize on this planet—that is, through which we matter (our brains, our tongues, our sex, our necks, our fingers)—are available to invest in building another reality. A wealthy Black feminist reality accrues in the preindividual potential that exists in being, lying in wait, available to be transduced through the structures we are creating together.[12] Individuation draws on this potential, which has been deposited by a shared imagination of Black feminism over time. This can be considered part of what Cedric Robinson describes as the "Black Radical Tradition": "an accretion, over generations, of collective intelligence gathered from struggle."[13] The assets over which any one individual is a steward— brain, tongue, neck, boob(s), finger(s)—are transindividual resources for a distributed, long-haul collective endeavor, a new world breathing here, now, perhaps.[14]

The sequences in Jafa's film featuring erotic dancers from Magic City, "Atlanta's premier Gentleman's Club," depict perceptibly Black female dancers, dimly lit. Some wear dresses; others have their naked breasts visible. They dance in slow motion in a sonic atmosphere that sounds like it has been muted and distorted through temporal manipulation. Portia Jordan, whom viewers have seen dancing in an earlier montage, is introduced through the repetition of an image of her dancing, slowly and suggestively, her body facing the camera and her head and eyes glancing first to one side, then to the other. She doesn't look directly into the camera. Her name and occupation, "Magic City Dancer," appear onscreen. As in the rest of the interviews relayed in *Dreams*, when a voice we believe is Portia Jordan's says over the image, "This costume is just a part of the nakedness 'cause how long am I really gonna have it on if someone starts throwing money? If someone likes how I look with this costume on and they want me to take it off and they're throwing the money, I'm gonna have to take it off. So, really I just feel like the nakedness is the uniform. The costume is just the accessary to it, kinda like a bracelet or some earrings," that voice is not synchronous with the image. The cut-away from the image of Jordan is to a medium close-up of a serving of chicken wings and sauce in a white Styrofoam container. A hand is slowly dipping the wings over and over into the sauce. By slowing down the sounds and images of Magic City, Jafa captures something of the base sensory allure of the place and associates Jordan's commentary about the deployment and value of her nakedness with the consumption of chicken wings and dipping sauce, a favorite and relatively affordable food to accompany a good time.

When Jordan says that, as a dancer at Magic City, her "nakedness" is her "uniform," she highlights how clothing can function as a form of enclosure that delineates public and private elements of any body. If her nakedness is her uniform, Jordan's role as a dancer might be characterized as one in which the boundaries between public and private—the distinction upon which notions of sexual propriety, self-determination, and ownership rest—are precisely where surplus value is generated in the strip club. The sequences shot in Magic City recur throughout *Dreams*. At one point in the film, they are placed into conversation via montage with Saidiya Hartman's insights into the anarchy in Black cultural practices of refusal and the attempts by race leaders in different historical periods to reign in "aesthetical negroes." The sequence featuring Portia Jordan described above includes voice over comments by Melvin Gibbs about how the ideas of "what money is" and of "what value is" are changing because of new technologies.

Through their placement in the film and the choices Jafa made in rendering them onscreen, the sequences shot in Magic City underscore that questions of sexual propriety are intimately connected with those of self-determination, self-definition, and ownership that have been central to Black American existence. These sequences pose questions regarding the differences class and gender make in Black American social and political life. Recurring throughout the film, they point to the condition of boundarylessness (both in the sense of excess and in the sense of an absence of enforceable sovereign boundaries) that, it might be argued, attends every feminine Black American's entry into some mode of legibility.[15] In the face of this, Jordan's insight that her clothing is just an accessory to her uniform, which is her "nakedness," is a profound statement of an alternative to ongoing struggles for ownership of the very elements through which we materialize on this planet.[16] Like the menacing boundarylessness of Grace Jones's digital skin in the music video for "Corporate Cannibal," Jordan's understanding of the role her nakedness plays in Magic City refuses to entertain the injunction that she seize control of her skin and enforce her ownership over it in a way that might be widely recognized as "proper." It is a refusal to posit her flesh as something that can be owned, by herself or by anyone else. As such, it makes possible a different configuration of self, other, and the world than that which demands that someone own each body, and it offers something like stewardship in place of enclosure.

What we recognize today as Black femininity, regardless of the official sex of the body that expresses it, has been a site of the oftentimes violent suturing of individuals to racial collectives over time. This process, as Cedric Robinson has proven, is entangled with the history of capitalism and European nationalism, wherein capitalism remains inseparable from the historical practice of enslaving Africans as legal forms of property, and nationalism is bound up with questions of sovereignty. Although the historical continuity of the identity category "Black women" has been unevenly associated with femininity, the nexus at which Black race meets feminine genders has been significant to the calculus involved in the distribution of property, profit, and power.[17] It is a store of value. The resulting figure, whom we might recognize today as "the Black woman," stitches processes of racialization to those of political economy, and thereby carries a potential to disrupt both.[18] Given this historical condition of Black women, what might it mean to take seriously Fannie Lou Hamer's assertion that "a Black woman's body is never hers alone"?[19] Instead of reinforcing a political stance and rhetoric that insist upon recuperating the historical situation of Black women's boundarylessness into the logics of enclosure, ownership, and privatization, a politics that embraces—as a condition of all enfleshment—the well-documented and much-discussed hypervisibility and heightened publicity of Black women's bodies might follow. Such a politics would demand a society which is bound together through a shared stewardship of all matter.[20]

Grace Jones's appearance is imbricated with these historical issues. The controversies about her participation in racist fantasies and the questions about the extent to which she has controlled her star image over time are pressure points in how her celebrity has navigated racial, national, gender, and sexual norms. Insofar as modulating the digital signal that indexes the star persona "Grace Jones" is a driving aesthetic strategy of the video, one of the questions "Corporate Cannibal" raises is a spatiotemporal one: Is the gendering of a legibly Black presence always yoked to the known past, its potential and significance captured in advance of its appearance as such? Are the forms it might take already anticipated, regardless of how they are modulated? To put the questions raised by "Corporate Cannibal" into a more direct conversation with this book's focus on technology, imagination, and liberation, in what follows I use terms from computer science, theories of ontopoiēsis, technics, and societies of control to ask: to what extent does any "modulation" of the form of appearance of the gendering of Black race already account for the Black feminist reality accruing in preindividual being? And, by extension, where might Black feminist praxis disrupt and/or redirect the modulation away from the reproduction of presently perceptible reality and toward the reality Black feminist praxis is presently assembling?

The concept and technique of "modulation" is a key element in any response to these questions about the video for "Corporate Cannibal." I am using the term "modulation" here in its senses as a technical term in computer science and as a description of a cultural logic with economic dimensions. As Shaviro explains about the music video for "Corporate Cannibal":

> "Corporate Cannibal" is about modulation. . . . Modulation requires an underlying fixity, in the form of a carrier wave or signal that is made to undergo a series of controlled and coded variations. . . . The modulations of "Corporate Cannibal" . . . imply that no matter what happens, it can always be contained in advance within a predetermined set of possibilities. Everything is drawn into the same fatality, the same narrowing funnel, the same black hole. There is no proliferation of meanings, but rather a capture of all meanings. Every event is translated into the same binary code, and placed within the same algorithmic grid of variations, the same phase space.[21]

Nick Hooker used digital video's capacity for modulation as an underlying aesthetic logic for a music video that seeks to capitalize on the allure of Grace Jones's black skin. For Shaviro, Hooker's choice means that the film can be read as being itself about modulation and that the meanings and events that might be generated through the modulations of the rendering of Jones's skin in the video are accounted for already. Shaviro argues that in "Corporate Cannibal," "Nick Hooker does not manipulate Jones's image, so much as he modulates, and actively recomposes, the electronic signals that she already is, and whose interplay defines the field of her becoming."[22] He therefore reads Jones's skin in the image as embodying "capital unbound" because Grace Jones has become "a pure electronic pulse. Just as the groundless figures of digital video are no longer tied to any indexical referents, so too the endlessly modulating financial flows of globalised network capitalism are no longer tied to any concrete processes of production."[23] Shaviro invokes Deleuze's notion that "a man [sic] is no longer a man confined but a man in debt" and claims that in the face of a foreclosure on the future we are experiencing a "fundamental failure of the imagination" because "we don't seem to be able to come up with anything concrete that would be independent of the logic of financial flows."[24] Shaviro and others read this as cause for despair because it means "the future" is merely a repetition of what exists—it is a modulation of the present (which is a mediation of the past); in this formulation the future has already been pre-mediated (to use Richard Grusin's word). It has been "accounted for, counted and discounted, in advance."[25]

Yet, this assessment of the situation misses the ways in which Jones's black skin indexes an incalculable debt that cannot be repaid.[26] This is one of the reasons why Alessandra Raengo can read Jones's image in "Corporate Cannibal" (and indeed what she calls "Blackness" more broadly) in terms of the money form.[27] Like money, the modulated digital image of Jones's black skin in the music video for "Corporate Cannibal" circulates as a mediation of social relations. In this case, those are relations historically managed through the production and reproduction of Black race or, to put this another way, through race as technology.

In this regard, "Corporate Cannibal" is an aesthetic accounting of the artistic risks Grace Jones has taken over the course of her career—an accounting that is impossible despite and because it is constantly modulated in ways that compound the already incalculable interest on a debt that can never be repaid. Jones's artistic space–clearing work has, as she puts it in the epigraph to this chapter, "created the space for others to be able to make it, without the pressure of being a pioneer. They can play the pioneer without taking the actual risk. Because to take the risk means to never soften enough that you can become truly successful."[28] Like other Grace Jones performances over the years, the music video for "Corporate Cannibal" already has proven to be generative for future generations of performers and other intellectuals. While it is clear that we are indebted to her, she gives knowing that what she's given can never be repaid. Like Portia Jordan's ephemeral performances in Magic City, the boundarylessness and impropriety of Grace Jones's performances are underwritten by the historical, socialized debt indexed by her black skin. To the extent that Jones can be read as embodying "Capital unbound" in the "Corporate Cannibal" video, as Shaviro would have it, this embodiment, menacing as it appears, exceeds its purpose of advertising the album *Hurricane*. It does that and then some, too.

Hooker's video seizes the digital image's capacity for modulation, "capturing all meanings" within what Deleuze calls, in reference to the language of modulation characteristic of control societies, a "numerical" language. About this aspect of his description of control societies, Deleuze clarifies that "numerical" here does not necessarily mean binary.[29] The clarification is important because it leads away from a strict attention to the ones and zeros of binary code and any presumptions about what that code has to do with the purported "content" of the music video and toward avenues for thinking algorithms, measurement, processes of commensuration, and what Wendy Hui Kyong Chun has referred to as "programmed visions."[30] Offering only Grace Jones's performance and emphasizing her dark skin, the video for "Corporate Cannibal" conceptualizes a digital Black image that prompts a confrontation with the relationships between Black skin, debt, and "wealth" as those become perceptible not only through calculation and measurement, but through (in)commensuration, impropriety, and opacity as well.

In this constellation, we encounter a force that attends Black existence, seething within and through the modulations of control, lying in wait.

Lying in wait is a spatiotemporal concept. To claim a force that attends Black existence lies in wait within the modulations of control means that we must consider digital media, financialization, and control societies within the broader historical arc offered in my discussion of Ian Baucom's work in the introduction. Here, "Corporate Cannibal" helps us to grasp (yet again) that "radically new ways of manufacturing and articulating lived experience" (in Shaviro's words) might also be the reinvigoration of older ways of manufacturing and articulating the lived experiences of Black existence. As a digital signal, Grace Jones displays the modulation of control societies in order to make the experience of a force that attends Black existence, heretofore felt primarily by Black people, more broadly perceptible and, perhaps, more widely distributed and felt. That "force" in this context refers to something that is more than what "race" usually means when it is invoked in the United States. I conceptualize it here along the lines sketched out in Fred Moten's question about "Blackness": "What is it to be an irreducibly disordering, deformational force while at the same time being absolutely indispensable to normative order, normative form?"[31]

This formulation also opens the force that attends Black existence to be conceptualized along the lines offered by Afro-German intellectual Fatima El Tayeb in her book *European Others: Queering Ethnicity in Postnational Europe*. El Tayeb offers different geographies of Black existence by anchoring her analysis in local relations and histories at the same time as she acknowledges its formation in anti-racist transnational political formations. El Tayeb explains:

> The focus on [the transatlantic slave trade] lets diasporic populations who have entered the West through different trajectories necessarily appear as less representative of the black condition. Accordingly, African diaspora studies have so far overwhelmingly focused on the black experience in the Americas and the methodological framework developed to grasp the particulars of that situation cannot necessarily be applied to other parts of the world. It can offer, however, an important foundation for further explorations of black communities, including those in continental Europe who so far play little role in transnational diaspora studies precisely because of their divergence from the U.S. norm.[32]

El Tayeb's significant intervention and contribution is an invitation to open conceptualizations of "Blackness" and Black existence by anchoring them in the specificity of Europe and other locations outside the United States. At the same time, El Tayeb builds on bodies of work that are themselves animated by a transnational impulse, such as women of color feminism and pan-Africanism. With El Tayeb's interventions in mind, the formulation I offer here—"a force that attends Black existence lies in wait within the modulations of control"—suggests something like the dispersed "mobile agent" with which Coleman ends her essay "Race as Technology." Geographically dispersed and temporally agile, this force, as Moten suggests, is simultaneously absolutely indispensable to the modulations characteristic of societies of control, and an abiding potential for disorder and deformation within those societies.

Confronting European racism is a central concern of El Tayeb's work, and Ruth Wilson Gilmore's definition of racism is instructive here: "Racism is the state-sanctioned and/or extra-legal production and exploitation of group-differentiated vulnerabilities to premature death, in distinct yet densely interconnected political geographies."[33] This definition calls attention to the fact that the production and exploitation of "group-differentiated vulnerabilities to premature death" is at the core of racism. Resting on a measurement of what counts as "premature death," it raises questions of calculation and computation and highlights the significance of the "distinct yet densely interconnected political geographies" in which such vulnerabilities to premature death are produced and exploited. Further, it raises the question carried by the word "premature" in the definition. If some deaths are premature and others are not, then a norm or an average death serves as a measure for this assessment. The empirical fact that premature deaths are differentiated by group must mean that these are accounted for in advance. We might ask, then, what modes of risk also are accounted for in this calculation? It must be assumed that those whose deaths are not premature accrue some level of risk simply because of the fact that others suffer deaths that are premature. The mere fact of group-differentiated inequities in life chances introduces a certain amount of risk to the entire structure. What range of events and circumstances have been accounted for already in the calculations regarding premature deaths? Here, again, the longue durée of modernity, the afterlife of slavery, and the present conditions of settler colonialism are fundamental. Within this broader historical context, some events and circumstances necessarily remain unaccountable to and within what Saidiya Hartman describes as the "measure of man and a ranking of life and worth" initiated with chattel slavery and modes of European colonization. These events are akin to the "Black Swan" events discussed in the introduction and bear in a significant way on Snead's analysis of repetition in Black culture, especially in reference to his discussion of culture as "coverage."

What interests Coleman about Snead's essay is the extent to which, for Snead, "Blackness" itself becomes mobile once it is understood in terms of its characteristic cultural form of repetition, rather than as a set of essential qualities of Black people. While Snead posits repetition as a source of the abiding potential within Black culture to undo the temporal logics of European culture, his analysis of Black culture is less of a celebration of its noise and speed (as in the painting by Italian Futurist Giacomo Balla to which Coleman compares Snead's essay) than a theorization of its mobility, dispersion, disruptive potential, and endurance.

For Coleman, Snead's essay offers a way to conceptualize "Blackness" as a kind of "sensibility," rather than as a property of any particular body or group. Coleman points out that Snead "discusses the structure of cultural transformation not in terms of progress (the standard Enlightenment concept), but in terms of repetition." She quotes Snead here: "Transformation . . . is culture's response to its own apprehension of repetition." Coleman points to Snead's use of "the cut" as a "disruptive modality that provokes a peculiarly late-modern self-consciousness, one that recognizes the randomness—or, even more threatening—the meaninglessness of the signifier." The cut for Snead is an aesthetic strategy, a temporal disruption that "behaves more like a break or a disruption of syntax, similar to the sensibility of the Italian futurists." Although she does not remark upon how this might also signal a crisis of value, for Coleman "the cut" suggests how "Snead thinks along a particular trajectory of race as technology."[34]

In Coleman's reading of Snead, "Blackness" bursts forth in itself—it is a poiētic mattering. That it has accrued to certain bodies over time as part of a hierarchical logic of classification and differentiation points to the historical significance of that which has been created under the sign of "Black": the ways it matters as a difference. Yet, as Coleman's essay highlights, "Blackness" also resists accretion and tends toward dispersion. It is generative and mobile which is why Coleman grants it agency. To the extent that it could be argued with Coleman via Snead that Black culture, as technē, is animated by a logic of "the cut," itself a disruption of syntax, this line of thinking is consistent with what I identified in the "Interlude" as one of the hallmarks of the digital regime of the image: the proliferation of irrational cuts.

This is a problem for European cultures in which, as Snead explains, the "dominant idea is material progress." He writes: "Such a culture is never 'immediate' but 'mediated' and separated from the present tense by its own future-orientation. Moreover, European culture does not allow 'a succession of accidents and surprises,' but instead maintains the illusion of progress at all costs."[35] A situation characterized by a proliferation of irrational cuts wreaks havoc on European culture's ability to maintain its illusion of progress. This is especially important in the discourse about capital in European economics, according to which "repetition must be seen to be not just circulation and flow but accumulation and growth."[36]

By contrast, in Black culture, according to Snead, "repetition means that the thing circulates (exactly in the manner of any flow, including capital flows) there in an equilibrium." The "thing (the ritual, the dance, the beat) is 'there for you to pick up when you come back to get it.'" European culture invests in accumulation and progress and must insure against accidents and surprises in such a way that at least the illusion of development is maintained (a process Snead calls "coverage"). On the other hand, as Snead explains, "Black culture, in the 'cut,' builds 'accidents' into its coverage, almost as if to control their unpredictability. Itself a kind of cultural coverage, this magic of the 'cut' attempts to confront accident and rupture not by covering them over but by making room for them inside the system itself."[37] In this way, "the cut" is a mechanism of modulation, a mode of social and cultural continuity, which does not rely upon commensuration. Instead, it makes "incommensurability" into a relation. It is wealth beyond measure, which is to say, following Moten and Harney, incalculable debt.[38] In so doing, "the "cut" is one of the aspects of Black culture that renders it "antifragile" (to invoke Nassim Nicholas Taleb's concept, discussed in the introduction). While European cultures have certainly been robust, they rest upon an illusion of progress, introduced most forcefully during their Enlightenment, which makes them, like much of the thinking about financial markets, especially susceptible to disruption due to the accidents and surprises characteristic of Black Swan events.

Although Taleb does not labor in the interest of Black liberation or toward the destruction of the existing structures that perpetuate racism, capitalism, misogyny, and/or heteropatriarchy, his diagnosis of and theoretical interventions in the assumptions undergirding prevalent methods of economic analysis are instructive for those of us who do. Where

Taleb's attitude is "nonmeek" and his stance is exceedingly macho and bent toward "conquering," "dominating," and "domesticating" "the unseen, the opaque, and the inexplicable," I humbly prefer not to dominate, conquer, or domesticate the fugitive flights of that which eludes capture and control, however fleetingly, enigmatically, and/or imperceptibly.

Taleb instructs economists "how to love the wind."[39]

Even as we labor to stop the wind from blowing always against our direction, we are fire and do already love the wind too.

For Taleb, the concept of "antifragility" allows economists and others who have an interest in managing the risks associated with time to assess whether something is antifragile, rather than trying to calculate and control for what is inherently unpredictable.[40] As the subtitle of his book *Antifragile: Things That Gain from Disorder* indicates, something is antifragile when it thrives rather than breaks in conditions of disorder and randomness. Indeed, things that are antifragile grow stronger under these conditions. In conversation with Snead, Taleb's work enables the insight that Black cultures are antifragile. They build accidents and surprises into the modulations that enable them to endure.

"Slave to the Rhythm of the Corporate Prison"

In musical terms, rhythm plays a primary role in theories of "the cut" in Black culture; and, importantly, as Martin Munro points out in his study of rhythm and race in the Americas: "If rhythmic repetition is the dominant mode of West African (and African diasporic) music, the repetitions are never quite identical: even as the music repeats itself, it introduces and highlights difference and variation. In the participatory mode of musical performance, repetition is less a static phenomenon than a dynamic, ongoing process of production."[41] Rhythm is one of the ways Black music insures the continuity of Black culture in the face of the accidents and surprises that inevitably assault it. As Snead points out, it encourages wandering by acknowledging that "the thing" will be there when and if one returns for it. Within the terms I have been using here, rhythm is a mechanism for transduction that works to establish continuities without necessarily positing equivalences. It functions as "a kind of continual re-petition, a re-appeal or request that requires a follow-up."[42]

"A man . . . eating machine," a cannibal, of the corporation, "Grace Jones" sings lyrics in the song "Corporate Cannibal" that both recall her earlier performances in ways that complicate the temporality of her appearance in Hooker's music video and help us to feel the allure and danger that lurk within financial flows. The lyrics to the song associate corporate cultures with cannibalism, one of the primitive foils Europeans constructed to advance themselves as more developed in comparison. By referencing her earlier performances (which also circulate as cultural commodities), Jones's lyrics underscore that the corporations about which she sings rely upon notions of progress and development and growth that often are illusory forms of coverage against the cut of repetition and other forces lying in wait. One of the most compelling references in "Corporate Cannibal" to Jones's previous performances is activated by the line "slave to the rhythm / of the corporate prison."

With these lyrics, Grace Jones references her 1985 album *Slave to the Rhythm*, which was released more than thirty years before *Hurricane*. Her seventh studio album, *Slave to the Rhythm* is a concept album consisting of eight tracks that riff on the theme of "slave to the rhythm," punctuated by interviews with Grace Jones and readings of passages from Jean-Paul Goude's controversial book, *Jungle Fever*. The title track is the biggest commercial hit from the album. The album is an astonishing sonic artifact of the transnational circulation, production, and consumption of subcultures, desire, and history during the 1980s. When Jones references it in "Corporate Cannibal" thirty-three years later, she re-calls it for her twenty-first-century listeners. When she sings "lost in this cell / in this hell / slave to the rhythm / of the corporate prison" in "Corporate Cannibal," she re-petitions her listeners to pick up her earlier work, prompting us to listen for the repetition of its thematic refrains in *Hurricane*, and adding a contemporary critique of the prison-industrial complex.

Jones's mention of "slave to the rhythm" suggestively occurs directly before distorted electronic sounds disrupt the rhythms that had organized the song to that point. In the music video, the moment is punctuated by rapid cuts between the two cameras Hooker used to capture Jones's performance. Much of the music video is of Jones's performance as captured on a camera directly facing Jones. The images from this camera are shiny, stretched, and morphed into different forms in the finished video. The second camera captures Jones from the side. Alessandra Raengo describes a spectatorial experience of the cut to the images from that camera:

> Suddenly, the image becomes grainy and fuzzy, low-fi and we become aware of its texture and its "failure" to fully render what it is an image of. These flashing images act almost as a return of the repressed in which the Grace Jones that stood before the cameras reasserts herself as something other than the image we are looking at. Her concrete corporeality cannot be undone. As much as her figure floats to and from the surface, at times lost in an image that absorbs her, the facial expressions, the tilting of the head are hers, and so is the movement of the wide-open mouth threatening to devour everything and anything.[43]

The images from the second camera are a re-petition of Grace Jones's errant presence and complex celebrity. Her existence before both cameras affirms that the modulation of the signal captured in one take during Jones's performance bears a materiality available within control societies—at some point, Jones was there, physically in front of the camera, to be captured by it. Although Jones has become digital signal circulating vis-à-vis Hookers's modulation of it for his music video, the materiality of Jones's and Hooker's labors to transduce Jones's performance into signal persists and, as Raengo would have it, threatens to return for the video's spectator with the cuts to the second camera. Hooker cuts from the shiny and fluid images from the first camera to the low-fi ones from the second at the very moment that Jones sings the words "slave to the rhythm," a repetition of the lyrics and title of her 1985 album. This refrain in "Corporate Cannibal" brings Jones's errant past collaborations with others into her present collaboration with Hooker for those who can recollect them. She petitions us to see and hear those collaborations differently. When we return to *Slave to the Rhythm*, which was produced by Trevor Horn, an influential music producer during the 1980s, we might listen again (or perhaps for the first time) to the song entitled "The Frog and the Princess." It consists almost entirely of an actor, Ian McShane, reading an excerpt from Goude's writing in *Jungle Fever* about his relationship with Jones over a steady electronic beat. The song begins:

> I was amazed when I first saw Grace Jones.
> She was the first to take radical fashion out of its predictable Parisian context and bring it into the music scene, where I had always thought it belonged.
> The first night watching her in Le Mouche, I had already decided to work with her.
> That night, she was singing her hit song "I Need a Man" to a room full of shrieking gay bobbysockses.
> The ambiguity of her act was that she herself looked like a man—a man, singing "I Need a Man" to a bunch of men.

The opening words in "The Frog and the Princess" reference the erotic appeal to the speaker, and possibly by extension to the song's listeners, of Jones's gender. Although Goude's account calls the fact that Jones looked like a man and was singing "I Need a Man" to a room full of men an "ambiguity," it also describes one of the modes of errantry that has propelled Jones's stardom, an errantry animated by experiments with(in) sex and gender, which has never been innocent of capitalism's flows. Jones's appearance has been described as androgynous, but here the narrator recollects it as decidedly male: she "looked like a man" and, because of this, the narrator (and perhaps others as well) read her performance of "I Need a Man" as gay. It was this combination of the gendered and sexual elements of Jones's performance that the narrator found ambiguous. It elicited in him a desire to "work with her."

The song continues:

> I could see how the average guy could get a little scared by her physical advance.
> It was so powerful. I thought she was . . . I thought she was great.
> I photographed her in different positions.
> I cut her legs apart, lengthened them, turned her body to face the audience.
> Soon, I found myself living to the very fast rhythm of Grace Jones.

Here, the narrative in "The Frog and the Princess" takes a turn, still driven by a desire for what Grace Jones re-presents to the speaker, from a fascination with the ambiguity in her performance of "I Need a Man" to an active effort to capture and manipulate Jones's appearance. The speaker here meets the thrill her "physical advance" elicits in him with an attempt to dictate and control how she appears to himself and to others. He seizes hold of her body through photography, cutting her legs apart and putting it on display. In turn, he associates Jones with "a very fast rhythm" that, over time, controls his life. As the song progresses, it becomes clear that Goude's embrace of Grace Jones seeks to thoroughly objectify her. The narrator says:

> I decided, deliberately, to mythologize Grace Jones.
> Black, shiny, muscular people . . . ahh, aerodynamic in design.
> 'Twas to emphasize this belief that I painted Grace Jones blue/black.
> I am no longer sure what I fell in love with; Grace or my idea of what
>   Grace should be.
> But in the two years following the birth of our son, there were
>   nothing else in my life.
> Grace let me take her over completely.

The self-reflexive statement, "I am no longer sure what I fell in love with; Grace or my idea of what Grace should be," pinpoints the slippery erotic terrain with which Grace Jones's stardom has tarried. Francesca Royster's keen observation (mentioned earlier) that Grace Jones is persistently explaining "what it is like to be an object" is relevant here, and Goude's sense that his "idea of what Grace should be" was enmeshed with Grace herself underscores the ways that as a pop star "Grace Jones" is what Steven Shaviro has characterized as an "alluring object." Shaviro explains, "Pop stars are slippery, exhibiting singular qualities while, at the same time, withdrawing to a distance beyond these qualities, and thus escaping any final definition. This makes them ideal commodities: they always offer us more than they deliver, enticing us with a 'promise of happiness' that is never fulfilled, and therefore never exhausted or disappointed."[44] In response to Goude's assertion in his book that he "created" her, Jones says in her memoirs, "And it was definitely not all Jean-Paul, even if his was the most illuminating expression of the creature creation. But the input of so many others was needed to get me to the point where Jean-Paul could focus his creativity, and the project definitely needed my active input."[45] Here, Grace Jones acknowledges that her star text is a

"project," a collaborative creation in which she has been an active partici-
pant. Certainly, the last two sentences in the quotation from "The Frog
and the Princess" offered above call into question who took over whom.[46]
If Grace and their son were the only things in Goude's life, Grace could
claim to have taken him over completely. Yet, he claims to have taken
her over completely. Keeping in mind this entanglement of Jones's celebrity with objectification and commodification by Jean-Paul, herself, and
others, it is remarkable that the one line Jones herself sings, or rather
screams, in "The Frog and the Princess" appears directly after the speaker
claims, "Grace let me take her over completely."

At this point, Jones yells—as though from somewhere beyond, out of
sync with, but oddly right on time in, the scene of the narrative unfolding through McShane's voice—"SLAVE!"

When Jones screams "Slave!" I hear rage and capitulation, a "resistance of the object" that, in this case, also participates in the ongoing
creation and commodification of "Grace Jones" through the repetition
of "slave to the rhythm," which gives the album its coherence as a cultural commodity.[47] With this word, she picks up the theme of the album
Slave to the Rhythm and associates it with the afterlife of slavery, offering
an echo of what it feels like to be a thing. The lyric "Slave!" ties "The Frog
and the Princess" to the themes of *Slave to the Rhythm* at the same time
as it functions as an assertion of Jones's acquiescence to Goude's fantasy
about her.[48] It is an objection to Goude's objectification of her even as it
participates in an erotics of domination and submission, driven by the
history of European anti-Black racism. In *I'll Never Write My Memoirs*,
Jones describes Goude's interest in her as follows:

> He could make me perfect by turning me into an illustration, a sculpture,
> a video, a special effect, a record sleeve, a stage show, a car commercial.
> He could create, and constantly modify, an illusion, plant me in a flaw-
> less phase of glamour midway between machine-ness and she-ness. He
> wanted me to be perfect. He wanted me to represent an Ideal.
>
> As with the church, it was an awful lot for me to live up to. Prick me,
> and I bleed.[49]

Jones does not state what counts here as perfection or as "an Ideal."
Elsewhere in her memoirs, she speculates on what her collaboration with

Goude on *One Man Show* might have been about for him.[50] Considering the products (such as the record sleeve, the car commercial) through which Goude expressed this "Ideal," if it is one, I think the "Ideal" Goude is after is an artifact of European racialization that satisfies his intense fascination with and objectification of Black women. He works to control Jones's appearance, attempting to make it conform to his desire for an Ideal Other. That racial Ideal hinges upon the production of Jones as a machine-like thing. While for Goude such performances may have been calibrated to shape what he can only unevenly control, for Jones the performances were about disrupting habitual ways of perceiving race and gender and sexuality. Jones explains, "I wanted to use my body to express how I had liberated myself from my background, ignored obstacles, and created something original, based on my own desires, fears, and appetites. I was using my body as a language. A language that comes from a dark continent. And dark is dangerous."[51]

Jones's description of Goude's objectification of her ("he wanted me to represent an Ideal") conveys a significant dimension of the material relations held in place by anti-Black racism by calling attention to the way Jones's "physical advance" animates a political economy that demands access to and control over what it imagines to be Black femininity, however masculine that might appear at times. Here, Black femininity is perceptible as an element in the allure of the object: the celebrity "Grace Jones." Yet, the inaccessibility of "Grace Jones" and the opacity of her performances are themselves part of the allure.[52] Goude sought to account for that opacity by wrenching it into some of the objectionable clichés through which Black femininity has been made to work in the interests of anti-Black racism. He accentuates her mouth and her ass; he calls attention to her dark skin. He heightens the hard, aerodynamic edges of her form. He puts her in a cage. Wielding race as technē in his art, Goude brings forth the erotic and sexual economy undergirding anti-Black racism.

When Jones screams "Slave!" in "The Frog and the Princess," she brings forth the history of chattel slavery and Euro-American anti-Black racism that informs her adventures with Jean-Paul Goude. She highlights the extent to which the position of the slave animated not only political economy but a sexual economy as well. I hear this moment in the song as a way Jones talks back to Goude's racist fantasy of her and, in that way, makes it do something else, too. At the same time, I hear it as Jones's insistence on making a contribution to the track, which, after all, is featured on her album with her approval. Jones plays with the boundaries between the personal and the political and the private and the public to the extent that interjecting "Slave!" during the narrative unfolding in "The Frog and Princess" is simultaneously an act of self-conscious critique and a way of flirting with danger. Like Portia Jordan, Jones acknowledges that her value, her "allure," derives from how her performances blur the boundaries between the public and the private, the indifferent and the intimate. This is not only because Jones is a pop star. It is also because she is perceptible as a Black woman and, as such, her appearance bears a fraught relationship to propriety, control, commerce, and privacy.[53]

Jones tarries with racist, homophobic, transphobic, and misogynistic clichés, in her personal relationships with both Goude and others as conveyed in her memoirs and in her professional oeuvre. Jones's work with and through these clichés is driven by a mode of errantry that is part of what Édouard Glissant refers to as a "poetics of Relation." Thinking Jones's celebrity in terms of errantry is consistent with Royster's observation: "As a subcultural icon, Jones forces us to think about the ways that black cultural traffic travels out from, as well as returns to, unpredictable, and unforeseen, directions."[54] Perhaps this is why technology and references to science fiction play such significant roles in Jones's oeuvre. She wields them as ways to open unexpected connections between the historically fraught categories and concepts her celebrity mobilizes. The errant connections she makes between parts of the world, groups of people, and our habitual ways of knowing them pass through the conceptualizations of alienness and animality that her physical appearance has been made to bear.

For Glissant, "errantry" marks a type of wandering that goes against a root. It is a mode through which to reject those certainties that origins and other anchors are assumed to secure. Betsy Wing, who translated *Poetics of Relation* from French into English, explains that Glissant's use of the word (in the original French, it is *errance*) "expresses overtones of sacred mission rather than aimless wandering."[55] For Glissant, errantry plays a role in the "poetics of Relation" because it is a way of establishing unexpected pathways to relation with the Other. The Black feminist world we are creating needs errant wanderers like Grace Jones. It seems to me her wandering is not "idle roaming." It seems to me that she "knows at every moment where" she "is—at every moment in relation to the other."[56] In this regard, Jones's errantry entails experimenting within and through the various modulations designed to control what her stardom can do vis-à-vis race, gender, sexuality, and nationality. Although it is cliché to say that errant wanderers like Jones are risk-takers, it must be said that errantry is a risky, but indispensable, mode of Relation.

At one point in her memoir, Jones recalls shaving her head as part of an experiment to try to find a niche as a fashion model. It backfired, and Wilhelmina, the woman who owned the modeling agency Jones was working with at the time, made her wear wigs until it grew back. Nonetheless, Jones conveys that she liked it because it caused a reaction. About this episode with her hair, Jones's memoir reads:

> The biggest reaction came when I cut it to the bone and revealed more of my black skin. It made me look hard, in a soft world. It made me look more like a thing than a person, but that was how I had felt I was treated growing up—as a thing, without feeling, an object, not even human. . . . Without fully understanding it at the time, I savored the response to what I did to myself, by breaking certain laws about how I was meant to behave and look, as a model, a girl, a daughter, an American, a West Indian, a human being.
>
> My shaved head made me look more abstract, less tied to a specific race or sex or tribe, but was also a way of moving across those things, belonging while at the same time not belonging. I was black, but not black; woman, but not woman; American, but Jamaican; African, but science fiction. It set me outside and beyond in some sort of slipstream, and instinctively, I liked that it was a way of expressing that I was flexible, that I could adapt to different situations, and that I was versatile, capable of changing who I was and what I was doing depending on who I was working with and in what contexts.[57]

Like "Grace Jones" the electronic signal that embodies finance capital in the music video for "Corporate Cannibal," Jones's celebrity persona is flexible, transversal, refusing to be pinned to any fixed state—Black, woman, West Indian, American, African. Her celebrity transduces fixed states, sometimes through their negatives—not Black, not woman—and sometimes through conjunctions—but Jamaican, but science fiction. In this passage from her memoir, Jones's shaved head gives expression to her errant wanderings through each of these concepts and the thick networks of sociality and history that congeal around and through them. The similarities between Jones's narration of how her career has been directed by her own desire to be flexible and adaptable and the flexibility and adaptability that describe the modulation of her image in "Corporate Cannibal" underscore that Jones's refusal to be bound to the terms the world has given to her is not foreclosed upon by the capitalist mode of production. She refuses to "go with the flow"; her errant wanderings feed those flows. Her errantry has created profitable spaces for others within those flows. As she says elsewhere in her memoir (in the longer quotation that serves as one of the epigraphs for this chapter), "I am to this day a radical about not going with the flow. . . . If I had followed the crowd, by now I would be as rich as people think I am."[58] For Grace Jones, errant wandering is its own reward.

Jones's errantry also assumes a norm or a standard of measure from or against which Jones's sexuality and gender wander or deviate in ways that open onto other connections, perhaps seemingly impossible before she forged them via her performances. Jones participates in Goude's racist fetishization of her, exploring its erotics and the power it wields. In this way, she wanders through dimensions of European racism like those of interest to Snead, who calls attention to the broad strokes through which Enlightenment logics authorize anti-Black racism and sometimes even make it feel good. Yet, according to Snead, to maintain these logics European cultural forms must persistently offer an illusion of progress and development.

When Jones interjects "Slave!" into "The Frog and the Princess," she pulls the past into the present so that it might have another hearing. Likewise, when, in "Corporate Cannibal," she intones, "Slave to the rhythm / of the corporate prison," she drags the album *Slave to the Rhythm* and the political and sexual economy of chattel slavery into the modulations that constitute the song's music video.[59] If those living beings through which various modes of Black femininity materialize figure the intersections between anti-Black racism and sexual and political economies (as suggested above), then Jones's ability to mix masculinity and femininity in her various performances introduces a kind of opacity into our consumption of her performances. Like other Black performers before her, Jones's errant wandering through the clichés that hold anti-Black racism and misogyny in place render those clichés themselves opaque (with varying degrees of success), and thereby frustrate their ability to function as a cliché, or as a sort of communicative short hand.[60] Her performances seek to explode from the inside the clichés that animate them by poking holes in them, insisting upon the opacity the clichés have been forged to finesse. This opacity short-circuits exchanges that rely upon the creation of equivalences and commensuration, upon fungibility; by so doing, it sparks other modes of connection and exchange.

If, historically, Black existence (that is, the material and cultural realities and expressions indexed but not wholly contained by the persistent presence of those we call "Black people" over time) is tethered to a notion of fungibility, as several people have argued, it might be grasped as itself speculative, characterized by an incommensurability that is inherent to it and has been finessed and managed by a variety of techniques and strategies of commensuration, measure, computation, and calculation.[61] In this context, Beth Coleman's conception of "Blackness" as a prosthesis tethered to the specific historical conjunctures that forged it underscores how it has functioned as a vehicle for creativity, fugitivity, and flight, as well as for capture, control, and exploitation. Coleman leaves her readers with a question and a provocation concerning the formulation of "Blackness" as technology. While Coleman accepts Snead's formulation of Black culture, she asserts the following about the implications of his analysis in a footnote: "In several respects, the argument proves quite alarming. Not only does Snead deconstruct Western culture, but in his dismantling of white subjectivity, he never constructs a Black subjectivity as anything other than the other of the white—a bad or absent reflection."[62] In other words, according to Coleman, while Snead is precise about "Black culture," he refuses to allow a Black subject to cohere as such. The "mobile agent" Coleman identifies in Snead's essay is a shadowy figure that results from the way that Snead claims "the Black" of modernity is a negation of Western subjectivity, without offering an alternative (Black) subject formation to replace the destroyed Western one. Coleman says Snead offers a "dispersed" subject, a spatially promiscuous, potentially disruptive presence, lying in wait. In Coleman's essay, the conceptualization of race as technology involves the production of a mobile agent that does not cohere as a subject. Such an agent is a "shadow" or a "dispersed being." In another footnote, she compares it to "the fate of human subjectivity in William Gibson's novel *Neuromancer*."[63] Coleman writes:

> Understanding black as negation, however, as Snead's essay does, leaves nothing with which to replace the fallen Western paradigm except for fragments of its past. Indeed, Snead thinks along a particular trajectory of race as technology. He locates an instrument, the cut of blackness, that possesses function, but not a particular identity. In lieu of an inherited formulation of subjectivity, Snead theorizes a dispersed being, one that relies on the action of motion to formulate itself. In a sense, we end up with a subject designed like a series of Joseph Cornell boxes—amalgamations of detritus that have been preciously assembled into a new order of meaning. Somehow, within the noise and speed of contemporary being, there is yet the silhouette, the dim figure of our mobile agent. The question remains: how does this subject find its way?[64]

The question with which Coleman leaves us is a spatiotemporal one—"how does this subject find its way?"—and it suggests there is a spatiotemporal confusion that attends the mobile agent unleashed by race as technology. The mobile agent, "the Black," lacks futurity. In Snead's account of it, it is simply "a dispersed being" in motion, comprised of "amalgamations of detritus that have been preciously assembled into a new order of meaning." As I have been suggesting throughout this book, rather than conceptualizing "the Black's" lack of a perceptible future as a problem to be solved or a crisis to be addressed, or a cause for pessimism or optimism, it might be understood as one of the crucial operations of what we might here grasp as the cut of Black existence: it might cleave an opening in the present order of meaning and being through which another structure, another world, perhaps, might be "preciously assembled." Rather than seeing this as any celebration of "the new," we can grasp this as an excavation of some of that which never was, but might have been. It accumulates. It refuses to(o). And still is, lying in wait.

Though Coleman's essay ends with a problem, a provocation to further thinking, it carries an optimistic strain. Wendy Hui Kyong Chun emphasizes this optimistic aspect in her own essay, inspired by Coleman's, entitled "Race and/as Technology: or, How to do Things to Race."[65] Chun asserts that unmooring "race" from specific subjects makes it available for different, perhaps even new, purposes. She poses it this way: "Could 'race' be not simply an object of representation and portrayal, of knowledge or truth, but also a technique that one uses, even as one is used by it—a carefully crafted, historically inflected system of tools, of mediation, or of 'enframing' that builds history and identity?"[66] The proposition "race as technology" means that what we have attributed to "race" as biological phenomena might also be understood otherwise. It also means that those things that have accrued to specific "races" historically might be set to challenge the existing organization of things. It means, in other words, that the roles played by "race" as a structuring element in the transduction of the transindividual (as discussed in chapter 1) may be more malleable than fixed.

Establishing a connection between race and mediation, Chun suggests that, like media, race is technology in its sense of poiēsis: "Race, like media, is also a heuristic, a way to understand, to reveal, the world around us."[67] She writes: "Thus the question becomes: to what extent can ruminating on race as technology make possible race as poiēsis, or at least as a form of agency?"[68] Chun acknowledges that conceptualizing race as technology is a risky proposition, since it suggests a use of race as a tool of domination (as in eugenics, for example) as well as a technology that "opens up the possibility that, although the idea and the experience of race have been used for racist ends, the best way to fight racism might not be to deny the existence of race, but to make race do different things."[69] Ultimately, Chun's essay asks, through a reading of Greg Pak's feature film *Robot Stories* (2003), and in language that suggests an affiliation with Black existence as I have been formulating it throughout this book, "Can the abject, the Orientalized, the robot-like data-like Asian/Asian American other be a place from which something like insubordination or creativity can arise?"[70]

While at the end of her essay Coleman turns with apprehension to Snead's formulation of Black culture and "the mobile agent" unleashed through it, Chun ultimately posits the abjection of Asians and Asian cultures vis-à-vis Europeans and European cultures as a site of possibility for "insubordination" or "creativity," as part of her broader formulation of the possibility that "race" might work as "poiēsis, or at least a form of agency." Both Coleman and Chun are interested in how thinking "race as technology" reveals that seemingly static formulations of "race" harbor a capacity for agency. Taking seriously Karen Barad's theory of agential realism involves acknowledging that agency is distributed throughout matter. Any capacity to "do things with race" or "make race do different things" therefore involves an individual agent, such as a filmmaker who might provide another expression, a different vision, or an alternative selection of audiovisual images, or a scholar who might assemble existing knowledge into new insights about race, or a philosopher who might create a different conceptualization of race; yet, more so, it would involve a transindividual effort.[71]

We can refer to the historical conjunctures in which Blackness has worked in divergent ways (and recall Ian Baucom's work discussed in the introduction) as those constitutive of the longue durée of modernity. In the neoliberal multicultural phase of racial capitalism, "Blackness" is available in various ways to those who are not immediately recognizable as "Black" according to existing common perceptual cues, and it also might wander, errantly, becoming perceptible, as of now, in a variety of places, terrestrial, extraterrestrial, and, through the work of the imagination, intergalactic and beyond. Here, "Blackness" as technology is African, and science fiction, like Grace Jones.

These certainly are queer times.

The De-American Bartleby

Archipelagoes, Refusal, and the Cosmic

Bartleby's silent immobility is a rhizomatic mode of erring that not only evades but decodes the American Way. Despite the continuing effort in much American literary criticism to settle with Bartleby by settling him in the disciplinary economy of the liberal democratic household, the vagabond scrivener "who refuses to budge" continues to elude the discourse that would codify and domesticate the spectral force of his mobile passivity. As Melville's great story clearly implies, the positivity of this errancy, of its enabling evasion of the disciplinary codes of the American Way through immobile silence, is, of course, minimal. But insofar as it compels thinking this spectral silence as a nascent form of language that has been paradoxically precipitated by the very fulfillment of the accommodational—read, now, codifying—language of the Wall Street lawyer, it is also a prelude to thinking the errant, the singular, the diverse, the migrant, the preterite—all that the prevailing language of America would encode and settle—different(ial)ly. It is in this sense that the Melville of "Benito Cereno" and "Bartleby" is our (global) contemporary.
—William V. Spanos, *Herman Melville and the American Calling*

If Melville had no use for phrases such as liberty, equality, or fraternity, he was at the same time, directly or indirectly, the mortal foe of any kind of program which laid down the road by which mankind should act to achieve salvation. If he were alive today, he would turn in horror from Socialists, Communists, Anarchists, Trotskyists and all who set

themselves up, not to do this or that particular task, but as the vanguard, the organizers, the educators, the leaders of the workers for the establishment of the Universal Republic. But he was writing in 1851. And what he was concerned with then is what we are increasingly concerned with now: what are the conditions of survival of modern civilization?
—C. L. R. James, *Mariners, Renegades, and Castaways*

In his essay on Melville, "Bartleby; or, The Formula," as we have seen, Gilles Deleuze writes: "There is nothing particular or general about Bartleby: he is an Original."[1] Deleuze claims that, like light, Originals can be characterized by their speed—that is, a calculation of their distance over time. Bartleby exists where stillness and motion become indiscernible, incalculable. Although the lawyer often characterizes Bartleby as "still" and "silent," these characteristics can be understood, following Deleuze and within the context of Melville's oeuvre, as consistent with one of the "two great original Figures that one finds throughout Melville, the panoramic shot and the tracking shot, stationary process and infinite speed."[2] "Stationary process" can be understood as a movement that remains constant over time, such as white noise, and "infinite speed" as an (im)possible proposition that confounds measure by hypothesizing something traveling so fast that its movement is imperceptible to humans. Deleuze continues: "And even though these are the two elements of music, though stops give rhythm to movement and lightning springs from immobility, is it not this contradiction that separates the originals, their two types?"[3]

Deleuze's introduction of film terms ("the panoramic shot and the tracking shot") in the context of Bartleby initially perplexes: Melville wrote Bartleby before the invention of film technology proper, and Deleuze's use of "the panoramic shot" and "the tracking shot" in his essay on Bartleby sweeps film as well as music into the discussion. Through the association of Bartleby with the immobility or the stops that give rhythm to movement, we can sense the extent to which Bartleby also figures a rhythm of the repetition that, in ways I discuss in chapters 3 and 4, is so important in Black culture according to James A. Snead. Deleuze's essay allows for a reading of Bartleby that associates him with the mode of agency of interest to Coleman in her "Race as Technology" essay: her mobile agent. Through his "mobile passivity" and by proliferating a contagious, queer formula, Bartleby is a figure for both the queerness that is autochthonous to time and the contagion that is Black culture when unleashed to render "race" technology. He is a figure of speed and white noise.

Deleuze suggests that the tracking shot and the panoramic shot offer two irreconcilable spatiotemporal orientations, and that "stationary process" and "infinite speed" exist at two different spatiotemporal poles. Stationary process and infinite speed are characteristics of strip photography, a kind of photography in which space and time can be mapped onto one another so that changes over time, motion, can be captured, while immobile spaces are rendered indistinct, or vice versa. It is a capacity of film, analogue video, and digital video that can be understood as a type of scanning; it has been used for military purposes as well as for artistic ones. It has proven especially well-suited to capturing panoramas.[4]

Whereas a tracking shot follows an object or subject through space, thereby establishing a set of relations motivated by movement, a panoramic shot provides an overview of space without necessarily establishing relations between particular coordinates. As scholars of the Western film genre have pointed out, however, panoramic shots have functioned ideologically to provide a sense of mastery over space and to project a "manifest destiny" orientation that encourages viewers to collude with the logic of settlers. This point of view anchors a perceptual schema through which what exists in the space shot in panorama, what is indigenous or autochthonous to that space, matters only to the extent it can support a perception of empty, open space.[5] This orientation toward a space in which "open," "empty," and "new" are coextensive underpins and rationalizes the conceptualization of "the New World" as such. It has contributed to the ontologies of settler colonialism and its attendant philosophies of being and the human, which have been criticized and resisted by Indigenous activism and scholarship, as well as by Black Studies, and now by many others, including "the new materialists."[6]

Deleuze associates Bartleby with the panoramic shot, asserting that he is "the immobile source" of "a livid white light" shone on his surroundings. Deleuze states that Bartleby reveals the "emptiness" of his world, "the imperfection of its laws, the mediocrity of particular creatures."[7] For Melville, Bartleby decodes the schemas of value through which his world has come to matter. Associated with "stationary process," Bartleby is also described by Deleuze earlier in the essay as an "autochthon," an original inhabitant of a place. The relationship between the lawyer and Bartleby that Deleuze perceives in Melville's short story hinges on what Deleuze describes as "a nearly acknowledged homosexual relation" secured by "a kind of pact" in which the lawyer wants to make this man without objective references, Bartleby, "a man of confidence who would owe everything to him." The lawyer wants to make Bartleby "*his* man."[8] Deleuze's references to Melville's novel *The Confidence Man* recalls that satirical novel about manifest destiny and American settler colonialism. Moreover, when the lawyer commands that Bartleby come into his office and check his legal copy—an instruction that breaks the terms of Bartleby's agreement with the lawyer, who had promised to leave Bartleby alone, hidden from view behind his screen—Bartleby pulls "from the debris" of that broken pact "a trait of expression, 'I prefer not to,' which will proliferate around him and contaminate the others, sending the attorney fleeing" and toppling language itself.[9] As the attorney flees, Bartleby remains in place. A "vagabond who refuses to budge," his is, as William Spanos puts it, a "mobile passivity."[10]

If, as Jean-Luc Godard claims (according to Deleuze), a moral problem lies in the conjunction of stationary process and infinite speed, it may have to do with the function of each type of shot in relation to the meaning of what it frames. A panoramic shot traditionally frames landscapes and seemingly takes a neutral stance vis-à-vis whatever movements occur within the frame (though, as I mention above, often the stance is not neutral in context), whereas a tracking shot designates an agent whose movements motivate the camera's. The conjunction between them might be understood as the work of an apparatus, which is generative and illustrative of value in process; a tracking shot selects an Agent from the range of possible agents framed by a panoramic shot, thereby assigning it value and possibility. The moral problem therefore lies in the selection of what from the range of potential movements is selected to initiate or continue a movement. Or, conversely, it lies in the selection of what is framed when movements are arrested or exhausted.

The inclusion of two Originals in the same picture involves adjudicating between very different movements, between their modes of agency and the interests those serve, and the challenge of arresting, modulating, commensurating, or transducing them by including them within the same frame. Or, it involves just allowing each to be in their "originality, that is, a sound that each one produces like a ritornello at the limit of language." According to Deleuze, allowing two Originals to be in their originality, and to be perceptible by their different sonic refrains, "requires a new perspective, an archipelago perspectivism that conjugates the panoramic shot and the tracking shot." Such a new perspective involves an acute perception that is visual and auditory, one that is perhaps not yet here but will arrive in time.[11]

Deleuze situates "Bartleby the Scrivener" within a reading of America's archipelagoes and the relationship between the Americas and sea exploration. He understands archipelagoes as a "world in process" and associates American pragmatism with this perspective. According to Deleuze, "Pragmatism is misunderstood when it is seen as a summary philosophical theory fabricated by Americans. On the other hand, we understand the novelty of American thought when we see pragmatism as an attempt to transform the world, to think a new world or new man insofar as they *create themselves*."[12] Deleuze claims that Melville, writing during the time in which American Transcendental philosophy was being generated by his contemporaries, Henry Thoreau and Ralph Waldo Emerson, "is already sketching out the traits" of pragmatism in his work. Deleuze presents American pragmatism as "first of all the affirmation of a world in process, an archipelago. Not even a puzzle, whose pieces when fitted together would constitute a whole, but rather a wall of loose, uncemented stones, where every element has a value in itself but also in relation to others: isolated and floating relations, islands and straits, immobile points and sinuous lines—for Truth always has 'jagged edges.'"[13] Reading pragmatism against its grain, Deleuze appreciates American pragmatism as a kind of radical empiricism.

In his essay on Bartleby, Deleuze is enamored of the open road and the open sea. He sees American pragmatism as a vehicle for becoming. He sees in it a possibility for a "new community;" yet, what troubles

Deleuze is "America's" consistent capacity to solidify into a nationalist project. With direct reference to D. W. Griffith's 1915 film, *The Birth of a Nation*, which helped revitalize the racist vigilante domestic terrorist group the Ku Klux Klan as a response to the First Reconstruction after the formal end of slavery, Deleuze explains about America's tendencies toward nationalism and white supremacy: "The birth of a nation, the restoration of the nation-state—and the monstrous fathers come galloping back in, while the sons without fathers start dying off again."[14] This aspect of Deleuze's reading of Bartleby troubles American investment in "the new"—"the new world," "the new man," and so on. Deleuze's reading itself is troubling for how it might support another variation on manifest destiny—a spatial reformation of "America," an American formation that exceeds the territory of the United States, taking instead the archipelago as its organizing spatial logic. Yet, Melville's short story might also be read as calling the American project itself into question.

"Bartleby the Scrivener" was written twenty-three years after US President Andrew Jackson signed the Indian Removal Act, two years after the Indian Appropriation Act of 1851 allocated federal resources to move Native peoples onto reservations, eight years after the phrase "manifest destiny" was coined, and seven years before the formation of the Confederate States of America and the beginning of the American Civil War. It is significant that at the end of the twentieth century and the beginning of the twenty-first, for several European philosophers, a character from a short story written in the United States in 1853 has become a touchstone from which to address themes salient to political and social philosophy today.

What Deleuze calls "America's promise to immigrants," the American dream that America become "a patchwork of small nations," is where Deleuze's discussion of Bartleby ends, with Bartleby himself offered as "the doctor of a sick America" and the writer, here, Melville, even in his failure, "the bearer of a collective enunciation, which . . . preserves the rights of a people to come, or of a human becoming."[15] "America" emerges in Deleuze's analysis as a concept to which Bartleby is tied in various ways, even though he remains unassimilable into it because he dies in jail. Deleuze claims about America: "Even in the midst of its failure, the American Revolution continues to send out its fragments, always making something take flight on the horizon, even sending itself to the moon, always trying to break through the wall, to take up the experiment once again, to find a brotherhood in this enterprise, a sister in this becoming, a music in its stuttering language, a pure sound and unknown chords in language itself."[16]

According to Deleuze's reading of Melville, we could say that the American enterprise, which relies upon a dissolution of the colonial bond with England—the father—forms a logic of alliance, a community of men, sisters and brothers without fathers. For Deleuze, the new man and his new world, "America," rely upon reconciling the inhuman with the human through exploration of the "open road" or the "open sea." It requires motion.

Picture the open road or the open sea framed in a stationary panoramic shot. The new man, the American, enters the frame, perhaps from the right, and the camera now follows him (tracking shot). In the panoramic shot, we mistake the open road for an empty space. The tracking shot following the American renders whatever or whoever was there already an indistinct blur, part of the landscape, eternal nature or backward savages or both at the same time within the time of the tracking shot. The selection of the Agent of the tracking shot is a moral problem because it involves a decision about what value(s) to extend through the attribution of motion, a decision that ultimately also involves one about what to suspend. It is a question of mattering. The tracking shot is a world-making venture that must select and cut a world and give it over to a spatiotemporal schema through which it can cohere as such.[17]

What Deleuze misses, therefore, in his acceptance of the story America tells about itself—that it is a "nation of immigrants" or a "patchwork of small nations"—is that this is a lie, or at best a half truth, meant to perpetuate American exceptionalism by burying and disavowing the United States' status as a settler society, the fact of Native American survivance, and the abiding presence of fungible Black bodies within and in excess of the national corpus and the official narratives through which that corpus is reproduced.[18]

Deleuze's insistence on reading Bartleby in the context of American pragmatism and, hence, in the context of the politics and poetics, the violences and possibilities, of "the New World" underscores that "Bartleby the Scrivener" advances a spatiotemporal logic attuned to the emergent, journeying, and open. Yet, "Bartleby the Scrivener" opens a line of flight from the violences of Bartleby's world. For Agamben, as for Žižek, that Bartleby might function in an ethically charged way is less compelling than that he might offer a way into thinking those concepts—"radical contingency" for Agamben, "ultimate parallax" for Žižek—through which what exists might be "decreated" and simultaneously rendered anew. In other words, what is of interest about Bartleby for these thinkers is what we might call, following Audra Simpson, Denise da Silva, and other scholars in Indigenous Studies and Black Studies, his "politics of refusal."[19]

For neither Agamben nor Žižek is Bartleby's formula merely a question of saying no to what exists. It is not a negation. It is instead a withdrawal from every mode of reproducing what exists (including saying "no" to it or negating it). It is a withdrawal, moreover, from the very terms of that withdrawal. Agamben describes it as a "decreation" in which "what could have not been but was becomes indistinguishable from what could have been but was not," and he insists that "a new creature" is what is at stake.[20] Žižek describes it as a parallax shift in which "the very frantic and engaged activity of constructing a new order is sustained by an underlying 'I would prefer not to' which forever reverberates in it."[21]

For Deleuze, Bartleby's formula is of interest for similar reasons: "Without a doubt, the formula is ravaging, devastating and leaves nothing standing in its wake."[22] By making Bartleby's formula, which Deleuze refers to as "a negativism beyond all negation,"[23] part of a discussion of Melville's America and of the American pragmatism that Deleuze claims Melville's oeuvre anticipates, Deleuze's essay prompts, but does not perform, a way to think about that which was set in motion with the colonization and settlement of the "New World" and a consideration of Bartleby's relationship to "the new" in the context of the American project. It could be said that Deleuze's Bartleby, in other words, shines "a livid light" on the attempted genocide of Indigenous peoples and of enslaved Africans underwriting the social orders of the "New World," and thereby calls attention to the violences and dangers that historically have attended radical social and economic experiments predicated on "the new."[24]

While Deleuze himself does not take the analysis that far, his reference to Bartleby as autochthonous and his considered attention to

American pragmatism and the American experiment in the context of Melville's literature points in that direction. For Deleuze, Bartleby marks, among other things, a way that Melville, along with his contemporaries, Emerson, and Thoreau, diagnosed "the American evil": "paternal authority and filthy charity," in the face of which Bartleby "lets himself die in prison."[25] William V. Spanos describes this as "the American Way," an extension of the doctrine of manifest destiny and a mode of American exceptionalism that holds that the United States is an exemplary democracy that ought to be spread to all corners of the globe. In the face of "the American evil," Bartleby prefers not to. The attempted genocide of American Indians and the enslavement of Africans constitutive of the settler colonial project that is "America" are among those American evils that preoccupied Melville in his time.[26]

We can understand Deleuze as interested at the end of the Bartleby essay in how "America" itself "conjugates the panoramic shot and the tracking shot," thereby giving a range of expressive actions to the yearnings perceptible in the space between stationary process and infinite speed.[27] We can approach this space now in the early twenty-first century as that held open by Coleman's mobile agent and unleashed through "repetition as a figure in Black culture" when race becomes perceptible as technology. It is a space that is "not nowhere"; it is another orientation toward space, place, and land.[28] Radical refusal might hold open that space. Yet, "America" here violently wrenches the yearnings coursing through that space into language and other symbolic regimes of value. It reterritorializes them into "the new world," a concept that has rationalized settler colonialism, chattel slavery, and the genocide of Indigenous peoples and enslaved Africans. It holds out the promise of "life, liberty, and justice for all" as a guarantor of the protections of citizenship it arrogates to itself the power to grant. It insists, as Spanos points out in the epigraph to this Intercession, that its version of democracy is the best socioeconomic and political structure for the rest of world to adopt and follow.

Gerald Horne recently revealed the extent to which the world-making venture of the American Revolution was at its inception in 1776 a "counter-revolution," which aimed to conserve the institution of slavery in "the New World."[29] His analysis helps us to understand that, during the American Revolution, not only Native American resistance but also

Black *existence* in the United States posed a radical refusal to the very idea of America. Following Horne's reading of it, American sovereignty at its inception was a means through which to continue the ontologies, epistemologies, and economies that sustain both settler colonialism and chattel slavery.[30]

As previously discussed, Saidiya Hartman has referred to our times as "the afterlife of slavery."[31] What recent scholarship about the history of chattel slavery such as Hartman's and Horne's, among others, makes perceptible is the extent to which "America" is a materialization of that afterlife today, a vehicle through which the white supremacist relations legalized during slavery are perpetuated today through other means, even as the official state narrative in the United States deploys a neo-liberal multicultural embrace of racial progress. Scholarship in Native and Indigenous Studies substantiate the salience of the ongoing settler colonial relation in the United States.[32] Bartleby's passive mobility, his radical refusal, carries a potential to de-create the American project. Like Coleman's mobile agent, however, Bartleby does not anchor a positive alternative. He dies in jail, unable to serve as a heuristic through which to continue any version of the American national project. Deleuze understands this as a "failure." As I explained above, he contextualizes Bartleby's relationship to Being and becoming within the context of American pragmatism, a philosophical tradition that he argues Melville's oeuvre anticipates and starts to create even before it exists as such.

Yet, Bartleby is not a pragmatic character. While American pragmatism minds those "jagged edges" of Truth, "Bartleby the Scrivener" is, as Agamben asserts, an "experiment without truth," one conducted in the context of a larger project having to do with "the American Dream," "the New World," and the philosophical traditions generated from the American Revolution and its failures. As we have seen, pragmatism, according to Deleuze, reaches an "affirmation of a world in process" through the coming into existence of what Deleuze refers to as "a community of explorers, the brothers of the archipelago, who replace knowledge with belief, or rather with 'confidence'—not belief in another world, but confidence in this one, and in man as much as in God." Deleuze asserts: "Pragmatism is this double principle of archipelago and hope."[33]

Bartleby is not a figure of hope. He is a figure, not of possibility or impossibility, but of potentiality. Bartleby confounds efforts to assign him to the position of "the Other," and the range of operations and phenomena reliant on the creation and existence of an Other. Bartleby is "an Original," who claims of himself that he is "not particular." He retains his originality, rather than melting into a Whole or succumbing to the calculations required to establish Universality. He does not found a people to come (though Deleuze and others such as Spanos argue that Melville anticipates them). Nor does he embrace the American Way or establish a collective. He is not a social being. We might say that Bartleby is a figure for preindividual being—pure potentiality. Not nothing, but the terms of his mattering remain unresolved at the end of the narrative, despite the fact that, as a gesture toward closure, the Wall Street lawyer passes along a "rumor" that Bartleby was formerly employed in the Dead Letter Office.

Bartleby's death directs us elsewhere. Rather than formulating "America" as a patchwork nation and understanding Bartleby's death as possibly redemptive of a failed American project, we might turn to the variety of other possible spatial formations of "the Americas" and study the experiments, with or without truth, that have been conducted there. As only one example of someone whose work has been with us throughout this book, Édouard Glissant conceptualizes myriad ways the space of "the Caribbean" has been transformed through a variety of contacts. Yet, his idea of Relation is not a nationalist project. What is important for Glissant is that the Middle Passage, the foundational narrative of the Americas, which marks the founding of a "new world," framed an encounter with "the Abyss," one that signified a beginning, not through the death of a Father, but by marking the erasure of a certain spatiotemporal trajectory and its possibilities.[34] Through catastrophe, the temporalities of African and Indigenous societies and their epistemologies and ontologies were severed, or at least profoundly threatened. That violent world-historical event inaugurated not a new world, but "the Diverse."[35]

Recently, Michelle Wright has argued that taking into consideration the new developments in physics demands that scholars of Black Studies no longer reify what she refers to as "the Middle Passage narrative," because space and time are not fixed, but in flux. For Wright, "the Middle Passage narrative" binds "Blackness" to an American context in ways that preclude other expressions of "Blackness" to register as such. She argues for other space-times of Blackness, in which World

War II marks a historical transformation in the geopolitical racial logics governing Blackness. Like Melamed, Wright understands the end
of World War II and the advent of the Cold War to mark a shift in the
global logics of race.

Thinking in the wake of that war in 1952, while held on immigration
charges at Ellis Island off the coast of New York City, the writer, activist,
and intellectual C. L. R. James, who was born in Trinidad, wrote a book
about Herman Melville entitled *Mariners, Renegades and Castaways:
The Story of Herman Melville and the World We Live In*. In it, James
argues that Melville, who was writing one hundred years earlier than
James, foresaw the basic relations that characterized the United States of
America in James's present, 1952, and that an analysis of Melville's now
classic novel *Moby Dick* is a literary exploration of the underlying human
characteristics of those relations. In addition to *Moby Dick*, James also
offers an analysis of Melville's novel *Pierre*, which, as James points out,
scandalized readers of its day, but offered premonitory insights into the
Freudian concept of "neurosis," which had become a dominant diagnosis of modern man in the 1940s and 1950s.

In its insistence on interrogating "the conditions of survival of modern civilization," James's book on Melville contributes to what Cedric
Robinson has characterized as the "aim of Black studies": a critique of
Western civilization.[36] Through an analysis of key texts in Melville's oeuvre, James advances an argument about the racial underpinnings of settler colonial nationalist projects and the possibilities for the creation of
alternatives to them.

In a chapter entitled "Neurosis and the Intellectuals," James points
out that Melville, bankrupt and outcast after the publication of *Pierre*,
wrote three short stories that stand "among the finest short stories that
have ever been written." The first of these is "Bartleby the Scrivener," to
which James devotes a brief three and a half pages. He presents it as a
story of "the revolt of white collar workers" and connects it to his reading of *Moby Dick*. Indeed, James points out that Melville uses a phrase
from *Moby Dick* when writing that Bartleby died "sleeping with kings
and counsellors."[37] James explains, "Kings and counsellors. It is the same
phrase used of the crew of the *Pequod* as they slept in the forecastle.
Somewhere this active go-getting Wall Street lawyer has recognized that
in Bartleby's life and death are some heroism and grandeur far above the

actual miserable existence of the clerk and his own worldly success."[38] In this way, James aligns Bartleby with the "mariners, renegades and castaways" that he claims are the heroes in *Moby Dick*.

The titular phrase of James's book on Melville refers to a passage in *Moby Dick* in which that novel's narrator, Ishmael, according to James, describes "the role the working man, i.e., the crew, will play in the book." James offers the following quotation from *Moby Dick* in support of his claim that "Melville intends to make the crew the real heroes of his book, but he is afraid of criticism":

> If, then, to meanest mariners, and renegades, and castaways, I shall hereafter ascribe high qualities, though dark; weave round them tragic graces; if even the most mournful, perchance the most abased, among them all, shall at times lift himself to the exalted mounts; if I shall touch that workman's arm with some ethereal light; if I shall spread a rainbow over his disastrous set of sun; then against all mortal critics bear me out in it, thou just Spirit of Equality, which hast spread one royal mantle of humanity over all my kind![39]

Although this passage from which James takes the title of his book on Melville can be read as consistent with the cliché of the simple-but-noble worker, and although indeed at times James himself replicates that cliché in his own efforts to valorize the "mariners, renegades, and castaways," James also takes pains to differentiate Melville's formulation of the crew, which is comprised of white Americans, Africans, Asians, and Indigenous people from different islands working alongside one another, from the conceptualization of "the primitive" or "the savage" that stands as the dichotomous Other against which are formulated civilization and its civilized man. James writes, for example, that Melville characterizes Queequeg, a cannibal from an island in the South Seas and a member of the crew of the *Pequod*, as having "mastery of one of the most important and authoritative positions in a great modern industry," in addition to "his splendid physique, unconquered spirit and spontaneous generosity."[40] With reference to Queequeg, James writes that "Melville does what he does all through the book, begins with the accepted practices, beliefs and even literary methods of his time, and then consciously and with the utmost sureness leaves them behind or rather takes them over into the world he saw ahead. He saw the future so confidently only because he saw so clearly all that was going on around him."[41]

Rather than indulging in the cliché of the noble savage or the primitive other, then, Melville, according to James, works with those clichés in order to transform them into concepts capable of generating futures of his present. Insofar as his positioning of Melville as an artist and *Moby Dick* as a novel of relevance to the world as James perceived it during the Cold War is a structuring logic of James's book, his claim that Melville's knowledge of his future came from his clarity about "all that was going on around him" is an assertion about the immanence of another world and another time in the existing ones. In the introduction to *Mariners, Renegades and Castaways*, Donald E. Pease explains that the temporality animating James's approach to Melville is that of the "future anterior," which "links a past event with a possible future upon which the past event depends for its significance."[42]

Melville's career as a writer lasted only eleven years, though Melville lived for twenty years after the publication of his final novel. He died in New York City in 1891. Much later, his work was recognized and hailed as among the best literature ever produced in the United States. Melville died without knowing that he was one of the greatest American writers ever to have found the courage to write. The story of Melville's career as a novelist and his posthumous rise to canonical status itself raises significant questions about the extent to which creative intellectual expressions can be apprehended in their time, and thereby calls attention to the complexities of temporal existence, the limits of contemporary standards of evaluation and measure, and the changing apparatuses of mattering. It also frustrates our ability to speculate on the future by tying it to what we can perceive in the present.

While *Moby Dick*'s Ahab and his crew on the *Pequod* are significant to James in 1952, Bartleby is the American literary character that has generated philosophical and political writing by thinkers, mostly European, in the last two decades of the twentieth century and at the beginning of the twenty-first. For James, Ahab offers an opportunity to delve into the human dynamics and relations underlying the rise of a variety of totalitarianisms during the first half of the twentieth century.[43] Yet, James asks that we "remind ourselves of Melville's view of his problem in 1851." About this, James writes:

The Pequod is taking a voyage that humanity has periodically to take into the open sea, into the unknown, because of the problems posed to it by life on the safe sheltered land. The Pequod set out on that voyage. But, as always on these journeys, mankind finds reflected in the water only the image of what it has brought with it. When the Pequod set out so bravely and boldly, it carried in its very heart, in the captain's cabin, the mono-maniacal Ahab, as genuine a part of that society as is Starbuck. Ahab will lead the vessel to inevitable destruction and those whose responsibility it is to defend the society will be completely incapable of doing so. . . . Melville took great pains to show that revolt was no answer to the question he asked. . . . If there had been a revolt on the Pequod . . . we would have been left in the end exactly where we had been at the beginning.[44]

James's insights regarding Melville's stance toward the possibility of revolt are worth considering in the context of both the historical moment in which Melville wrote *Moby Dick* and of the Cold War and its aftermath. It also bears re-petition now. *Moby Dick* was published in the social, cultural, and political milieu leading up to the American Civil War, directly after the passage of the Fugitive Slave Act (1850), which conscripted Northerners to the perpetuation of the institution of chattel slavery. As I mentioned about the publication of "Bartleby the Scrivener" in 1853, this was also when the reservation system for Native Americans was being established (1851). This context is important, because it situates the issues James identifies in Melville regarding revolt and insurrection within the broader set of concerns James raises about race, class, and nation. Melville's sense that, in James's words, "a revolt was no answer to the question he asked," because it would have left things exactly as they were, can be understood as an insight about the extent to which white supremacy, capitalist accumulation, and the basic relations between the Northern and the Southern states in Melville's time would be radically transformed by a revolt.

Melville's Bartleby offers another form of resistance: a passive resistance that is not a revolt, but, as we have been exploring throughout this book, a significant upheaval of the surety of equivalences and correspondences. Bartleby's resistance is to insist on opacity. For Glissant, "opacity" refers to a group's right to remain illegible to other groups or otherwise imperceptible according to the dominant terms through which things become perceptible. During a conversation with Manthia

Diawara, as we have seen, Glissant explains that opacity ought to be a right because it insists upon the power of a group's own modes of valorization and their own systems of signification rather than insisting that they conform to others' systems.[45] Rather than insisting upon a politics that can only be one of reform, because it reifies rather than challenges existing structures, a politics of opacity offers a way for groups to assert a right to self-determination, even when that hinges on improprieties and anarchy, and to assemble structures of belonging, valorization, and significance that are indifferent to existing ones.

As we have seen, Bartleby, with his "queer formula" and his ability to make language cease to signify, is opaque to the lawyer who narrates his story. Bartleby's ability to remain opaque to the lawyer throughout the story is one of the elements of the scrivener's story that has made it appealing to thinkers during the latter decades of the twentieth century and the early ones of the twenty-first. Bartleby's opacity is what opens the story to contexts and interests beyond its own. Allowing for that opacity is what enables philosophers to conceptualize Bartleby's resistance as a radical refusal within existing structures. Bartleby's opacity, his refusal to signify in accountable and politically meaningful ways, is the story's greatest resource. By the last decades of the twentieth century, the unaccountable Bartleby had become a significant figure through which to address the modalities of power characteristic of control societies, including the transformation of individuals into what Deleuze calls "dividuals," subjected to quantification and measurement.[46]

In the middle of the twentieth century, James claims that Melville had the ability to speak to the future because he saw so clearly what was happening around him. If this is the case, it could be argued that the elements of the types of financialization and control salient today were perceptible during Melville's career as a writer—that is, in the decades leading up to the American Civil War and the formal end of chattel slavery in the United States. In the face of the calculations characteristic of chattel slavery and settler colonialism, including, as we have seen in the discussion of Baucom's work earlier in this book, the emergence of the spatiotemporal logics of finance capital and speculation, "Bartleby the Scrivener" portends the financialization of everyday life.

Donald E. Pease points out that James's *Mariners, Renegades, and Castaways* can be read as an appeal for the immanence of a different form of citizenship within the logics of the United States, one that might be understood in the terms available to James as an "international" citizenship. Pease's discussion of the criticism that American Studies scholars have lodged against James is compelling because it reveals the extent to which American Studies has participated in a Cold War project of American nationalism and, more interestingly (since the origins and initial aims of American Studies already are well established), it resituates a prior history of transnational American studies with James as an early progenitor.[47]

Pease identifies the intimations of a transnational American Studies within James's reading of *Moby Dick*, which is taken by most American Studies scholars of James's day to be a novel that ideologically authorizes American imperialism. Following along the lines laid out by Pease, we can turn our attention back to "Bartleby the Scrivener," recalling that Bartleby is identified by James through that character's association with the "mariners, renegades, and castaways" invoked in *Moby Dick*. James is writing about *Moby Dick* in the Cold War period, which Melamed associates with the emergence of racial liberalism as an official national stance of the United States that preserves the socioeconomic, if not the formally political, material relations of white supremacy and advances American imperialism. In that context, James reads Melville's novel as a way to challenge the ideological underpinnings of US imperialism and the protocols of citizenship that had relegated James to a holding cell at Ellis Island. Reading James's *Mariners, Renegades, and Castaways* along the lines offered by Pease opens formulations of "America" onto other relations than those that have defined the United States domestically. Taking Pease's reading of James a step further by centering Bartleby rather than Ahab, Ishmael, or Queequeg and the rest of the crew hunting the formidable whale Moby Dick, attention shifts from the question of the racial, ethnic, class, and national composition of the crew to the very conditions of possibility for the transformation of "the new world" into an ethical and political formation that might undo its own survival as such. Indeed, this is the provocation with which James's reading of Melville leaves us today.

Through the interests and insights laid out by a variety of European theorists, alongside a sustained consideration of the experiments and freedom dreams found in various Black cultural products, my readings of "Bartleby the Scrivener" seek to offer ways to think the present (im)-possibilities of not only a transnational form of citizenship, but, perhaps also a cosmic mode of voluntary or other logics of belonging. They strive to offer a way to release Coleman's figure, the "mobile agent" generated by neoliberal racial capitalism's official embrace of multiculturalism, through which "race" becomes perceptible as technology, from its duty to represent or to anchor a collective and/or from the injunction to become perceptible according to existing codes. A queer technology, the mobile agent need not anchor an alternative way to be nor be of any use to us whatsoever. It need only *matter*. Now. Even if in ways that elude our methods of assessment.

5

"World Galaxy"

Throughout this book, I have considered examples of artists and other intellectuals who engage primarily with aspects of Black American culture and/or with Black American history, thought, and/or politics. In addition, I have worked with Herman Melville, a canonical figure in American literature. From this decidedly American focus, *Queer Times, Black Futures* tries to reach, however clumsily, beyond national formations, to touch a cosmic perspective.

Such a "cosmic perspective" has been a dimension of various cultural imaginaries for a long time. Science is catching up with our collective imagination. Many physicists, technologists, and other scientists have been inspired by speculative fictional scenarios, and many of us in the humanities are beginning to incorporate in systematic ways the new insights scientists have gained from their glimpses into a cosmic perspective. Doing so is challenging how we approach several of the concepts long considered foundational to Western thought, including "time," "temporality," "subjectivity," "the human," "the Other," and "agency." Working with and through scientific and technical knowledge in the service of humanistic inquiry is a challenge of world historical significance. I believe that if the species life that has enabled a book such as this to be written is to continue on this planet, the inequities "the human" has fostered and maintained over time must be redressed. A cosmic orientation can underscore the profound interrelatedness of matter(s) presently governed by race, class, gender, sexuality, disability, nationality, and so on, with other urgent material questions posed to, for, and in our times, such as global climate change, the Anthropocene, artificial intelligence, big data, computation, the potential and dangers of and in the human genome, epigenetics, and CRISPR (Clustered Regularly Interspaced Short Palindromic Repeat), space travel and the colonization of other planets, cryptography, cryptocurrency, and other technology used in societies of control.

"In the Dark"

With these world-historical entanglements in mind, a cosmic imagination is possible today, one that embraces what Édouard Glissant has called the "poetics of Relation": a mobile, fugitive perception of the interconnectedness of all things, which does not insist upon a universal system of commensuration, but instead allows for every thing's right to opacity. The "poetics of Relation" carries with it, indeed is fueled and enabled by, the violence of modernity and its characteristic contacts between groups of people. Yet, for Glissant, that poetics also allows for a fundamental transduction of selves, societies, and values into a multiplicity that, though open and changing, remains powerfully connected to the historical contexts of its production. Glissant does not call for a rupture in historical time (indeed, as I discussed in chapter 1, for Glissant, catastrophe has already occurred); rather, he calls for a sense of time as an opening up to, or, to put this another way, a caving in to another world we might feel is (im)possible now.[1] Though it may be imperceptible, that other world is accruing value (if there will be such a thing) here and now. "Contentless and simple," everything is.[2]

"At Home"

Glissant's formulation of the "poetics of Relation" hinges on the French word *relation*, as he explains: "To the extent that our consciousness of Relation is total, that is, immediate and focusing directly upon the realizable totality of the world, when we speak of a poetics of Relation, we no longer need to add: relation between what and what? That is why the French word Relation, which functions somewhat like a transitive verb, could not correspond, for example, to the English term relationship."[3] In the chapter entitled "Poetics" in his book *Poetics of Relation*, Glissant narrates his "poetics of Relation" as part of a series of transformations within the French language made by poets who confronted or encountered various Others along their journeys from their native lands. These poets were distinguished by the ways in which they registered "the shock of elsewhere"—the impact of their travels and geographic wanderings—in their work.

"Toward the World"

Glissant claims that the earlier movements of Relation that accompanied the journeying of European language, as part of the European territorial expansion into other parts of the world, operated according to a series of arrow-like trajectories, which "link the places of the world into a whole made up of peripheries, which are listed in function of a Center."[4] What he calls the first "itinerary" led from the Center toward the peripheries and included "all those who, whether critical or possessed, racist or idealist, frenzied or rational, have experienced passionately the call of Diversity."[5] After that, "a second itinerary then began to form, this time from the peripheries toward the Center." This movement included "poets who were born or lived in the elsewhere" and "dream" of the Center as a source of their "imaginary constructs and, consciously or not, 'make the trip in the opposite direction,' struggling to do so."[6] Glissant continues, "In a third stage the trajectory is abolished; the arrowlike projection becomes curved" in such a way that the poet's word "abolishes the very notion of center and periphery."[7]

Glissant names exemplary French and Francophone poets from each of the three stages he identifies. After characterizing the third stage, Glissant explains:

> The time came, then, in which Relation was no longer a prophecy made by a series of trajectories, itineraries that followed or thwarted one another. By itself and in itself Relation exploded like a network inscribed within the sufficient totality of the world.[8]

That Glissant uses a metaphor of the network here reminds us of the centrality of "networks" to the logics of social connection and communication prevalent today, and it brings to mind the importance of computational media technologies in producing and sustaining those networks. Within the repetitions and circularity of the totality in which a "poetics of Relation" inscribes itself, the dispersed mobile agent of interest to Beth Coleman through her reading of James A. Snead (discussed at length in the previous chapters) is also perceptible here. Glissant writes, "Every expression of the humanities opens onto the fluctuating complexity of the world. Here poetic thought safeguards the particular, since only the totality of truly secure particulars guarantees the energy of Diversity," where "Diversity" can be understood, according to Glissant, as "the quantifiable totality of every possible difference."[9]

In the third stage, Relation, no longer journeying and future-facing, explodes "like a network inscribed within the sufficient totality of the world" and reveals its depth, a dimension within ourselves that may be approached through duration. It signals a spatiotemporal shift experienced in common. Again, Glissant explains:

> We no longer reveal totality within ourselves by lightning flashes. We approach it through the accumulation of sediments. The poetics of duration (another leitmotiv), one of the first principles of the sacred, founding books of community, reappears to take up the relay from the poetics of the moment. Lightning flashes are the shivers of one who desires or dreams of a totality that is impossible or yet to come; duration urges on those who attempt to live this totality, when dawn shows through the linked histories of peoples.[10]

For Glissant, then, the ethical challenge of duration involves attempting to live the totality of the world as a temporal layering of the "linked histories of peoples." Over time, knowledge, including intuition, reaches into the sediment that has accumulated in time to assemble a living poetics that strives toward a totality comprised of Diversity. This is no longer a poetics of the moment in which a perception of the Whole arrives in quick flashes through which we dream of what yet, still might be one day. It is a poetics of duration in which the Whole is perceptible as an opening in which we live, here and now.

Relation anchors us in the queerness that is autochthonous to time. The "poetics of Relation" is a method of transduction, in Simondon's sense of "the operation whereby a domain undergoes information."[11] Stubborn forms, such as nations and peoples, can be transduced into different forms, perhaps unrecognizable as such, through errant and unanticipated connections with other sediment. Glissant states: "In addition, the poetics of Relation remains forever conjectural and presupposes no ideological stability. It is against the comfortable assurances linked to the supposed excellence of a language. A poetics that is latent, open, multilingual in intention, directly in contact with everything possible."[12] An upheaval within language, with material force.

The "poetics of Relation" is speculative. The spatial logics of "trajectory" no longer apply. Instead, "this poetics of Relation interweaves and no longer projects."[13] The "poetics of Relation" acknowledges the dense entanglement of matter(s). A modulation within Black culture, the "poetics of Relation" thrives on surprises and accidents as it "safeguards . . . the totality of truly secure particulars." It is antifragile.[14]

"World Galaxy"

As I mentioned in chapter 1, the first chapter of *Poetics of Relation* provides an impressionistic rendering of the experience of the Atlantic slave trade linking Europe, Africa, the Americas, and the Caribbean, which evokes something of what must have been the horrors of experiencing what Glissant calls "the abyss." Glissant characterizes the experience of the abyss that was the slave's journey into the European's "new world" as an "asceticism of crossing" in a closed boat (as opposed to the open boat, which Glissant says characterized an African politics).[15] Glissant asks his reader to imagine "the land-sea that, unknown to you, is the planet Earth, feeling a language vanish, the word of the gods vanish, and the sealed image of even the most everyday object, of even the most familiar animal, vanish."[16] Offering a poetic rendering of an experience of forced crossing, Glissant argues that Africans, especially those in the Europeans' "new world," carry a dimension of the abyss within.

Glissant understands "being" as in a constant process of change, a permanent process that he refers to as "creolization," which he identifies specifically with the Caribbean, but in such a way that it becomes "valid" for everybody. Glissant explains that he sees the history of the Caribbean as exemplary of this creolization: "What took place in the Caribbean, which could be summed up in the word 'creolization,' approximates the idea of Relation for us as nearly as possible. It is not merely an encounter; a shock . . . , a *métissage*, but a new and original dimension allowing each person to be there and elsewhere, rooted and open, lost in the mountains and free beneath the sea, in harmony and in errantry."[17] According to Glissant, the history of the Caribbean takes "into account the history of the world, because in this very moment the whole world is creolizing itself, and there are no longer nations or races that are untouched by others."[18] I think of a world that is creolizing itself as a "World Galaxy," a phrase I take from the title of a 1972 album by Alice Coltrane.

Coltrane, born Alice McLeod in Detroit, Michigan, in 1937, was married to and had four children with renowned jazz musician John Coltrane. A talented pianist, harpist, organist, and composer, she released seventeen albums between 1968 and 2004. In 1972, she founded a Vedantic Center. Later, she became a Hindu swami, established an ashram, and added "Turiyasangitananda" to her name, becoming known as Alice Coltrane Turiyasangitananda or A. C. Turiyasangitananda. She served as spiritual director of the ashram until her death in 2007.[19] Thinking about her life and work opens up another route through Afrofuturist concerns with "imagination, technology, the future, and liberation"[20] by acknowledging that intercultural sonic connections and mixings, in this case between African American and Asian cultural forms and practices, are a significant part of the prehistory of Afrofuturism.[21]

If Afrofuturist progenitor Sun Ra experimented with the tropes and sounds of space travel and imagined Black people colonizing other planets as a solution to the spatial restrictions placed on Black Americans during Jim Crow segregation and to the psychic and material toll anti-Black racism takes on the imagination and consciousness of Black people, his contemporary, Alice Coltrane, forged a line of flight out of American anti-Black racism via errant wandering to the East. Where Sun Ra claimed to be from Saturn, evoked the spiritual beliefs of ancient Egypt, and invested in presently impossible futures, Coltrane founded a spiritual community in the Santa Monica Mountains outside of Los Angeles, where she created a syncretic music out of the vibrant sonic traditions of African American gospel music and Indian devotional music in the Hindu tradition.[22] Sun Ra was preoccupied with how technology enables an exploration of outer worlds. Alice Coltrane forged sonic and spiritual technē to search for liberation within.

During the mid- to late 1960s, when Sun Ra, John Coltrane, Alice Coltrane, and other musicians were experimenting with form, jazz functioned as an engine of creolization. Many scholars have pointed out the influence of African music and traditions on the distinctly African American cultural form of jazz, but few have discussed the extent to which Asian, particularly Indian and Japanese, musical forms and spiritual logics were also significant currents flowing into jazz during this period. A wide range of sonic material influenced John Coltrane's own original compositions.[23] In 1969, after John Coltrane's death, bassist Vishnu Wood, hoping to lift Alice Coltrane out of her grief and depression, introduced her to Swami Satchidananda, who had been giving lectures on Manhattan's Upper West Side. Swami Satchidananda's lectures in New York City were part of a broader cultural preoccupation in the United States at the time with what Jane Iwamura has called "the icon of the Oriental monk." Iwamura refers to how, between 1950 and 1975, television and film in the United States put into circulation an iconic image, "the Oriental monk," that was representative of "an otherworldly (though perhaps not entirely alien) spirituality that draws from the ancient wellsprings of 'Eastern' civilization and culture."[24] Alice Coltrane's turn to "otherworldly" Eastern musical and spiritual forms happened during the broader American Orientalist embrace of Eastern religions and philosophies of the 1960s. While these intercultural exchanges certainly involved cultural appropriation, there is a crucial difference in the case of Alice Coltrane from the kind of cultural appropriation in which the value that has accrued to the cultural innovations of one group of people are made to serve the interests of another group that is in a position of power vis-à-vis the innovative group.[25]

Alice Coltrane's embrace of the philosophical and spiritual teachings of the Vedas unsettles a unitary notion of African American selfhood, pushing it beyond the parameters of nation-state belonging and its structures of citizenship and into a terrain of belonging on the scale of what she refers to as a "world galaxy" and, in the title of another album from the same time period, a "universal consciousness." In her life and music, the errantry driving her entanglements with Asian musical, cultural, and spiritual forms was animated by a quest for liberation, the abolition of war, and dreams of different kinds of connection inconsistent with a simple will to arrogate the value of Asian culture for herself, for African Americans, or for another group with which one could claim she was affiliated. By forging generative, errant connections from those avenues available to her during the late 1960s, she created a new musical form.[26] It could be said that Coltrane's turn to Asian cultural forms is a type of "Black Orientalism." Following Helen Jun, I use the phrase

"Black Orientalism" to designate "a heterogeneous and historically vari-
able discourse in which the contradictions of black citizenship engage
with the logic of American Orientalism." In Jun's usage, Black Orientalism "is in no way an accusatory or reductive condemnation that seeks
to chastise black individuals or institutions for being imperialist, racist,
or Orientalist." It does not have "a singular meaning or manifestation."
Here, "Black Orientalism encompasses a range of black imaginings of
Asia that are in fact negotiations with the limits, failures, and disap-
pointments of black citizenship."[27]

For Coltrane, the Orientalist elements of "world galaxy" tap into the
way that "the Orient" historically constitutes a geopolitical and ontological position that serves as an alternative to, if not a contestation of, Western or European hegemonies. It is a way of working from within existing
logics and structures in order to imagine another set of possibilities immanent to them. Coltrane's sonic Black Orientalism is inspired most directly by the Indian musical traditions popularized in the United States
by Ravi Shankar, which also significantly influenced her husband John
Coltrane, and, as I mentioned, by the relationship she established in
1969 with Swami Satchidananda, two years after John Coltrane's death.

Following Glissant, Alice Coltrane's experiments with(in) Asian musical forms, as well as her travels to India and Japan, can be understood
as sonic and spiritual errantry. Glissant understands "errantry" as a
way of refusing the specificity of a particular root or sense of an origin.
When it shows up in African American jazz in relation to Asian musical
traditions, it can work as a mode of critique that pushes beyond already
existing analyses of forms of exploitation and domination and, through
its structures of feeling, participates in a creolization that today can be
understood metaphorically as the hyphen in Afro-Asian. Perhaps it also
anticipates a more radical upheaval of the logics in which "Black" and
"Asian" cohere as such.[28]

As in my discussion of Sun Ra, my focus on Alice Coltrane's music
routes my analysis and arguments through jazz, a distinctly African
American cultural form that has achieved an expressive validity and relevance well beyond the particularities of Black existence in the United
States. During a discussion with Manthia Diawara, Glissant highlights
the efforts of Black American jazz musicians in a way relevant to my
discussion here of Sun Ra and Alice Coltrane, who were progenitors of

Afrofuturism.[29] Glissant argues that Africa's specific calling is to move from Unity to multiplicity, and that Africans have in part accomplished this through cultural and other forms of mixing. He explains that when African culture mixes with other cultures, what is produced tends to be "valid" for all. He gives jazz and reggae as two musical examples:

> The Africans had lost everything; they had nothing, not even a song. In jazz, black Americans had to recompose, through memory and through extraordinary suffering, the echo of what Africa had for them. Jazz came about not through a book but through a flight of memory. That's why jazz is valid for everybody, because it's a reconstruction within a distraught memory of something that had disappeared and had now been regained. It required a terrifying effort. That's why jazz at the beginning was so tragic. If you look at the faces of the great jazz musicians, they are very tragic, and that's something everyone can see. The same goes for Bob Marley and reggae: it's valid for everyone.[30]

In other words, jazz issues from the dimension of the abyss at the core of diasporic Black culture. Jazz musicians confronted the abyss and recomposed a past through it. From his specific location in the Caribbean, Glissant helps us to understand that, in the face of natal alienation and the psychic and other violent upheavals that characterize the abyss, jazz seeks to forge new modes of being that apply to everyone. In the case of Alice Coltrane, Black Orientalism was part of the "terrifying effort" required to create a new musical form that might call everyone into Relation.[31] The core impulse in Coltrane's mode of Black Orientalism is cosmic; that is, it seeks to re-Orient humanity toward and within a vast imagined universe. As Kodwo Eshun writes, "With Alice Coltrane, the jazz composer becomes the electric transmitter. In her Galactic Tetralogy, recording becomes a primaudial technology. The cosmos is an infinity of endlessly reverberating vibrations. The universe begins in sound. Therefore new sound engines can amplify new universes into resonance."[32]

Alice Coltrane's work after John Coltrane's death can be understood within the context of the transformations taking place in the social and political landscape of the United States and elsewhere after 1967–1968. Coltrane's errant turn to an Eastern spiritual tradition during this time is part of a broader cultural turn inward to an exploration of self, fueled by American Orientalism. Coltrane's turn to inner worlds as a way to address the present limitations of American society takes its rationale and logic from within the jazz music that preceded it, and from within a trajectory of American thought consistent with the logics of liberal multiculturalism. Nonetheless, it also is a rejection of the dominant institutions in the United States during a time when they were increasingly allowing more access and recognition to Black people and people of color. Coltrane's creation of a sonic "world galaxy" was in the interest of producing a set of affective, if not entirely politically operational, conditions for a new humanism. It is a creolization between African and Asian that tends toward what I call "errant futures" because it brings together seemingly disparate logics and paradigms in relatively unpredictable ways.

Today, in a moment when the citizenship gains of the civil rights era are being rolled back, when Black life continues to be deemed negligible, when uprisings against neoliberalism are palpable and increasingly powerful worldwide, and when the representational paradigms that previously underwrote our political logics no longer or only tenuously apply, I purposively wander back to Alice Coltrane's Black Orientalism in order to explore the "world galaxy" she created with sound, listening for and within the hyphen between African and American and Asian that is part of our now.

Speculations on Africa

Within this spatiotemporal catastrophe we call modernity, I also wander to narratives of Africa. Sometimes these offer an anchor for imagining reconnection. Other times, they posit "Africa" as a vibrant site of dispersal and contagion. As I discussed in the introduction, for Shell and other transnational corporations, "Africa" is a site of economic and geologic exploitation in the name of shareholders' profits and maintaining present forecasts for global energy futures. A formulation of "Africa" also figures centrally in Afrofuturism, whether as an anchor for a "Black Atlantic" or as a setting for speculative fiction. A formulation of "Africa" functions within corporate scenarios as well; as Kodwo Eshun points out, "If global scenarios are descriptions that are primarily concerned with making futures safe for the market, then Afrofuturism's first priority is to recognize that Africa increasingly exists as the object of futurist projection. . . . Africa is always the zone of the absolute dystopia. There is always a reliable trade in market projections for Africa's socioeconomic crises. Market dystopias aim to warn against predatory futures, but always do so in a discourse that aspires to unchallengeable certainty."[33] In the introduction, I discussed the global scenarios of the type Eshun mentions here, taking as exemplary those produced by Shell Oil to inform their product development, planning, and assessments of risk and profits. In the face of corporate speculations on "Africa," the Afrofuturisms of interest throughout *Queer Times, Black Futures* narrate alternative, fantastic, unpredictable responses to potential futures for "Africa" and for peoples of the African diaspora.

To understand this valence of Afrofuturism, I turn to Wanuri Kahiu's short film *Pumzi* from 2009 and Nnedi Okorafor's third novel, *Who Fears Death,* published in 2010. The fantastic and irrational futures imagined in these cultural productions are animated by queer, unpredictable connections between things. Although there is much that could be said about both of these remarkable texts, I focus here on the way each of them depicts the active creation of dreams, myths, and stories as responses to the quotidian violence of their story's present. As I explained in the introduction and chapter 1, quotidian violence maintains a temporality and a spatial logic that is hostile to the queerness in time. In the speculative narratives of *Pumzi* and *Who Fears Death*, dreams, myths, and stories are precisely what must be managed by those in power so that present relations are rendered logical, viable, and sustainable. In order for existing relations to survive as such, dreams, myths, and stories must not accrue material force. As I discuss most directly in chapter 3, but have been arguing throughout *Queer Times, Black Futures*, the digital regime of the image facilitates a more widespread acknowledgment of the separation of indices from their material referents. Under these conditions, the stories we tell, the myths we believe, and the dreams through which, as Audre Lorde explains, insights and revelations, new knowledge, might enter and inform existing structures are some of the reservoirs for the transduction of present relations into another organization of things.[34]

In Wanuri Kahui's short film *Pumzi*, the protagonist's dreams provide access to insights capable of supporting radical transformations in the material world. In the film's speculative global scenario, set in the "Maitu Community, East African Territories, 35 years after World War III, the water war," the Maitu Community exists in a compound sealed off from the seemingly dead world outside. They make their own energy (the signs on the wall read: "One hundred percent self-powered community. Zero percent pollution.") and recycle all their bodily and other fluids, including their urine and sweat. Even their thoughts and dreams are monitored. Kahiu's film highlights the role of technology in the structures of control that characterize the film's speculations about a future "Africa," set in the cultural context of historical Kenya. This speculative scenario is the element of the film about which Kahiu receives questions; in interviews, she explains: "People ask if it's difficult to blend science fiction and Africa. . . . As far as I know, science and Africa have never been separate."[35]

The society *Pumzi* depicts is one of seemingly complete control; it is a closed system in which the community's collective energies and bodily expenditures are channeled back into the reproduction of the community itself. It is predictable and manageable. The mode of control presented in the Maitu Community relies upon a medical management of dreams and, it could be argued by extension, the imagination. The society proves to be actively hostile to the protagonist's success in the activity the society seems to be set up to help foster and discover—namely, the quest for water that would support plant and other life outside of the compound.

The film's protagonist, Asha, is a researcher analyzing soil samples for their water content.[36] She receives a sample with unusually high water content, but when she brings it to the attention of the authorities, she is told not to pursue it and is subsequently punished for trying to follow up on the evidence she has uncovered. Ultimately, she chooses to break out of the compound, with help from a cleaner who appears to be of a different racial and class background than Asha. After arduously navigating the rocky and dusty world outside the compound, which the governing council of the Maitu Community tells her is "dead," Asha sacrifices her own life in order to test her theory that the soil sample contains enough water to support vegetation. The film ends as Asha breathes her last breath while sheltering the bulb she planted into the ground and nurtured with her own sweat and the last of her potable water. The camera pans out as a tree grows from the spot on which she died. The sound of thunder can be heard as the camera continues its pan, taking a bird's eye view of the terrain, and the film's title, *Pumzi*, is revealed on the screen.[37] As a wider view becomes apparent, it is clear that Asha died some distance from, but not a great distance from, what appears to be a dense forest.

The aerial shot at the end of the film recalls the establishing aerial shot of the compound at the beginning, which slowly pushes in until a cut to a close-up shot and a pan to reveal jars in a lab space inside the compound. These contain samples of seeds and other forms of plant life, as well as glass cases displaying newspaper clippings and other artifacts chronicling the scarcity of and quest for water. There is a close up of the descriptive title on one of the jars. It reads "Maitu (Mother) Seed. Kikuyu language. 1. Noun—Mother. Origin: Kikuyu Language from MAA (Truth) and ITU (Ours). OUR TRUTH." The word "Maitu" already is familiar to viewers from the opening text that references the "Maitu Community" in East Africa. This context situates the film within "a Gikuyu (Kikuyu) centric modern African feminist paradigm."[38]

In its first frames, *Pumzi* re-petitions the matrilineal origin story for the Agikuyu people (who speak the Bantu language Kikuyu), translating an oral tradition into film. In so doing, it anchors the science fictional society of its speculative future within a set of references to an ethnic group who presently exist in the nation we know today as Kenya. For those viewers who are familiar with Kikuyu and the myths and history of Agikuyu culture, *Pumzi* offers a futuristic heroine who resists the demand that she stop listening to her dreams and accept existing conditions. By the end of the film, she is associated with the mighty tree that she has been seeing in her dreams and that calls to her from across the desert once she escapes. This tree recalls the Mugumo tree, or Mukuyu tree, which "is central to Gikuyu culture as a sacred tree" and is used in this monotheistic culture "as a place of worship and communing with God and collectively."[39] For that segment of its audience who lack knowledge of Agikuyu culture, *Pumzi* provides a feminist vision of activism in the face of environmental devastation in East Africa, perhaps recalling the efforts of environmentalist Wangari Maathai, who was Gikuyu, to found the Green Belt Movement and work to reverse the environmental destruction threatening rural Kenyans. In 2004, Maathai won a Nobel Peace Prize for this work, which she undertook even in the face of great danger to herself and those who worked with her. Around the time that she was making *Pumzi*, Kahiu directed a documentary film about Maathai entitled *For Our Land* (2009).[40]

Pumzi's speculation on "Africa" posits its future as dystopian, "after World War III, the water war," but its investments are in the risky actions of the main character, in fugitivity, and in errant connections, such as those between Asha and the cleaner. Before she knows she will find the fertile soil (and therefore before she has any clear motive to help the cleaner), Asha leaves some of her water for the cleaner in the restroom. Later, the cleaner helps Asha to escape in order to pursue her dream of finding the tree. *Pumzi*'s narrative hinges on the main character's action of withdrawing her consent from the terms of control and pilfering the soil sample (in which a seed she'd planted has started to grow) and water out of a structure and system that would control their circulation. She steals these riches so that they can be invested in a different project. *Pumzi* infuses a speculative scenario about future disasters in Africa with the unpredictability of fugitivity, errantry, and criminality, all of which are here efforts toward the freedom and survival of a collective, not of the society that exists in *Pumzi*, but of another, already held in escrow, that might grow out of work and other action undertaken today.

Pumzi's director, Wanuri Kahiu, was born in Nairobi, Kenya, and has a bachelor's degree of science from the University of Warwick in the United Kingdom, and an MFA in film directing from the University of California, Los Angeles, in the United States. Her first film, *From a Whisper* (2008), won five African Movie Academy Awards and helped to bring her to the attention of African American producer Kisha Cameron-Dingle while Cameron-Dingle was program director of the Focus Features Africa First Short Film Program. Cameron-Dingle's film production company, Completion Films, optioned the film rights to Nnedi Okorafor's novel *Who Fears Death* and signed Wanuri Kahiu onto the project as its director. Although that project never materialized, Okorafor and Kahiu have collaborated on several other projects since then, including short stories and an animated film entitled "The Camel Racer."[41]

Okorafor's *Who Fears Death* carries an epigraph by Patrice Lumumba, identified there as the "first and only elected Prime Minister of the Republic of the Congo." The epigraph begins with a salutation—"Dear friends,"—and continues with a question, "are you afraid of death?" "Dear Friends, are you afraid of death?" This question sounds like an invitation—a challenge and incitement to risk and revolution. While it begins with this epigraph from a hopeful, revolutionary, now dead and decaying past, *Who Fears Death* ends with an illustration of the material force of the stories we tell.

Sola, the narrator of "Chapter One: Rewritten," the novel's last chapter, has not previously served as narrator. Sola writes the story of what happens after Onyesonwu, the novel's protagonist, fulfills prophesy by rewriting the Great Book and being stoned to death for it. In "Chapter One: Rewritten," rather than dying from the stoning she endures after rewriting the Great Book, Onyesonwu rewrites the Great Book and, in the midst of the stoning, takes to the sky as a Kponyungo (a giant flying lizard that is thought to be mythical but that Onyesonwu and her mother, among other sorcerers, can transform into).

As Onyesonwu flies through the air to meet her lover Mwita, below her to the South, West, and East, a wave of change, unleashed when Onyesonwu succeeded in fulfilling her destiny to rewrite the Great Book, transforms relationships between people. Both Mwita and Onyesonwu are Ewu, the name given to the children of a Nuru and an Okeke parent. When the novel opens, the Nuru and the Okeke have been at war for a long time, and Nuru men regularly rape Okeke women as a weapon of war. Onyesonwu fulfills a prophecy to end the war. When she does, new abilities, such as the capacity for flight, are bestowed upon people. It is a historical rupture with spatial coordinates. It creates another world.

Yet, though change spreads throughout the rest of the world, "directly below" a mob still waits. At the end of the novel, this waiting is a bloodthirsty inertia. To conclude the novel, Sola writes:

> If Onyesonwu had taken one last look below, to the south, with her keen *Kponyungo* eyes she'd have seen Nuru, Okeke, and two Ewu children in school uniforms playing in a schoolyard. To the east, stretching into the distance, she'd have seen black paved roads populated by men and women, Okeke and Nuru, riding scooters and carts pulled by camels. In

downtown Durfa, she'd have spotted a flying woman discreetly meeting up with a flying man on the roof of the tallest building. But the wave of change was yet to sweep by directly below. There, thousands of Nuru still waited for Onyesonwu, all of them screaming, yelling, shouting, laughing, glaring . . . waiting to wet their tongues with Onyesonwu's blood. Let them wait. They will be waiting for a long long time.[42]

The mob's waiting reinscribes the violent temporality of the present in which the mob waits. It is not normal waiting, nor is it lying in wait. Lying in wait is subterranean, indecipherable. This waiting is part of the old organization of things. It is waiting that seeks to anchor and perpetuate the logics and narratives of genocide, rape, and exploitation through which the characters in this novel have come to be who they are. The mob wants Onyesonwu's blood because in fulfilling the prophecy in which she rewrites the Great Book and thereby creates a new world, she also killed all the virile men within a Nuru town and impregnated all the women. And she killed their general, her father, the Nuru sorcerer named Daib, who raped Onyesonwu's Okeke mother and in that way fathered Onyesonwu.

The rupture narrated in *Who Fears Death* is, then, predicated simultaneously on a patricide and a radical interruption of social reproduction on the level of biological reproduction. Killing all the virile men and impregnating all the pregnable women, Onyesonwu sires a generation without fathers—a prophetic generation is coming. It arrives. Still, directly below Onyesonwu, surrounded by a new world that is breathing and becoming within the wave of change, the mob waits, impervious to that wave of change, seeking its own survival as such—brutal, genocidal, necropolitical, and authorized by the Great Book before Onyesonwu rewrote it.

Caught within the image of waiting that concludes *Who Fears Death* is an organization of time that resonates with the temporality of a variety of religious and religiously inflected systems of thought, among them the Jewish apocalyptic and rabbinic traditions about which Giorgio Agamben comments in *The Time that Remains*, his reading of the Apostle Paul's "The Letter to the Romans." For Agamben, the Pauline texts are "the fundamental messianic texts of the West." The invocation of messianic time in Okorafor's novel calls our attention to the fact that messianic and apocalyptic time have spatial implications, and it calls attention to the spatial politics of the temporality that undergirds "the fundamental messianic texts of the West."[43] These spatial implications complicate how we might think the politics and possibilities for radical transformations in existing conditions. In *Who Fears Death*, there is a point at which the fictional land the characters inhabit is revealed to have a referent in the world of the reader of the novel in 2011. After Onyesonwu rewrites the Great Book and is stoned to death, her supporters, the witnesses to her death, burn her body on a funeral pyre. Sola mentions for the first time the name of the place in which the novel's action has unfolded: "It was the most we could do for the woman who saved the people of the Seven Rivers Kingdom, this place that used to be part of the Kingdom of Sudan."[44]

The wave of change described at the end of *Who Fears Death* has material spatial implications. The transduction of one organization of things into another, however rapidly or gradually that occurs, involves an entanglement with existing matter(s). As in all mattering, ethical questions of evaluation, measurement, and adjudication are brought to the fore when chapter 1 of the Great Book is rewritten. As a fantastic speculative fiction, *Who Fears Death* invests in the impossible possibility that the geopolitics and historical conflicts that fuel the violence in Sudan might succumb to the logics of a different authorizing narrative shaped by a Black radical imagination invested in liberation.

Radical changes (whether in terms of the founding of new nations as in the case of the Americas I discussed in the "Intercession," where I considered Deleuze's reading of Bartleby, or of the imaginative positing of a colony for Black people "up under different stars" as in Sun Ra's *Space Is the Place*, or of other fundamental changes in the existing organization of things) raise ethical questions about spatial relations. *Who Fears Death* invokes "the Sudan" as that kingdom whose authorizing myths, legends, and stories Onyesonwu was prophesied to rewrite. In so doing, the novel imaginatively unmoors their capacity to shape reality, and it upends the quotidian violence holding that reality in place. Sola, an apostle, we might say, risks dreaming that the rapes, genocide, and exploitation that were taking place in 2010 in the Sudan in the material world familiar and accessible to the novel's readers might give way to a different organization of things, a different system of signification and value, another world there now, and that it might give way to this other world through the power carried in stories, myths, and legends. This dream is dangerous and productive of many valences of risk in the time that remains between what Onyesonwu was (as anchored by the angry mob of the Kingdom of Sudan so far immune to the wave of change that is enveloping the space around them) and what she would become (the woman who saved the people of Seven Rivers Kingdom).

Yet, invoking a place, Sudan, which has an objectively verifiable existence in our world, *Who Fears Death* anchors its freedom dreams for another future in a here and now with complex geopolitical coordinates and stubborn historical entanglements. Released one year before the founding of South Sudan, *Who Fears Death* evinces no foreknowledge of that jubilant moment, or of the tragic disappointment that stains what it would mean in hindsight today (at the time of this writing, it is 2017) or in your today, dear reader. Still, *Who Fears Death* asks us to acknowledge the injustices and violence that have characterized a place in our world and the beliefs that authorize them. It provides a mythical hero, created by Okorafor and unmoored from tradition, but not unlike those saviors with whom we already are familiar. Although it does not provide a program for change, *Who Fears Death* calls attention to the roles that myths, beliefs, dreams, and imagination play in changing material conditions. Re-calling its readers to the violence in their world at the end of the novel, *Who Fears Death* establishes a connection between the world of the novel and the world of its readers. It calls attention to its readers' entanglements in existing matter(s) and to the stories, micro- and macro-, through which those entanglements have materialized.

Among the entanglements this move calls attention to, I would include Nnedi Okorafor, the author of *Who Fears Death*, and Wanuri Kahiu, the director of *Pumzi* and Okorafor's collaborator, as well as myself and perhaps you, because our biographies, known and hidden, might help to better map the sets of investments, mobilities, and interests that are brought to bear upon what was called "Sudan" in 2010 through the analyses we offer, the stories we tell about it, and the amount of belief we invest in those stories.

"In the Dark"

Still, within this here and now exist yearnings and openings, experiments, errant wanderings, radical refusals, and creative projects; here and now are echoes from a hopeful past—Patrice Lumumba addresses us as "friends," "Dear friends, are you afraid of death?"—and in our responses to him, are futures that fly in defiance of even the most scientifically sound speculations about them. The fantastic queer times of our lives support unpredictable alliances, theories, knowledges, and connections that might operate on a register that is incommensurate with the calculated risks speculative capital already assumes through its investments in existing relations, even as, perhaps, such unpredictable and random connections have been anticipated, domesticated, dominated, and conquered in advance.

Perhaps.

"At Home"

In the context of the algorithms and relations characteristic of finance, poetic knowledge returns the body to the living organism and upends the rationale for the violences of finance capital. It prefers not to. By introducing desire and the senses into knowledge production, it disrupts the common, habitual relations of signification that allow for prediction and reconciliation between things. It insists that how we come to know what we know is as significant as what we know, and, in these ways, it provides a queer way of knowing that flies in the face of calculation and commensuration—an empiricism that invites surprises.

"Toward the World"

ACKNOWLEDGMENTS

I finish this project deeply indebted to many amazing thinkers, artists, and friends. I started working on the ideas contained in this book before my first monograph was published ten years ago. Due to the amount of time that has passed and the inadequacy of my accounting, I am not able to name everyone who has contributed to *Queer Times, Black Futures*. So, I want to begin by acknowledging the many people who have impacted this work in some way, but are not mentioned by name below. I regret that I did not keep a more careful record of my intellectual debts over the years.

My colleagues at the University of Southern California over the years have been intellectually generous and supportive, professionally and personally. In no particular order, they are: my colleagues in Cinema and Media Studies—Tara McPherson, Priya Jaikumar, Akira Lippit, Ellen Seiter, Nitin Govil, Anikó Imre, Curtis Marez, Marsha Kinder, Michael Renov, Laura Serna, David James, Bill Whittington, Rosa-Linda Fregoso, Drew Casper, Rick Jewell, Todd Boyd, and the late Anne Friedberg; Dean Elizabeth Daley and the School of Cinematic Arts full faculty; my colleagues in American Studies and Ethnicity—Jack Halberstam, Macarena Gomez-Barris, Fred Moten, Ruth Wilson Gilmore, Robin Kelley, Stan Huey, Chris Finley, Juan De Lara, Shana Redmond, Sarah Gualtieri, Edwin Hill, Dorinne Kondo, Viet Nguyen, Manuel Pastor, Karen Tongson, Nayan Shah, John Carlos Rowe, Lanita Jacobs, Francille Wilson, and the late María Elena Martínez-López; those in other parts of the university—Sarah Banet Weiser, Robeson Taj Frazier, Josh Kun, and Neetu Khanna; all of the graduate students who took my courses and came to my office hours, including Adam Bush, who gave me an Afrofuturism playlist; and the staff in the two departments in which I worked at USC, especially Alicia White, Jujuana Preston, Sonia Rodriguez, Kitty Lai, and Linda Overholt.

I also had the great fortune to have a wonderful intellectual community outside of USC in Los Angeles and elsewhere. The feminists of the

LOUD Collective, including Maylei Blackwell, Yogita Goyal, Mishauna Goeman, Tiffany Willoughby-Herard, Erica Edwards, Deb Vargas, Sarah Haley, and Arlene Keizer all provided intellectual and spiritual sustenance (and excellent food, too!) at crucial moments when those seemed to be in short supply. I also want to acknowledge: D. Soyini Madison, Rod Ferguson, Herman Gray, Jennifer Brody, Alexandra Juhasz, Fatima El-Tayeb, Mariam Lam, Arthur Jafa, Alessandra Raengo, Lynne Joyrich, Phil Rosen, Bonnie Honig, Amy Villarejo, Lisa Parks, Lisa Nakamura, Wendy Hui Kyong Chun, Alexander Weheliye, Huey Copeland, Wangui wa Goro, Peggy Piesche, Maisha Auma, Henriette Gunkel, Alondra Nelson, Raimi Gbadamosi, Akosua Adomako Ampofo, and Nana Adusei-Poku.

This book also has benefited from conversations with people at the Institute for Advanced African Studies in Bayreuth, Germany, Brown University, the Society for Cinema and Media Studies annual conference, the University of California at Los Angeles, the University of California at San Diego, the University of California at Santa Cruz, Indiana University, the University of California at Riverside, the College Arts Association conference, Yale University, Princeton University, the University of Chicago, Northwestern University, the American Studies Association annual conference, Humboldt University in Berlin, Goldsmiths University in London, the Association for Cultural Studies conference in Hong Kong, Wayne State University, Georgia State University, Georgia Tech University, the Inter-Asia Cultural Studies conferences in Singapore and in Seoul, the Witte de With in Rotterdam, and elsewhere.

I learned a great deal from all of the amazing people I had the pleasure of working with for the six years that I had the honor to serve as a board member for the Highlander Center for Research and Education.

Queer Times, Black Futures has been enriched by the care, comradery, and intellectual generosity shown to me by Grace Kyungwon Hong, Jodi Kim, Jacqueline Najuma Stewart, Daphne Brooks, Meaghan Morris, and Wangui wa Goro. Wangui kindly provided relevant translations for chapter 5.

Gabriel Karagianis generously agreed to create original artwork for this book's cover. At a late stage in the writing process, this manuscript benefitted from editorial help by Colleen Jankovic. The editorial staff at New York University Press have been diligent and devoted to this project from the beginning. I especially appreciate Eric Zinner's advice, expertise, and patience. Jose Muñoz believed in this project early on and encouraged me to publish it with NYU Press. I wish I would have published it during his lifetime. Tavia Nyong'o picked it up when Jose passed away.

Chandra Ford read every chapter in this book several times, and she patiently offered me crucial feedback and encouragement each time. Her fiercely creative intellect is matched only by her beauty, love, and kindness.

While this book has been strengthened by my encounters with many people over the years, all of its faults can be attributed only to me.

* * *

An earlier version of parts of chapter 2 is in Kara Keeling, "Looking for M—: Queer Temporality, Black Political Possibility, and Poetry from the Future," GLQ: A Journal of Lesbian and Gay Studies 15, no. 4 (2009): 565–582.

Parts of the introduction and chapter 1 have been reworked from their earlier appearance in Kara Keeling, "Electric Feel," Cultural Studies 28, no. 1 (2009): 49–83.

Parts of the "Interlude" have been adapted from Kara Keeling, "Sounds of Time/Image," in Time / Image Exhibition Catalogue, ed. and curator Amy Powell (Houston: Blaffer Art Museum at the University of Houston, 2015).

NOTES

PREFACE

1 Audre Lorde, "A Litany for Survival," *The Black Unicorn* (New York: W.W. Norton, 1978), 31. For a more sustained discussion of the concept of "survival" in Lorde's poem, see Alexis Pauline Gums and Julia Roxanne Wallace, "Something Else to Be: Generations of Black Queer Brilliance and the Mobile Homecoming Experiential Archive," in *No Tea, No Shade: New Writings in Black Queer Studies*, ed. E. Patrick Johnson (Durham, NC: Duke University Press, 2016), 380–393.

2 Giorgio Agamben, *The Time that Remains: A Commentary on the Letter to the Romans* (Palo Alto, CA: Stanford University Press, 2005).

3 I use the phrase "organization of things" throughout this book to reference a broad conceptualization of politics. I take from the phrase from Fred Moten's *In the Break: The Aesthetics of the Black Radical Tradition* (Minneapolis: University of Minnesota Press, 2003). After claiming "the tragic in Baraka is political despair," Moten writes, "Have you ever suffered from political despair, from despair about the organization of things?" He continues, "What does it mean to suffer from political despair when your identity is bound up with utopian political aspirations and desires?" (93).

4 Under the rubric of "new materialisms," I include vital materialism, feminist materialism, object-oriented ontologies, and emergent thinking focused on the urgent need to reverse, if not undo, trends in climate change.

5 Frantz Fanon, *Black Skin, White Masks*, trans. Charles Lam Markmann (New York: Grove Press, 1967), 229.

6 See, for example, André Breton, *What Is Surrealism?: Selected Writings* (Atlanta, GA: Monad, 1978).

7 Franklin Rosemont, *Revolution in the Service of the Marvelous* (Chicago: Charles H. Kerr Publishing Company, 2004), 17.

8 Ibid., 139.

9 Audre Lorde, "Poetry is not a Luxury," in *Sister Outsider: Essays and Speeches* (Freedom, CA: Crossing Press, 1984), 39.

10 Ibid., 37.

11 Jane Bennett, *Vibrant Matter: A Political Ecology of Things* (Durham, NC: Duke University Press, 2010).

12 Afropessimism and the debates regarding the ontology of Blackness generated by scholarship claiming and claimed by that body of work serve as a

valuable interlocutors for *Queer Times, Black Futures*. See, for example, Frank B. Wilderson III, *Red, White & Black: Cinema and the Structure of US Antagonisms* (Durham, NC: Duke University Press, 2010); Frank B. Wilderson III, "Gramsci's Black Marx: Whither the Slave in Civil Society?" *Social Identities* 9, no. 2 (2003): 225–240; Frank B. Wilderson III, *Incognegro: A Memoir of Exile and Apartheid* (Durham, NC: Duke University Press, 2015); Frank B. Wilderson III, "Grammar & Ghosts: The Performative Limits of African Freedom," *Theatre Survey* 50, no. 1 (2009): 119–125; Jared Sexton, *Amalgamation Schemes: Antiblackness and the Critique of Multiracialism* (Minneapolis: University of Minnesota Press, 2008); Jared Sexton, "People-of-Color-Blindness: Notes on the Afterlife of Slavery," *Social Text* 28, no. 2 103 (2010): 31–56; Jared Sexton, "The Social Life of Social Death: On Afro-Pessimism and Black Optimism," *InTensions* 5, no. 1 (2011): 1–47; Fred Moten, *In the Break*; Fred Moten, "The Case of Blackness," *Criticism* 50, no. 2 (2008): 177–218; Fred Moten, "Black Op," *PMLA* 123, no. 5 (2008): 1743–1747; Saidiya V. Hartman, *Scenes of Subjection: Terror, Slavery, and Self-Making in Nineteenth-Century America* (Oxford, UK: Oxford University Press, 1997); Hortense J. Spillers, "Mama's Baby, Papa's Maybe: An American Grammar Book," *Diacritics* 17, no. 2 (1987): 65–81.

13 For a formulation of the Bartleby industry, see Dan McCall, *The Silence of Bartleby* (Ithaca, NY: Cornell University Press, 1989), and Andrew Knighton, "The Bartleby Industry and Bartleby's Idleness," *ESQ: A Journal of the American Renaissance* 1, no. 2 (2007): 184–215.

14 For a theorization of a politics of refusal, see Audra Simpson, *Mohawk Interruptus: Political Life across the Borders of Settler States* (Durham, NC: Duke University Press, 2014).

15 "Freedom dreams" here invokes Robin D. G. Kelley's formulation in *Freedom Dreams: The Black Radical Imagination* (Boston: Beacon Press, 2003).

16 This is an adaptation of a phrase from a conversation between Paolo Friere and Myles Horton, as conveyed in the book *We Make the Road by Walking: Conversations on Education and Social Change* (Philadelphia, PA: Temple University Press, 1990). There, referring to how to start their talking book, Friere states: "I think that even though we need to have some outline, I am sure that we make the road by walking. It has to do with this house [Highlander], with this experience here. You're saying that in order to start, it should be necessary to start." To which, Horton replies: "I've never figured out any other way to start" (6). A footnote to that exchange states: "The phrase 'we make the road by walking' is an adaptation of a proverb by the Spanish poet Antonio Machado, in which one line reads "se hace camino al andar," or "you make the way as you go." See Antonio Machado, *Selected Poems*, trans. Alan S. Trueblood (Cambridge, MA: Harvard University Press, 1 982), 143.

17 Robin D. G. Kelley, *Freedom Dreams: The Black Radical Imagination* (Boston: Beacon Press, 2003).

INTRODUCTION

1 Shell, "Join the Taxi Ride to a Sustainable Energy Future," YouTube, 3 min., 39 sec, November 14, 2008, www.youtube.com.

2 Shell Oil, "People and Connections: Global Scenarios to 2020, Public Summary," (2002), 6, www.shell.com/. The full introduction reads:

> Scenarios are a tool for helping managers plan for the future—or rather for different possible futures. They help us focus on critical uncertainties: the things we don't know about that might transform our business, and the things we do know about that might involve unexpected discontinuities. They help us understand the limitations of our "mental maps" of the world—and to think the unthinkable, anticipate the unknowable, and utilize both to make better strategic decisions. Scenarios are alternative stories of how the world may develop. They are not predictions, but credible, relevant, and challenging alternative stories that help us explore "what if" and "how." Their purpose is not to pinpoint future events, but to consider the forces that may push the future along different paths. They help managers understand the dynamics of the business environment, recognize new possibilities, assess strategic options, and take long-term decisions. Shell companies pioneered the use of scenarios for strategic planning in the 1970s and since then, have applied them to a wide range of decision-making situations. Shell planners have also been involved in developing scenarios with such bodies as the World Business Council for Sustainable Development and the Intergovernmental Panel on Climate Change, as well as in using scenarios to help build a shared vision of the future in divided societies, such as South Africa in the early 1990s. There is no limit to the stories we could tell about the future. Some scenario exercises create a wide range of alternative scenarios. But Shell's experience is that for developing our strategic thinking, it is more productive to focus on just two thought-provoking scenarios—such as the two we present in People and Connections.

3 Mark Dery, "Black to the Future: Interviews with Samuel R. Delany, Greg Tate, and Tricia Rose" in *Flame Wars: The Discourse of Cyberculture,* ed. Mark Dery (Durham, NC: Duke University Press, 1994), 180.

4 Ytasha L. Womack, *Afrofuturism: The World of Black Sci-Fi and Fantasy Culture* (Chicago: Chicago Review Press, 2013), 9.

5 Kodwo Eshun, "Further Considerations of Afrofuturism," *CR: The New Centennial Review* 3, no. 2 (2003): 287–302.

6 Reading Eshun's claim sparked my research into corporate futures scenarios. See Kodwo Eshun, "Further Considerations of Afrofuturism," 291. That impulse was further affirmed by a member of the audience for my 2010 presentation of this topic at the College Art Association conference, who told me more about corporate scenarios. I regret that I cannot recall her name.

7 Shell Oil, "People and Connections," 6.

8 See John Maynard Keynes. *General Theory of Employment, Interest and Money.* New York: St. Martin's Press, 1936.

9 Ian Cummins and John Beasant, *Shell Shock: The Secrets and Spin of an Oil Giant* (Edinburgh, UK: Mainstream Publishing, 2005), 75.

10 Daniel Yergin, *The Prize: The Epic Quest for Oil, Money & Power* (New York: Free Press, 2008), 57; 105. Cummins and Beasant explain that oil "had been known to exist for more than 400 years" in Sumatra when Zijlker "discovered" it there (*Shell Shock*, 64).

11 Cummins and Beasant, *Shell Shock*, 109.

12 Ibid., 117.

13 Ibid., 120.

14 Yergin, *The Prize*, 528–529.

15 Shell, "Shell Scenarios."

16 Quoted in Ike Okonta and Oronto Douglas, *Where Vultures Feast: Shell, Human Rights, and Oil in the Niger Delta* (London, UK: Verso, 2003), 118.

17 Bronwen Manby, *Shell in Nigeria, Corporate Social Responsibility and the Ogoni Crisis: Case Study #20* (N.p.: Carnegie Council on Ethics & International Affairs, 2000).

18 This is an extremely condensed version of a complex set of events recounted in Okonta and Douglas, *Where Vultures Feast*, 116–156.

19 According to Jad Mouawad's *New York Times* report, "Royal Dutch Shell, the big oil company, agreed to pay $15.5 million to settle a case accusing it of taking part in human rights abuses in the Niger Delta in the early 1990s, a striking sum given that the company has denied any wrongdoing. The settlement, announced late Monday, came days before the start of a trial in New York that was expected to reveal extensive details of Shell's activities in the Niger Delta." See Mouawad, "Shell to Pay $15.5 Million to Settle Nigerian Case," *New York Times*, June 8, 2009, B1. Ken Saro-Wiwa, Jr., a respected journalist, died in 2016.

20 See "Royal Dutch Shell on the Forbes List," https://www.forbes.com (accessed August 21, 2018). The figures are updated each year.

21 Manby, *Shell in Nigeria*.

22 Cummins and Beasant, *Shell Shock*, 12.

23 Ibid.

24 Bloomberg, "Shell Inflated Reserves by 41%," *New York Times*, March 8, 2005, www.nytimes.com.

25 Ibid.

26 Ibid.

27 Shell, *Scenarios: An Explorer's Guide* (2008). It continues:
When we plan for the future, we need to try to build a comprehensive picture of the context in which we operate. However, we can't do this alone—our blind spots impose limitations on our understanding—so we need to combine our knowledge and thinking with that of others. Scenario building can address this problem in a number of complementary ways: It

is a collaborative, conversation-based process that facilitates the interplay of a wide variety of ideas; it enables different fields of knowledge and ways of knowing to be combined; it reframes questions, prompting the generation of ideas across disciplines rather than going over old ground; it encourages the involvement of different perspectives on an issue or question; unlike forecasting, scenarios do not demand consensus, but rather respect and accommodate differences, seeking only to define them clearly; the story form of scenarios enables both qualitative and quantitative aspects to be incorporated, so ideas are not excluded on the basis that they can't be measured; by building sets of scenarios we assemble several different versions of the future at the same time. This trains us to keep thinking of the future as full of possibilities.

28 Lawrence Grossberg, *Cultural Studies in the Future Tense* (Durham, NC: Duke University Press, 2010), Kindle ed.

29 Ibid., loc. 106.

30 As a caution against an easy celebration of Cultural Studies' history and methods, it is worth mentioning that Max Haiven points out, but does not elaborate, that the "rise to institutional prominence" of Cultural Studies "eerily mirrors the acceleration of financial speculation and the rise of neoliberalism over the past forty years." See Haiven, "Finance as Capital's Imagination?: Reimagining Value and Culture in an Age of Fictitious Capital and Crisis," *Social Text* 29, no. 3 (2011): 95.

31 Stuart Hall, "The Emergence of Cultural Studies and the Crisis of the Humanities," *October* 53, no. 3 (1990): 16; cited in Grossberg, *Cultural Studies in the Future Tense*, loc. 1525.

32 Hall, "The Emergence of Cultural Studies," 11–23.

33 See also Roderick Ferguson's analysis of what he calls "the rise of the interdisciplines" in *The Reorder of Things: The University and Its Pedagogies of Minority Difference* (Minneapolis: University of Minnesota Press, 2012).

34 Gilles Deleuze, "Postscript on the Societies of Control," *October* 59 (1992): 4.

35 See Ferguson, *The Reorder of Things*.

36 Deleuze's comments suggest this line of argumentation as well. See "Postscript on the Societies of Control."

37 Ibid., 4.

38 Fred Moten and Stefano Harney have offered a conceptualization of "the undercommons" as a way to address the fact that many intellectuals who work in universities and colleges enter those institutional spaces with an interest in disrupting their relationship to control and the maintenance of existing power relationships. See Fred Moten, Stefano Harney, and J. Jack Halberstam, *The Undercommons: Fugitive Planning & Black Study* (New York: Autonomedia, 2013).

39 Seth Godin, *Linchpin: Are You Indispensible?* (New York: Portfolio [Penguin], 2010).

40 Franco Bifo Berardi, "Precariousness, Catastrophe and Challenging the Blackmail of the Imagination," *Affinities: A Journal of Radical Theory* 4, no. 2 (2010): 1–4.

41 Ibid.
42 Berardi offers this definition of "the radical imagination": "Radical imagination is the ability to recombine the contents of our experience of exploitation, of suffering, of exhaustion, in a way that Felix Guattari would label creation of a new retournelle, Chaosmose, calling forth of a new relationship between the environment and the human organism" ("Precariousness," 3).
43 Ibid.
44 I discuss Berardi's conceptualization of an "after the future" later in this chapter, and the formulation "poetry from the future" in the next chapter.
45 Karl Marx, Grundrisse: Foundations of the Critique of Political Economy, trans. Martin Nicolaus (New York: Vintage Press, 1973), 487; also cited in Fred Moten, "The Case of Blackness," Criticism 50, no. 2 (2008): 177–218. I discuss this quotation again later in this chapter and in chapter 4.
46 Édouard Glissant, Poetics of Relation, trans. Betsy Wing (Ann Arbor: University of Michigan Press, 1997).
47 Ibid.
48 Ibid.
49 See, for example, the introduction to Meaghan Morris, Identity Anecdotes: Translation and Media Culture (Thousand Oaks, CA: Sage Publications, 2006), 1–28, for a discussion of the role anecdotes can play in Cultural Studies scholarship.
50 It is not important to rehearse here how scholars are returning to the work of Immanuel Kant, Benedictus de Spinoza, and Gilles Deleuze, among others, in order to recalibrate philosophical thought about the Imagination in ways that underscore and valorize, rather than dismiss, its association with the body and its senses. Yet, it is worth pointing out here that much of this scholarship, especially that on Kant and Spinoza, reads well-known work in a new way in order to address today's pressing intellectual and political problems. In this way, they make perceptible currents within modernity relevant to the imagination, offering avenues for thinking and action today that seemed foreclosed when those ideas initially appeared.
51 Octavia E. Butler, Parable of the Sower (New York: Warner Books, 1993), 3.
52 Here, one might think of theories of temporality such as Walter Benjamin's, which posits a possibility for something new to appear; see "Theses on the Philosophy of History," in Illuminations, ed. Hannah Arendt, trans. Harry Zohn (New York: Harcourt Brace Jovanovich, 1969), 253–264.
53 Eve Kosofky Sedgwick, Tendencies (Durham, NC: Duke University Press, 1993), 8. It is important to note that the capaciousness of Sedgwick's definition of "queer" has not always informed the use of "queer" in practice. Heather Love puts the scholarly critique of this succinctly, writing, "In her important account of the exclusions of queer politics, 'Punks, Bulldaggers, and Welfare Queens,' Cathy J. Cohen . . . indicts queer as a false universal, one that claims to address the situation of all marginal subjects but in fact is focused on the concerns of gays and lesbians. One can see a similar critique

of queer among some trans scholars, who have argued that Queer Studies has not engaged fully with the material conditions of transgender people but has rather used gender nonnormativity as a sign of allegory of queerness" ("Queer," *TSQ: Transgender Studies Quarterly* 1, nos. 1–2 (2014): 172–176; Cohen's article is in *GLQ: A Journal of Lesbian and Gay Studies* 3, no. 4 (1997): 437–465).

54 As I discuss in chapter 2, José Muñoz recently described this valence of "queer" as operating according to the temporality of the "not-yet" in *Cruising Utopia: The Then and There of Queer Futurity* (New York: New York University Press, 2009). In addition to work on "becoming" by or inspired by Gilles Deleuze, the rich body of work on queer feelings and affect also is relevant here—though, in my work, "affect" is understood, following Deleuze's reading of Spinoza, as a marker of a body's capacity to be affected.

55 See "About the Collective," at The Nest Collective website: www.thisisthenest.com (accessed August 23, 2018).

56 The Nest Collective, *Stories of Our Lives: Queer Narratives from Kenya* (Nest Arts Collective, 2015), xi. Thank you to Wangui wa Goro for gifting me this special book.

57 For an account of how "queer" is being made to work as part of a speculative economy calibrated to perpetuate an anti-black neoliberal geopolitical order, see Anna M. Agathangelou, "Neoliberal Geopolitical Order and Value," *International Feminist Journal of Politics* 15, no. 4 (2013): 453–476.

58 Deleuze, "Postscript on the Societies of Control," 4.

59 Nassim Nicholas Taleb, *The Black Swan: Second Edition: The Impact of the Highly Improbable Fragility* (New York: Random House, 2007), Kindle loc. 376–377.

60 Ibid., 382–385.

61 Ibid.

62 Ibid., 398–399.

63 Ibid., 413–415.

64 Ibid.

65 James Owen Weatherall, *The Physics of Wall Street: A Brief History of Predicting the Unpredictable* (Boston, MA: Mariner Books [Houghton Mifflin Harcourt], 2013), Kindle ed.

66 Ibid.

67 Nassim Nicholas Taleb, *Antifragile: Things that Gain from Disorder* (New York: Random House, 2014), Kindle loc. 341–346.

68 Edward E. Baptist, *The Half Has Never Been Told: Slavery and the Making of American Capitalism* (New York: Basic Books, 2014), Kindle loc. 1340–1342.

69 Among the works that have influenced my thinking here the most are: C. L. R. James, *The Black Jacobins: Toussaint L'Ouverture and the San Domingo Revolution* (New York: Vintage, 1989), and Susan Buck-Morss, "Hegel and Haiti," *Critical Inquiry* 26, no. 4 (2000): 824–865.

70 Buck-Morss, "Hegel and Haiti," 845.

71 Buck-Morss argues that the silences in historical analyses of the significance of the Haitian Revolution to Hegelian thought are due in part to the rigidity of the disciplines. About Trouillot's arguments (quoted above), she writes, "Of course he is correct to emphasize the incapacity of most [of Hegel's] contemporaries, given their ready-made categories, 'to understand the ongoing revolution on its own terms.' . . . But there is a danger in conflating two silences, the past and the present one, when it comes to the Haitian story. For if men and women in the eighteenth century did not think in nonracial terms of the 'fundamental equality of human-ity,' as 'some of us do today,' at least they knew what was happening; today, when the Haitian slave revolution might be more thinkable, it is more invisible, due to the construction of disciplinary discourses through which knowledge of the past has been inherited" ("Hegel and Haiti," 845).

72 George G. Szpiro, *Pricing the Future: Finance, Physics, and the 300-year Journey to the Black-Scholes Equation: A Story of Genius and Discovery* (New York: Basic Books, 2011).

73 Ian Baucom, *Specters of the Atlantic: Finance Capital, Slavery, and the Philosophy of History* (Durham, NC: Duke University Press Books, 2005), 16.

74 See also Baptist, *The Half Has Never Been Told*.

75 Baucom, *Specters of the Atlantic*, 17.

76 Dick Bryan and Michael Rafferty, "Financial Derivatives and the Theory of Money," *Economy and Society* 36, no. 1 (2007): 142.

77 Ibid., 145.

78 Lawrence Grossberg, "Modernity and Commensuration," *Cultural Studies* 24, no. 3 (2010): 295–332.

79 Ibid., 317.

80 Randy Martin, Dick Bryan, and Michael Rafferty, "Financialization, Risk and Labour," *Competition & Change* 12, no. 2 (2008): 122.

81 Ibid., 130.

82 Baucom, *Specters of the Atlantic*, 22.

83 M. Nourbese Philip, *Zong!* (Middletown, CT: Wesleyan University Press, 2008).

84 Ian Baucom writes with reference to Glissant's "poetics of Relation":
Crucially, however, what enables this passage (from endings to beginnings, from terror to promise, from exception to relation) is a second, implied reversal: a reversal of what, with reference to the slave trade, we must un-derstand exchange to entail. For if, in this context, "exchange" continues to suggest not only a generically formal logic of dematerialization (a stripping away of the exceptional quality of things in their transit from use value to exchange values), but also a historically particular absolutization of such dedifferentiating protocols (an apocalyptic stripping away of the exceptional quality of persons in their speculative transit from humanness to money), then, however counterintuitive this might seem, Glissant suggests that exchange must be apprehended, in precisely such moments, not only as

a word for loss but as a word for gain. Exchange, in this sense, once more names a form of substitution, though here what replaces exceptionality is not fungibility but relation, where relation is a word for what I have been calling an interested politics of the abysmal event (an anti-transcendent and recognizably counter-Kantian habit of holding to "the deeds and crimes" from which Kant's sublimely disinterested theory of the event seeks to detach itself), and a word for those "transverse" forms of culture, identity, and solidarity that emerge from the act of holding to, enduring, relating, and avowing our (present's) relational complicity with modernity's most violent scenes of exchange. (*Specters of the Atlantic*, 311)

85 Saidiya Hartman, *Lose Your Mother: A Journey along the Atlantic Slave Route* (New York: Farrar, Straus and Giroux, 2008), 6.

86 I consider this formulation in greater detail in chapter 3, where I discuss the relationship between Blackness, digital technologies, representation, and computation.

87 Grossberg, "Modernity and Commensuration," 319–320.

88 Martin, Bryan, and Rafferty, "Financial Derivatives and the Theory of Money," 141; emphasis in original.

89 Bryan and Rafferty, "Financial Derivatives and the Theory of Money," 141.

90 Ibid., 140.

91 Glissant, *Poetics of Relation*, 190.

92 Ibid.

93 Bryan, and Rafferty, "Financial Derivatives and the Theory of Money," 145.

94 Kara Keeling, *The Witch's Flight: The Cinematic, the Black Femme, and the Image of Common Sense* (Durham, NC: Duke University Press, 2007).

95 For relevant discussion of this debate in Film Studies, see, for example, Alice Maurice, *The Cinema and Its Shadow: Race and Technology in Early Cinema* (Minneapolis: University of Minnesota Press, 2013); Tom Gunning, "Moving Away from the Index: Cinema and the Impression of Reality," *differences* 18, no. 1 (2007): 29–52; Philip Rosen, *Change Mummified: Cinema, Historicity, Theory* (Minneapolis: University of Minnesota Press, 2001).

96 I have taken up these questions from at least two different directions already. See "Passing for Human: Bamboozled and Digital Humanism," *Women & Performance: A Journal of Feminist Theory* 15, no. 1 (2005): 237–250, and "I=Another: Digital Identity Politics," in *Strange Affinities: The Gender and Sexual Politics of Comparative Racialization*, ed. Grace Kyungwon Hong and Roderick A. Ferguson (Durham, NC: Duke University Press, 2011), 53–75. For a related approach to these questions, see Herman Gray, "Subject(Ed) to Recognition," *American Quarterly* 65, no. 4 (2013): 771–798.

97 See Randy Martin, "After Economy? Social Logics of the Derivative," *Social Text* 31, no. 1 (2013): 83–106.

98 Baucom, *Specters of the Atlantic*, 309–333.

99 For a critique of the Left and the liberal embrace of the saying "We are the ones we have been waiting for," see Jodi Byrd, *The Transit of Empire: Indigenous Critiques of Colonialism* (Minneapolis: University of Minnesota Press, 2011), 15.

100 Max Haiven and Alex Khasnabish, "What Is the Radical Imagination? A Special Issue," *Affinities: A Journal of Radical Theory, Culture, and Action* 4, no. 2 (2010): 3.

101 Robin D. G. Kelley, *Freedom Dreams: The Black Radical Imagination* (Boston: Beacon Press, 2002), ix.

102 Toni Morrison, *Sula* (New York: Random House, 1998). For other references to and discussions of this phrase from *Sula*, see Roderick A. Ferguson, *Aberrations in Black: Toward a Queer of Color Critique* (Minneapolis: University of Minnesota Press, 2004); Alexis Pauline Gumbs and Julia Roxanne Wallace, "Something Else to Be: Generations of Black Queer Brilliance and the Mobile Homecoming Experiential Archive," in *No Tea, No Shade: New Writings in Black Queer Studies*, ed. E. Patrick Johnson. (Durham, NC: Duke University Press, 2016), 380–394.

103 Franco Bifo Berardi, *After the Future* (Chino, CA: AK Press, 2011), 24–25.

104 Gary Wilder, *Freedom Time: Negritude, Decolonization, and the Future of the World* (Durham, NC: Duke University Press, 2014), 16.

105 David Marriott recently elucidated a way of reading Frantz Fanon's assertion that "the real leap consists of introducing invention into life" (Marriott, "Inventions of Existence: Sylvia Wynter, Frantz Fanon, Sociogeny, and 'the Damned,'" *CR: The New Centennial Review* 11, no. 3 [2012]: 45–89).

106 For my earlier thinking on Fanon's formulation of the temporality of the "hellish cycle," see my book *The Witch's Flight*.

107 Marx, *Grundrisse*, 487.

108 See Marriott, "Inventions of Existence."

109 Marx, *Grundrisse*, 487.

110 I synthesized these ideas from my reading of Moten's "The Case of Blackness," *Criticism* 50, no. 2 (2008): 177–218, as well as his short piece, "Black Op," *PMLA* 123, no. 5 (2008): 1743–1747.

111 I take up these issues in a different context in chapter 3. For a reading of "the Black" in Western philosophy, which posits that he is "always there already" in the human, see James A. Snead, "On Repetition in Black Culture," in *Racist Traces and Other Writing: European Pedigrees / African Contagions*, ed. Kara Keeling, Colin MacCabe, and Cornel West (London: Palgrave Macmillan, 2003), 11–33. For one of my earlier engagements with Snead's formulation, which is of relevance to the present discussion see "Passing for Human: Bamboozled and Digital Humanism," *Women & Performance: A Journal of Feminist Theory* 15, no. 1 (2005): 237–250.

112 Recall here Baucom's formulation about the production of value during the transatlantic slave trade as a process underpinned by "belief" in his *Specters of the Atlantic*.

INTERREGNUM

1 For a reading of what this particular temporality has to do with feminism, see Meaghan Morris, *Too Soon, Too Late: History in Popular Culture* (Bloomington: Indiana University Press, 1998).

2 Saidiya V. Hartman, "Venus in Two Acts," *Small Axe: A Caribbean Journal of Criticism* 12, no. 2 (2008): 1.

3 Ibid., 3.

4 Ibid., 4.

5 See Katherine McKittrick and Sylvia Wynter, "Unparalleled Catastrophe for Our Species, or To Give Humanness a Different Future: Conversations," in *Sylvia Wynter: On Being Human as Praxis*, ed. Katherine McKittrick, (Durham, NC: Duke University Press, 2015), 9–89.

6 Hartman, "Venus," 9.

7 Ibid., 1.

8 Ibid., 13.

9 Ibid., 14.

10 Scholars have argued that "Bartleby" was Melville's response to the critical and popular failure of *Moby Dick* and *Pierre*. Barbara Foley argues that "a familiarity with mid-nineteenth century class struggles in New York—and with the contemporaneous discourse about these struggles—is indispensable to a complete understanding of 'Bartleby'" (Foley, "From Wall Street to Astor Place: Historicizing Melville's 'Bartleby,'" *American Literature* 72, no. 1 [2000]: 87–116).

11 Herman Melville, *Bartleby and Benito Cereno*, ed. Stanley Appelbaum (Mineola, NY: Dover, 2012), 1.

12 Ibid., 1.

13 Ibid., 2.

14 Ibid.

15 Ibid., 7.

16 Ibid., 8.

17 Ibid., 9.

18 Ibid.

19 Naomi C. Reed, "The Specter of Wall Street: 'Bartleby, the Scrivener' and the Language of Commodities," *American Literature* 76, no. 2 (2004): 263.

20 Ibid., 265.

21 David Norman Rodowick, *Reading the Figural, or, Philosophy after the New Media* (Durham, NC: Duke University Press, 2001), xi.

22 Ibid.

23 As I will discuss in chapter 3, this operation within systems of signification has another vector, traversed by what James A. Snead refers to as "the cut" in Black culture. See James A. Snead, "On Repetition in Black Culture," in *Racist Traces and Other Writing: European Pedigrees / African Contagions*, ed. Kara Keeling, Colin MacCabe, and Cornel West (London: Palgrave Macmillan, 2003), 11–33.

24 See David Marriott, *Haunted Life: Visual Culture and Black Modernity* (New Brunswick, NJ: Rutgers University Press, 2007) for reflections on the Black image, representation, and the "unwilling delegate."

25 Manthia Diawara, "One World in Relation: Edouard Glissant in Conversation with Manthia Diawara," *Nka Journal of Contemporary African Art* 28 (2011): 4–19.

26 Giorgio Agamben, *Potentialities: Collected Essays in Philosophy* (Palo Alto, CA: Stanford University Press, 1999), 260.

27 Ibid., 260–261.

28 Ibid., 261.

29 Ibid., 261–266.

30 Ibid., 266.

31 Ibid., 267.

32 Ibid.

33 David Scott, *Conscripts of Modernity: The Tragedy of Colonial Enlightenment* (Durham, NC: Duke University Press, 2004).

34 Agamben, *Potentialities*, 268.

35 Ibid., 270.

36 Ibid.

37 Édouard Glissant, *Poetic Intention*, trans. Nathalie Stephens (Callicoon, NY: Nightboat, 2010), 176.

38 Agamben, *Potentialities*, 271.

39 It also animates Gilles Deleuze's analysis of cinema in *Cinema 1: The Movement Image*, trans. Hugh Tomlinson and Barbara Habberjam (Minneapolis: University of Minnesota Press, 1986), and *Cinema 2: The Time Image*, trans. Hugh Tomlinson and Barbara Habberjam (Minneapolis: University of Minnesota Press, 1989).

40 Gilles Deleuze, *Essays Critical and Clinical* (Minneapolis: University of Minnesota Press, 1997), 70.

41 Slavoj Žižek, *The Parallax View* (Cambridge, MA: MIT Press, 2009), 382.

42 Deleuze, *Essays Critical*, 73.

43 Ibid.

44 Ibid.

45 Jodi A. Byrd, *The Transit of Empire: Indigenous Critiques of Colonialism* (Minneapolis: University of Minnesota Press, 2011), Kindle loc. 17.

46 Deleuze, *Essays Critical*, 73.

47 Ibid., 74.

48 Melville, *Bartleby*, 27.

49 Deleuze, *Essays Critical*, 73–74.

50 Ibid., 76.

51 Ibid., 81.

52 See Jane Bennett, *A Vibrant Matter: A Political Ecology of Things* (Durham, NC: Duke University Press, 2010).

53 Hartman, "Venus," 14.

54 Žižek, *The Parallax View*, 384.

55 As Žižek explains, "the difficulty of imagining the New is the difficulty of imagining Bartleby in power" (ibid., 382).

CHAPTER 1. "IT'S AFTER THE END OF THE WORLD (DON'T YOU KNOW THAT YET?)"

1 John Coney, dir., *Space Is the Place* (New York: Plexifilm, 2003 [1974]), DVD.
2 Gilles Deleuze and Feliz Guattari, *A Thousand Plateaus: Capitalism and Schizophrenia* (Minneapolis, MN: University of Minnesota Press, 1987), 311.
3 Édouard Glissant, *Poetics of Relation*, trans. Betsy Wing (Ann Arbor: University of Michigan Press, 1997), 8–9.
4 Fred Moten, "Black Op," *PMLA* 123, no. 5 (2008): 1744.
5 Meaghan Morris, *Identity Anecdotes: Translation and Media Culture* (New York: Sage, 2006), 190.
6 See my essay "Electric Feel: Transduction, Errantry and the Refrain," *Cultural Studies* 28, no. 1 (2014): 49–83, for another iteration of this method.
7 Conversation with the author.
8 Coney, *Space Is the Place*.
9 Daniel Kreiss, "Appropriating the Master's Tools: Sun Ra, the Black Panthers and Black Consciousness, 1952–1973," *Black Music Research Journal* 28, no. 1 (2008): 57. Such a call for a new relationship between the living organism and its environment resounds throughout *Queer Times, Black Futures*.
10 Kreiss, "Appropriating," 57, 65. John F. Szwed, *Space Is the Place: The Lives and Times of Sun Ra* (Cambridge, MA: Da Capo Press, 1998), 175.
11 See Kodwo Eshun, *More Brilliant than the Sun: Adventures in Sonic Fiction* (London: Quartet Books, 1998).
12 See Alexander G. Weheliye, *Phonographies: Grooves in Sonic Afro-Modernity* (Durham, NC: Duke University Press, 2005).
13 William Edward Burghardt Du Bois, *The Souls of Black Folk* (Oxford: Oxford University Press, 2008 [1903]), 15.
14 Kara Keeling, *The Witch's Flight: The Cinematic, the Black Femme, and the Image of Common Sense* (Durham, NC: Duke University Press, 2007).
15 Gilles Deleuze, *Cinema 2: The Time-Image*, trans. H. Tomlinson and R. Galeta (Minneapolis: University of Minnesota Press, 1989), 3.
16 Ibid., 18.
17 Ibid., 261.
18 The last sentence reads, "In spite of the narrator's attempt at closure, the black femme function persists . . . insisting on the existence of a radical Elsewhere" (Keeling, *The Witch's Flight*, 158).
19 Deleuze, *Cinema 2*, 261.
20 I have begun thinking about this elsewhere as "the digital regime of the image." See Kara Keeling, "'I=Another': Digital Identity Politics," in *Strange Affinities*, ed. Roderick Ferguson and Grace Hong (Durham, NC: Duke University Press, 2011), 53–75; "Passing for Human: Bamboozled and Digital Humanism," *Women & Per-*

formance: A Journal of Feminist Theory 15, no. 1 (2005): 237–250; and "Queer Os," *Cinema Journal* 53, no. 2 (2014): 152–157.

21 J. Melamed, *Represent and Destroy: Rationalizing Violence in the New Racial Capitalism* (Minneapolis: University of Minnesota Press, 2011). I return to this idea in chapter 3.

22 Even though Sun Ra experimented primarily with analog sound technologies, the more recent digitization of his work, along with his abiding interest in creating other-worldly, alien sounds through technologically enhanced music, lend to considering how the "the digital regime of the image" is instrumental to efforts to make sonic Afrofuturisms' gestures towards liberation felt anew. I offer "the digital regime of the image" while keeping in mind that "the image" includes sound-images and a variety of other images. The language of "the regime" is important because it calls attention to the ways that the perceptual apparatus is imbricated in the workings of power and hegemony, including consent, coercion, violence, and force.

23 For analysis and debates about the differences and similarities between articulations of "social death" and "social life," see, for example, Fred Moten, "The Case of Blackness," *Criticism* 50, no. 2 (2008): 177–218, "Blackness and Nothingness (Mysticism in the Flesh)," *South Atlantic Quarterly* 112, no. 4 (2013): 737–780, and "Black Op"; as well as Jared Sexton, "The Social Life of Social Death: On Afro-Pessimism and Black Optimism," *InTensions* 5, no. 1 (2011): 1–47; Frank Wilderson III, "Gramsci's Black Marx: Whither the Slave in Civil Society?" *Social Identities* 9, no. 2 (2003): 225–240; Frank B. Wilderson III, "Grammar & Ghosts: The Performative Limits of African Freedom," *Theatre Survey* 50, no. 1 (2009): 119–125; Terrion L. Williamson, *Scandalize My Name: Black Feminist Practice and the Making of Black Social Life* (Oxford: Oxford University Press, 2016).

24 Lisa Yaszek, "Afrofuturism, Science Fiction, and the History of the Future," *Socialism and Democracy* 20, no. 3 (2006): 53.

25 See Grace Kyungwon Hong, *The Ruptures of American Capital: Women of Color Feminism and the Culture of Immigrant Labor* (Minneapolis: University of Minnesota Press, 2006), 3–30.

26 Frantz Fanon, *Black Skin, White Masks*, trans. Richard Philcox (New York: Grove Press, 2008 [1952]), 205. Although a full consideration of the merits of Philcox's translation compared to Charles Lam Markmann's is beyond my present abilities, it is worth noting that this is a sentence where Philcox's translation differs from Markmann's 1967 translation. According to Philcox's translation, Fanon wrote: "The black is not. No more than the white man."

27 Some of this passage is also included in my essay "Looking for M—: Queer Temporality, Black Political Possibility, and Poetry from the Future," *GLQ: A Journal of Lesbian and Gay Studies* 15, no. 4 (2009): 565–582.

28 Of course, one might also understand that title to mean that music from the world will sound like this tomorrow, but even this seeks to posit a break from the world today.

29 Coney, *Space Is the Place.*

30 Graham Lock, *Blutopia: Visions of the Future and Revisions of the Past in the Work of Sun Ra, Duke Ellington, and Anthony Braxton* (Durham, NC: Duke University Press, 1999).

31 Ibid., 2.

32 Ibid., 3.

33 Eshun, *More Brilliant than the Sun,* 00[-003].

34 Octavia E. Butler, *Parable of the Sower* (New York: Warner Books, 1993), 3; Kindle loc. 2876 of 4538.

35 Ibid., 2876.

36 Ibid., 2948.

37 See Eve Tuck, Allison Guess, and Hannah Sultan, "Not Nowhere: Collaborating on Selfsame Land," *Decolonization: Indigeneity, Education & Society* 26 (June 2014): 1–11.

38 Octavia Butler, *Parable of the Talents* (New York: Warner Books, 1998), 1.

39 See Agamben, *Potentialities.*

40 Recent research into and analyses of Negritude underscore the extent to which Francophone thinkers and artists such as Leopold Senghor and Aimé Césaire advanced conceptions of the world that provide another corpus from which subterranean energies continue to flow. This scholarship makes newly available a vision of the decolonization that might have been, but was not (yet). See Gary Wilder, *Freedom Time: Negritude, Decolonization, and the Future of the World* (Durham, NC: Duke University Press, 2014).

41 The quotation "we stay with poetry" is a reference to Glissant, *Poetics of Relation,* 9.

42 Branka Arsić, "Active Habits and Passive Events or Bartleby," in *Between Deleuze and Derrida,* ed. Patton, Paul, and John Protevi (New York: Continuum, 2003), 154.

43 See James A. Snead, "On Repetition in Black Culture," in *Racist Traces and Other Writing: European Pedigrees / African Contagions,* ed. Kara Keeling, Colin MacCabe, and Cornel West (London: Palgrave Macmillan, 2003), 11–33.

44 Muriel Combes, *Gilbert Simondon and the Philosophy of the Transindividual,* trans. Thomas LaMarre (Cambridge, MA: MIT Press, 2013), xxi.

45 Ibid., 1.

46 For discussions of Wynter's work on ontogenesis and autopoeisis, see McKittrick, Katherine, ed., *Sylvia Wynter: On Being Human as Praxis* (Durham, NC: Duke University Press, 2015); for Sylvia Wynter's thinking about film and aesthetics, see her "Rethinking 'Aesthetics': Notes Towards a Deciphering Practice," in *Ex-iles: Essays on Caribbean Cinema,* ed. Mbye B. Cham (Trenton, NJ: Africa World Press, 1992), 237–279.

47 Katherine McKittrick, Denise Ferreira Da Silva, Zakiyyah Jackson, and Alexander Weheliye are among the many other scholars taking seriously the challenges Sylvia Wynter's oeuvre poses to the tendency of those of us working with and

against poststructuralist theories and critiques to privilege the theories of white Europeans and Americans over those whose work, like Wynter's, might open different genealogies of and insights into abiding poststructuralist concerns. For essays by these authors that are especially relevant to the concerns of this book, see, for example, the following: Denise Ferreira Da Silva, "Toward a Black Feminist Poethics: The Quest(ion) of Blackness Toward the End of the World," *Black Scholar* 44, no. 2 (2014); Zakiyyah Iman Jackson, "Animal: New Directions in the Theorization of Race and Posthuman," *Feminist Studies* 39, no. 3 (2013): 669–685; and Katherine McKittrick, "Plantation Futures," *Small Axe: A Caribbean Journal of Criticism* 17 (November 2013): 1–15. See also Alexander G. Weheliye, *Habeas Viscus: Racializing Assemblages, Biopolitics, and Black Feminist Theories of the Human* (Durham, NC: Duke University Press, 2014).

48 Ytasha L. Womack, *Afrofuturism: The World of Black Sci-Fi and Fantasy Culture* (Chicago: Chicago Review Press, 2013), 9.

49 Combes, *Gilbert Simondon*, 2.

50 Ibid.; emphasis in original.

51 Ibid.

52 Ibid., 6.

53 Ibid., 7.

54 Ibid., 3.

55 Ibid. In the quotation, Combes cites Simondon's original texts: *L'individu et sa genèse physico-biologique* (Grenoble: Éditions Jérôme Millon, 1995 [1964]), 30, and *L'individuation à la lumière das notions de forme et d'information* (Grenoble: Éditions Jérôme Millon, 2005), 32.

56 See the preface for a discussion of Audre Lorde's and Franklin Rosemont's insights regarding poetry.

57 For "sympoiesis," see Donna J. Haraway, *Staying with the Trouble: Making Kin in the Chthulucene* (Durham, NC: Duke University Press, 2016).

58 Beth Coleman's foundational formulation of race as technology and Wendy Hui Kyong Chun's extension of that work are the key texts I consider in this regard. See Beth Coleman, "Race as Technology," *Camera Obscura: Feminism, Culture, and Media Studies* 24, no. 1(70) (2009): 177–207; and Wendy Hui Kyong Chun, "Race and/as Technology or How to Do Things to Race," in *Race after the Internet*, ed. Nakamura, Lisa and Peter A. Chow-White (New York: Routledge, 2012), 38–60.

59 The choice of the word "vestibular" here is meant to invoke Hortense Spillers's formulation in "Mama's Baby, Papa's Maybe: An American Grammar Book," *Diacritics* 17, no. 2 (1987): 64–81.

60 Joy James, "'Concerning Violence': Frantz Fanon's Rebel Intellectual in Search of a Black Cyborg," *South Atlantic Quarterly* 112, no. 1 (2013): 57–70.

61 Ibid., 57; emphasis in original. James refers to the translation by Constance Farrington. A more recent translation by Richard Philcox of the passage reads: "Personal interests are now the collective interest because in reality *everyone* will be discovered by the French legionnaires and consequently massacred or else

everyone will be saved" (Frantz Fanon, *The Wretched of the Earth*, trans. Richard Philcox [New York: Grove Press, 1963], 11–12).

62 James, "'Concerning Violence,'" 58; emphasis in original.

63 Ibid., 61.

64 Ibid., 63.

65 Ibid., 60.

66 While I do not adhere to the language James offers of "the cyborg" because of the specificity of that term in media studies and its particular genealogy within feminist studies, I am interested throughout this book in attending to the senses in which decolonization and liberation for all entails an effort to create "a new creature," a wealthy thing, or, perhaps, it entails the creations of a they and a them presently accruing in pre-individual being. In Fanon's original formulation, "Decolonization is truly the creation of new men" (Frantz Fanon, *The Wretched of the Earth*, trans. Constance Farrington [New York: Grove Press, 1963], 2).

67 Saidiya V. Hartman, "Venus in Two Acts," *Small Axe: A Caribbean Journal of Criticism* 26 (June 2008): 1–14.

68 See John E. Drabinski, "What Is Trauma to the Future?: On Glissant's Poetics," *Qui Parle: Critical Humanities and Social Sciences* 18, no. 2 (2010): 296. The quotation appears in Drabinski's discussion of Glissant's formulation of abyss. Drabinski explains that "there can be no birth out of trauma without abyss" (298). He goes on to assert: "Bodies do not mark this traumatic birth, as they do for Benjamin in 'Theses on the Philosophy of History'; there are not bodies—decaying or ashen—in the shackles. Only the shackles— gone green—remain. Drown at the sea's bottom. Lost. Salt, as treated in the *Black Salt* cycle, sits in the wound of those who survive, but it is also what destroys what cannot remain, what cannot even be conceived as loss: the body of the slave thrown overboard. Roots set and fail to take up in what is less than the remainder. There are not even the privileges of loss, namely, the object of mourning. Indeed, loss itself is stolen in the Middle Passage. So roots do not cling even to traces" (300). In this context, "Memory seals abyssal beginnings by locating the movement, not from Africa to America, but from having already lost Africa and being conceived as a people in the boat's belly" (301).

69 Ibid., 296.

70 Ibid., 297.

71 Ibid., 296.

72 Fred Moten, *In the Break: The Aesthetics of the Black Radical Tradition* (Minneapolis: University of Minnesota Press, 2003), 7–8.

CHAPTER 2. YET STILL

1 Quoted in Frantz Fanon, *Black Skin, White Masks*, trans. Richard Philcox (New York: Grove Press, 2008 [1952]), 198.

2 Kara Keeling, *The Witch's Flight: The Cinematic, the Black Femme, and the Image of Common Sense* (Durham, NC: Duke University Press, 2007), and Kara Keeling, "'In the Interval': Frantz Fanon and the 'Problems' of Visual Representation," *Qui Parle: Critical Humanities and Social Sciences* 13, no. 2 (2003): 91–117.

3 See Keeling, *The Witch's Flight*.

4 Gilles Deleuze, *Cinema 2: The Time Image*, trans. Hugh Tomlinson and Barbara Habberjam (Minneapolis: University of Minnesota Press, 1989), 66; Henri Bergson, *Matter and Memory*, trans. Nancy Margaret Paul and W. Scott Palmer (Courier Corporation, 2004), 61–63.

5 Since I finished writing *The Witch's Flight*, the relevant scholarship on affect has grown considerably. My thinking here is informed by and in conversation with that more recent work, including: Patricia Ticineto Clough and Jean Halley, eds., *The Affective Turn: Theorizing the Social* (Durham, NC: Duke University Press, 2007); Melissa Gregg and Gregory J. Seigworth, eds., *The Affect Theory Reader* (Durham, NC: Duke University Press, 2010); Patricia Ticineto Clough, Greg Goldberg, Rachel Schiff, Aaron Weeks, and Craig Willse, "Notes towards a Theory of Affect-Itself," *Ephemera: Theory and Politics in Organization* 7, no. 1 (2007): 60–77.

6 Marcia Landy, *The Folklore of Consensus: Theatricality in the Italian Cinema, 1930–1943* (Albany: State University of New York Press, 1998).

7 See Keeling, *The Witch's Flight*.

8 Robin D. G. Kelley, *Freedom Dreams: The Black Radical Imagination* (Boston, MA: Beacon Press, 2002), 9.

9 Ibid., 10.

10 Ibid., 11.

11 For a critique of the liberal and progressive appropriation of this phrase from Native Americans, see Jodi A. Byrd, *The Transit of Empire: Indigenous Critiques of Colonialism* (Minneapolis: University of Minnesota Press, 2011). I invoke it here as an example of a phrase that has become a popular shared articulation of the temporality of radical change.

12 For work on the difference between "perception" and "preception" in vitalist thought, see Laura U. Marks, "Cinema and Transcultural Process Philosophy," in *Film Theory Handbook*, ed. Hunter Vaughn and Tom Conley (London: Anthem Press, forthcoming).

13 Gilles Deleuze, *Cinema 1: The Movement Image*, trans. Hugh Tomlinson and Barbara Habberjam (Minneapolis, MN: University of Minnesota Press, 1986); Deleuze, *Cinema 2*; Frantz Fanon, *The Wretched of the Earth*, trans. Constance Farrington (New York: Grove Press, 1963); and Karl Marx, *The Eighteenth Brumaire of Louis Bonaparte* (IndyPublish, 2003). See *The Witch's Flight* for my earlier work on the temporality of the cinematic. In addition, the critique of the official temporality of sociology offered by Dipesh Chakrabarty in the essay "Time of History and Times of Gods," in *The Politics of Culture in the Shadow of Capital*, ed. Lisa Lowe and David Lloyd (Durham, NC: Duke University Press,

1997), 35–60, is relevant here, as is Chakrabarty's embrace of an alternative temporality and the epistemologies it supports. Chakrabarty's work on temporality offers a way to acknowledge the existence of epistemologies that are at odds with official ones.

14 Elizabeth Freeman, *Time Binds: Queer Temporalities, Queer Histories* (Durham, NC: Duke University Press, 2010); José Esteban Muñoz, *Cruising Utopia: The Then and There of Queer Futurity* (New York: New York University Press, 2009); Lee Edelman, *No Future: Queer Theory and the Death Drive* (Durham, NC: Duke University Press, 2004).

15 Muñoz, *Cruising Utopia*, 1.

16 Ibid.

17 Ibid., 32. For relevant work by Ernst Bloch, see *The Principle of Hope and the Utopian Function of Art and Literature: Selected Essays*, trans. Jack Zipes and Frank Mecklenberg (Cambridge, MA: MIT Press, 1989).

18 Muñoz, *Cruising Utopia*, 32.

19 I thank Colleen Jankovic for calling the connection to Sara Ahmed's work to my attention. See Sara Ahmed, *Queer Phenomenology: Orientations, Objects, Others* (Durham, NC: Duke University Press, 2006).

20 Freeman, *Time Binds*, xvi.

21 Muñoz, *Cruising Utopia*, 26; Freeman, *Time Binds*, xvi.

22 Freeman, *Time Binds*, xvi.

23 This formulation is also meant to highlight the points of contact between Freeman's, Muñoz's, and my own formulations of temporality and queerness. See Keeling, *The Witch's Flight*. For other, earlier, analyses of queerness that link it with surplus and the detritus of history, see Matthew Tinkcom, *Working like A Homosexual: Camp, Capital, Cinema* (Durham, NC: Duke University Press, 2002), and Amy Villarejo, *Lesbian Rule: Cultural Criticism and the Value of Desire* (Durham, NC: Duke University Press Books, 2003).

24 Leo Bersani, *Homos* (Cambridge, MA: Harvard University Press, 1995).

25 Muñoz, *Cruising Utopia*, 10.

26 Freeman, *Time Binds*, xiii.

27 Ibid.

28 Fanon, *The Wretched of the Earth*, trans. Richard Philcox (New York: Grove Press, 2005), 6.

29 See Fred Moten, *In the Break: The Aesthetics of the Black Radical Tradition* (Minneapolis: University of Minnesota Press, 2003), and my essay, "'In the Interval.'" See also the discussion of Édouard Glissant and the abyss in chapter 1.

30 My analysis of *The Watermelon Woman* is informed by the following publications about it: Matt Richardson, "Our Stories Have Never Been Told: Preliminary Thoughts on Black Lesbian Cultural Production as Historiography in *The Watermelon Woman*," *Black Camera* 2, no. 2 (2011): 100–113; Laura L. Sullivan, "Chasing Fae: *The Watermelon Woman* and Black Lesbian Possibility," *Callaloo* 23, no. 1 (2000): 448–460; C. Zimmer, "Histories of *The Watermelon Woman*: Reflexivity

Between Race and Gender," *Camera Obscura: Feminism, Culture, and Media Studies* 23, no. 2 68 (2008): 41–66.

31 For a discussion of this phrase, see David Marriott, *Haunted Life: Visual Culture and Black Modernity* (New York: Rutgers University Press, 2007), 113. See also Stuart Hall, "The Neo-Liberal Revolution," *Cultural Studies* 25, no. 6 (2011): 718.

32 *The Watermelon Woman* also makes available this reading of history because it is concerned with a search for a past that is absent from the archives. Its look backward is clearly an interested one, which does not pretend to be objective.

33 Walter Benjamin, "Theses on the Philosophy of History," in *Illuminations*, ed. Arendt, Hannah (New York: Harcourt Brace Jovanovich, 1968), 255.

34 Grace Kyungwon Hong, *Death beyond Disavowal: The Impossible Politics of Difference* (Minneapolis: University of Minnesota Press, 2015), 124.

35 Benjamin, "Theses," 255.

36 I note that my interest in M— is "problematic" in order to underscore the inevitably historical and contingent nature of my own interests in this project. I also call attention to it to make visible the aporia from which M— is projected here; to mark my interest in and construction of M— as a possible site for subsequent deliberations, evaluations, and recalibrations; to highlight the contradictions in any investment in present appearances; and to underscore the problem of representation in general. For more of my thinking about these issues, see Keeling, *The Witch's Flight* and "'In the Interval.'" My thinking here also has been influenced by that of Rinaldo Walcott's essay on *The Aggressives*. See, in particular, "Reconstructing Manhood; or, The Drag of Black Masculinity," *Small Axe*, no. 1 (2009): 86.

37 See, for example, Dean Spade, *Normal Life: Administrative Violence, Critical Trans Politics, and the Limits of Law* (Durham, NC: Duke University Press, 2015).

38 The designation trans* has come into more widespread use since *The Aggressives*. It aims to resolve some of the issues raised by aggressives.

39 Hear Big Pun, featuring Joe, "Still Not a Player," on the album *Capital Punishment* (Loud Record, LLC, 1998).

40 See Judith Jack Halberstam, *In a Queer Time and Place: Transgender Bodies, Subcultural Lives* (New York: New York University Press, 2005) for a formulation of subcultural time and its relationship to queer life cycles.

41 Dylan Rodriguez explains that "the prison is a place—a facility, in the clinical and experimental sense—in which experiences prior to and outside of the prison's proper domain disappear from both the official record and the institutional landscape" (*Forced Passages: Imprisoned Radical Intellectuals and the U.S. Prison Regime* [Minneapolis: University of Minnesota Press, 2006], 212). Also of relevance to this conversation is Rodriguez's corrective assessment of the relevance of Antonio Gramsci's formulations of hegemony, including the "war of position" and the "war of maneuver," in the context of imprisoned intellectuals (in chapter 4 of *Forced Passages*). See also Frank Wilderson's critique of the use of Gramsci's notion of hegemony in "Grams-

ci's Black Marx: Whither the Slave in Civil Society?" *Social Identities* 9, no. 2 (2003): 225–240.

42 See Fanon, *The Wretched of the Earth* (2005 ed.), 3–4.

43 Ruthie Gilmore's influential statement that racism "is the state-sanctioned or extralegal production and exploitation of group-differentiated vulnerability to premature death" is relevant here (*Golden Gulag: Prisons, Surplus, Crisis, and Opposition in Globalizing California* [Berkeley: University of California Press, 2007], 28). I discuss Gilmore's definition in chapter 4.

44 Halberstam, *In a Queer Time and Place*, 158.

45 See Audre Lorde, "The Erotic as Power," in *Sister Outsider: Essays and Speeches* (Berkeley, CA: Crossing Press, 2007).

46 José Esteban Muñoz, *Cruising Utopia: The Then and There of Queer Futurity* (New York: NYU Press, 2009), 96.

47 After writing this chapter, I read Rinaldo Walcott's reading of *The Aggressives* in "Reconstructing Manhood."

48 See Moten, *In the Break*, where he writes: "Have you ever suffered from political despair, from despair about the organization of things?" (93).

INTERLUDE

1 Herman Melville, *Bartleby and Benito Cereno*, ed. Stanley Appelbaum (Mineola, NY: Dover, 2012), 33.

2 Ibid., 10.

3 Ibid., 8–9.

4 Ibid., 18, 20–21, 25.

5 Ibid., 4.

6 Ibid., 629–630.

7 Gilles Deleuze, *Cinema 2: The Time Image*, trans. Hugh Tomlinson and Barbara Habberjam (Minneapolis: University of Minnesota Press, 1989), 280.

8 Gilles Deleuze, "Bartleby; or, The Formula," in *Essays Critical and Clinical* (Minneapolis, MN: University of Minnesota Press, 1997), 72.

9 Ibid., 82–83.

10 Ibid., 83.

11 Slavoj Žižek, *The Parallax View* (Cambridge, MA: MIT, 2009), 382.

12 Giorgio Agamben, *The Coming Community* (Minneapolis: University of Minnesota Press, 1993), 37.

13 Gilles Deleuze, *Cinema 1: The Movement Image*, trans. Hugh Tomlinson and Barbara Habberjam (Minneapolis: University of Minnesota Press, 1986), 206.

14 In this regard, the designation "minorities" is misleading, since the individuals that comprise the groups to whom Deleuze refers are more numerous than those in the groups whose power they were contesting.

15 Gilles Deleuze, *Cinema 2: The Time Image*, trans. Hugh Tomlinson and Barbara Habberjam (Minneapolis: University of Minnesota Press, 1989), 3.

16 Ibid., 18.

17 Ibid., 261.

18 See David Norman Rodowick, *Gilles Deleuze's Time Machine* (Durham, NC: Duke University Press, 1997) and David Norman Rodowick, *The Virtual Life of Film* (Cambridge, MA: Harvard University Press, 2009).

19 Deleuze, *Cinema 2*, 279. About irrational cuts between images, Deleuze writes: "And yet there is a relation between them, a free indirect or incommensurable relation, for incommensurability denotes a new relation and not an absence." (279)

20 Deleuze, *Cinema 2*, 265.

21 Ibid.

22 Gilles Deleuze, *Negotiations, 1972–1990* (New York: Columbia University Press, 1995), 177–182.

23 Ibid.

24 Deleuze, *Cinema 2*, 265–266.

CHAPTER 3. BLACK CINEMA AND QUESTIONS CONCERNING FILM/MEDIA/TECHNOLOGY

1 Kara Keeling, *The Witch's Flight: The Cinematic, the Black Femme, and the Image of Common Sense* (Durham, NC: Duke University Press, 2007), 1.

2 John Akomfrah, "Digitopia and the Spectres of the Diaspora," *Journal of Media Practice* 11, no. 1 (2010), 21–29.

3 Jodi Melamed, *Represent and Destroy: Rationalizing Violence in the New Racial Capitalism* (Minneapolis: University of Minnesota Press, 2011), xv–xvi. If it turns out that the election of Donald Trump marks the end of the third phase and the beginning of another that we will be working to better understand and characterize over the coming years, 2017 could be an end date for neoliberal multiculturalism. Such a shift will not be incidental to those I am tracing within Black film production. Indeed, Arthur Jafa's short *Love Is the Message, the Message Is Death*, discussed later in this chapter, may be a prescient part of this next phase.

4 Ibid., xix; see also 93.

5 Ibid., xv.

6 The seminal Cultural Studies text *Policing the Crisis* offers an important analysis of how the American phenomenon of "mugging" was imported into the British context in the late 1960s, carrying with it certain assumptions about and understandings of race, class, and urban space that, though inflected differently in the United Kingdom, nonetheless connect the logics animating the socioeconomic relations of the two countries. For example, Stuart Hall, Chas Critcher, Tony Jefferson, John Clarke, and Brian Roberts write: "In general this slow translation of 'mugging' from its American setting to British ground was shaped and structured by what we might call 'the special relationship' which exists between the media in Britain and the United States. In general this coverage is sustained by the continual search for *parallels* and *prophecies*: will what is happening in the United States happen here?" (*Policing the Crisis: Mugging, the State and Law and Order* [New York: Palgrave Macmillan, 1978], 25).

7 Philip Rosen's *Change Mummified: Cinema, Historicity, Theory* (Minneapolis: University of Minnesota Press, 2001) points out that this was a common formulation of the digital regime of the image within Cinema Studies as digital technologies were challenging basic assumptions within the field concerning film's specificity as a medium. Rosen's analysis reverberates throughout my discussion of Akomfrah's *The Last Angel of History* in this chapter.

8 Akomfrah, "Digitopia," 24.

9 See Kara Keeling, "Passing for Human: Bamboozled and Digital Humanism," *Women & Performance: A Journal of Feminist Theory* 15, no. 1 (2005): 237–250. The debate about the significance of the digital to the questions that have animated Cinema and Media Studies and Film Theory continues. Among the most interesting outcomes of this debate so far are the way that it is reinvigorating Film Theory by calling attention to what is changing in what film theorists have conceptualized as "the apparatus," as well as the pressure it puts on Film and Media History and historiography to excavate alternative histories of cinema and media. The renewed interest in "the apparatus," for example, offers an opportunity to reconceptualize the materiality of film and media technologies in ways that might extend the insights of feminist film theory and contribute to scholarship about race and sexuality in film and media, while at the same time putting them into conversation with relevant insights from science and technology studies. Indeed, this is one aim of the present study.

10 For example, we might also put Akomfrah's formulation of "digitopia" into conversation with the excitement expressed by early French film theorists such as Jean Epstein for the concept of *photogénie* as the art of cinema. It could be argued that what Akomfrah identifies as the capacity of digital film formats to realize the promise of cinema vis-à-vis Black images can be understood as signaling the belated arrival of *photogénie* as an inherent possibility within a renewed Black cinema aesthetic. See Jean Epstein, "On Certain Characteristics of Photogénie," in *Jean Epstein: Critical Essays and New Translations*, ed. Jason N. Paul and Sarah Keller, (Amsterdam: Amsterdam University Press, 2012), 292–296.

11 These issues have been taken up in film studies from a variety of angles and avenues. See, for example: Tom Gunning, "Moving Away from the Index: Cinema and the Impression of Reality," *Differences: A Journal of Feminist Cultural Studies* 18, no. 1 (2007): 29–52; Daniel Morgan, "Rethinking Bazin: Ontology and Realist Aesthetics," *Critical Inquiry* 32, no. 3 (2006): 443–481; David Norman Rodowick, *The Virtual Life of Film* (Cambridge, MA: Harvard University Press, 2009); as well as the aforementioned Rosen, *Change Mummified*, and Alice Maurice, *The Cinema and Its Shadow: Race and Technology in Early Cinema* (Minneapolis: University of Minnesota Press, 2013).

12 Akomfrah, "Digitopia," 28.

13 It is salutary in this context to think, for example, about movement as a constitutive element of cinema, as Tom Gunning prompts us to do, or to enrich our

understanding of realism in cinema, as Dan Morgan and others have done by returning us to the work of Andrè Bazin.

14 D. Fox Harrell, *Phantasmal Media: An Approach to Imagination, Computation, and Expression* (Cambridge, MA: MIT Press, 2013), 45.

15 Walter Benjamin, "Theses on the Philosophy of History," in *Illuminations*, ed. Hannah Arendt (New York: Harcourt Brace Jovanovich, 1968), 263.

16 Harrell, *Phantasmal Media*, 45.

17 Wendy Hui Kyong Chun, *Programmed Visions: Software and Memory* (Cambridge, MA: MIT Press, 2013).

18 For example, in my book *The Witch's Flight*, in following Gilles Deleuze's reading of Henri Bergson's work, especially in *Matter and Memory*, I argued that present reality appears in its entirety and we habitually perceive less than what appears. This also applies to memory-images, sensory images of and from the past that appear in the present, including what we call "memories." Memories and the past can be formed and re-formed each time they appear. In *The Witch's Flight* I presented this in terms of the sedimented layers of common sense that accrue over time in the struggle for hegemony. Because I was concerned with how things could be different than they presently are—how they might actually support alternative socialites such as Black lesbian butch/femme—it was important there for me to engage with a past that is not finished, one that we are constantly creating and recreating by accessing elements deposited within it, even if those are presently imperceptible, rather than a past from which anything that can reach us is already pre-formed. I think about this conceptualization of temporality along the lines offered by Deleuze, who sees cinema as "the organ for perfecting the new reality" (*Cinema 1: The Movement Image*, trans. Hugh Tomlinson and Barbara Habberjam [Minneapolis: University of Minnesota Press, 1986], 8).

19 Benjamin, "Theses," 257.

20 Ibid., 254.

21 Ibid., 262.

22 The rather well-known thesis to which I refer reads:

A Klee painting named "Angelus Novus" shows an angel looking as though he is about to move away from something he is fixedly contemplating. His eyes are staring, his mouth is open, his wings are spread. This is how one pictures the angel of history. His face is turned toward the past. Where we perceive a chain of events, he sees one single catastrophe which keeps piling wreckage upon wreckage and hurls it in front of his feet. The angel would like to stay, awaken the dead, and make whole what has been smashed. But a storm is blowing from Paradise; it has got caught in his wings with such violence that the angel can no longer close them. This storm irresistibly propels him into the future toward which his back is turned, which the pile of debris before him grows skyward. This storm is what we call progress. (Benjamin, "Theses," 258).

In a personal conversation, Alondra Nelson offered a critique of the masculinization of this version of Afrofuturism and a discussion of the extant alternatives to it.

23 Martin Heidegger, *The Question Concerning Technology and Other Essays*, trans. William Lovvitt (New York: Harper & Row, 1977).

24 Upon the introduction of the word "essence," William Lovvitt, the translator of Heidegger's essay, writes in a footnote: "'Essence' is the traditional translation of the German noun *Wesen*. One of Heidegger's principal aims in this essay is to seek the true meaning of essence through or by way of the 'correct' meaning. He will later show that *Wesen* does not simply mean what something is, but that it means, further, the way in which something pursues its course, the way in which it remains through time as what it is. Heidegger writes elsewhere that the noun *Wesen* does not mean *quidditas* originally, but rather 'enduring as presence' (*das Währen als Gegemoart*)" (3fn.).

25 Heidegger, *The Question*, 4.

26 Ibid., 10–11.

27 Ibid, 13.

28 Ibid, 33.

29 Angelica Nuzzo, "What Are Poets For?" *Philosophy Today* 59, no. 1 (2015): 40.

30 Ibid., 41.

31 Ibid., 43.

32 Christian Fuchs, "Martin Heidegger's Anti-Semitism: Philosophy of Technology and the Media in the Light of the Black Notebooks. Implications for the Reception of Heidegger in Media and Communication Studies," *TripleC* 13, no. 1 (2015): 55–78. See also Jean Luc Nancy, *The Banality of Heidegger*, trans. Jeff Fort (New York: Fordham University Press, 2017).

33 See James A. Snead, "On Repetition in Black Culture," in *Racist Traces and Other Writing: European Pedigrees / African Contagions*, ed. Kara Keeling, Colin MacCabe, and Cornel West (London: Palgrave Macmillan, 2003), 11–33. Also see Ronald Judy, "Kant and the Negro," *Surfaces* 1, no. 8 (1991): 4–70.

34 Jürgen Habermas, "Martin Heidegger: On the Publication of the Lectures of 1935," in *The Heidegger Controversy*, ed. Richard Wolin (Cambridge, MA: MIT Press, 1992), 186–197.

35 Likewise, that these logics linger in our thinking and scholarship after the revelations about Nazi Germany at the end of World War II and in the face of scholarship and other efforts that have elucidated the racism undergirding the European Enlightenment adds further support to the salience and continuing importance of critiques of official and state-recognized liberal anti-racisms.

36 See Alexander G. Weheliye, *Phonographies: Grooves in Sonic Afro-Modernity* (Durham, NC: Duke University Press, 2005).

37 See Simone Brown, *Dark Matters: On the Surveillance of Blackness* (Durham, NC: Duke University Press, 2015), for an analysis of how digital technologies of surveillance extend and enhance older technologies of surveillance and disci-

pline vis-à-vis Black bodies. See also Kodwo Eshun, "Further Considerations on Afrofuturism," *CR: The New Centennial Review* 3, no. 2 (2003): 287–302.

38 Beth Coleman, "Race as Technology," *Camera Obscura: Feminism, Culture, and Media Studies* 24, no. 1(70) (2009): 177–207.

39 Ibid., 178.

40 Herman Gray, "Subject(Ed) to Recognition," *American Quarterly* 65, no. 4 (2013): 771.

41 See Jodi Melamed, "The Spirit of Neoliberalism from Racial Liberalism to Neoliberal Multiculturalism," *Social Text* 24, no. 4 (2006): 1–24; and Melamed, *Represent and Destroy*.

42 Gray, "Subject(Ed) to Recognition," 771.

43 Lawrence Grossberg, "Modernity and Commensuration," *Cultural Studies* 24, no. 3 (2010): 315.

44 Karen Barad, *Meeting the Universe Halfway: Quantum Physics and the Entanglement of Matter and Meaning* (Durham, NC: Duke University Press), Kindle loc. 829.

45 Ibid., 1007–1008; and Keeling, *The Witch's Flight*.

46 Barad, *Meeting the Universe Halfway*, Kindle loc. 2741–2743. While a full discussion of Barad's theories is beyond the scope of the present book, it is worth pointing out here that Barad's formulation of "the apparatus" within "agential realism" shares with my understanding of "the cinematic" and "cinematic reality" an insistence that, as Barad puts it, "apparatuses are not mere observing instruments but boundary-drawing practices—specific material (re)configurings of the world—which come to matter" (ibid., 2811–2813).

47 Ibid., 2845–2846.

48 Ibid., 3412–3413.

49 Ibid., 2963–2964.

50 In the terms of my earlier work, it might be said that what I have called "the black femme function" indexes a "poetics of Relation" within cinematic reality. Insofar as it courses through the cinematic, it also names one of the reservoirs for a "bursting forth." It is not the only one available in cinematic reality, nor does it rely upon any specific, recognizable mode of embodiment. It marks, as I stated in *The Witch's Flight*, "a potential for creativity and self-valorization within affectivity" (144). The Black femme function marks a distributed capacity to affect reality coursing through the cinematic.

51 Barad, *Meeting the Universe Halfway*, Kindle loc. 3578–3581.

52 Melamed, *Represent and Destroy*, xvii.

53 James Snead, "Repetition as a Figure of Black Culture," in *Black Literature and Literary Theory*, ed. Henry Louis Gates and Sunday Ogbonna Anozie (New York; Routledge, 1984), 59–79. Snead's essay is part of a broader effort to reassess the inheritance of the Enlightenment in the context of theories of Blackness and Black identity. For another engagement, see Paul Gilroy, *The Black Atlantic:*

Modernity and Double Consciousness (Cambridge, MA: Harvard University Press, 1993).

54 Coleman, "Race as Technology," 200.

55 See also Paul Gilroy, *Against Race: Imagining Political Culture beyond the Color Line* (Cambridge, MA: Harvard University Press, 2000).

56 Coleman, "Race as Technology," 177.

57 Ibid., 179.

58 See, for example, Richard Iton, *In Search of the Black Fantastic: Politics and Popular Culture in the Post-Civil Rights Era* (Oxford: Oxford University Press, 2010).

59 Akomfrah, "Digitopia and the Spectres of Diaspora," 21–29.

60 Ibid.

61 Deleuze, *Cinema 2*, 265.

62 See Louis Althusser, "Ideology and Ideological State Apparatuses" in *On the Reproduction of Capitalism: Ideology and Ideological State Apparatuses* (New York: Verso Books, 2014), 232–272.

63 See Allyson Nadia Field, *Uplift Cinema: The Emergence of African American Film and the Possibility of Black Modernity* (Durham, NC: Duke University Press, 2015).

64 Entry for "algorithm" in *Oxford English Dictionary Online* (JSTOR, 2007).

65 The longer quotation by Glissant referenced here concerns errantry and opacity: "In the poetics of Relation, one who is errant (which is no longer traveler, discoverer or conqueror) strives to know the totality of the world yet already knows he will never accomplish this and knows that is precisely where the threatened beauty of the world resides" (Édouard Glissant, *Poetics of Relation*, trans. Betsy Wing [Ann Arbor: University of Michigan Press, 1997], 20).

66 YouTube user Luca Graziani, "DEAD GIVEAWAY Charles Ramsey ORIGINAL interview, rescuer of Amanda Berry," YouTube.com, May 8, 2013, www.youtube.com.

67 For the full text, see Martine Syms, "The Mundane Afrofuturist Manifesto," *Rhizome*, December 13, 2013, http://rhizome.org.

68 It is not surprising that Jafa and Akomfrah share a desire to make Black film more like Black music since they have been in conversation and communication with one another for many years.

69 This is an adaptation of language from Giorgio Agamben, "Bartleby, or on Contingency," in *Potentialities: Collected Essays in Philosophy*, trans. Daniel Heller-Roazin (Palo Alto, CA: Stanford University Press, 1999), 253–256.

70 See Herman Gray, "The Feel of Life: Resonance, Race, and Representation," *International Journal of Communication* 9, no. 1 (2015): 1108–1119.

71 Glissant, *Poetics of Relation*.

72 Here, I am thinking about *Love Is the Message* along the lines Gray suggests might be helpful for television scholars interested in questions of race within a media ecology characterized by media convergence and modes of neoliberal governance and self-crafting. In "The Feel of Life," Gray writes, "Methodologically, we might ask what sort of sentiments find expression in different arrangements and parts of

the race machine, and what these sentiments might tell us about the failures, gaps, and tensions in the machine. Put another way, can we read these practices of sentiment and the media through which they circulate and resound for the different intensities, velocity, duration, and sensations that they express and for what they tell us about the liberal project of capitalist progress, liberal tolerance, and liberal subject making?" (1117).

CHAPTER 4. "CORPORATE CANNIBAL"

1 Francesca T. Royster, *Sounding like a No-No* (Ann Arbor: University of Michigan Press, 2013), ProQuest Ebook Central.
2 James Snead, "Repetition as a Figure of Black Culture," in *Black Literature and Literary Theory*, ed. Henry Louis Gates and Sunday Ogbonna Anozie (New York; Routledge, 1984), 59.
3 Ibid., 60.
4 Ibid.
5 Ibid.
6 Ibid., 67.
7 Grace Jones, as told to Paul Morley, *I'll Never Write My Memoirs* (New York: Gallery Books, 2015), 15.
8 Ibid.
9 Steven Shaviro, "Post-Cinematic Affect: On Grace Jones, Boarding Gate and Southland Tales," *Film-Philosophy* 14, no. 1 (2010): 12.
10 Daphne Brooks, "'Ain't Got No, I Got Life': #OscarsSoWhite and the Problem of Women Musicians on Film," *Los Angeles Review of Books*, February 28, 2006, https://lareviewofbooks.org.
11 Karl Marx, *Grundrisse: Foundations of the Critique of Political Economy*, trans. Martin Nicolaus (New York: Vintage Press, 1973), 488. See the discussion of this in the introduction.
12 See the discussion of Simondon's formulation of the "preindividual" and the "transindividual" in chapter 1.
13 Cedric Robinson, *Black Marxism: The Making of the Black Radical Tradition* (Chapel Hill, NC: University of North Carolina Press, 1983).
14 I am thinking here of this aspect of Adrian MacKenzie's reading of Gilbert Simondon: "The notion of the transindividual forms a crucial part of Simondon's alternative account of psychosocial experience because it links the emergence of collectives to something that is not fully experienced or perceived by individuals. A collective is a process of individuation emerging from beings who are not entirely themselves since they are transductive" (MacKenzie, *Transductions: Bodies and Machines at Speed* [New York: Continuum, 2002], 117). Here, I aim to describe a process through which the resources accumulating in preindividual being are transduced through matter (brains, hands, and so on) as part of a collective endeavor to realize a radical Black feminist vision.

15 I am indebted to a conversation with Jacqueline Stewart for this insight.

16 A discussion of the politics of sex work is beyond the scope of this chapter. But the question of the extent to which Jordan can claim sovereignty over the resources available to her and the potential that lies in refusing to do so in recognizable ways could be a factor in any discussion of it that might follow from here.

17 For an account of the role of sexual violence in the European settlement of the United States, see Andrea Smith, *Conquest: Sexual Violence and American Indian Genocide* (Durham, NC: Duke University Press, 2015). For a formulation of "the black woman" as "the figure that crystallizes the arrangement between capital and the event of captivity," see Rizvana Bradley, "Living in the Absence of a Body: The (Sus)Stain of Black Female (W)Holeness," *Rhizomes: Cultural Studies in Emerging Knowledge*, no. 29 (2016).

18 The primary role that enslaved cis-gender women played in the reproduction of the slave economy is but one example of this. As the epigraph to *At the Dark End of the Street: Black Women, Rape, and Resistance—a New History of the Civil Rights Movement from Rosa Parks to the Rise of Black Power* (New York: Vintage Books, 2011), for example, Danielle L. McGuire gives the following quotation from Gunnar Myrdal (1944): "Sex is the principle around which the whole structure of segregation . . . is organized."

19 As cited in McGuire, *At the Dark End of the Street*, xix.

20 Wendy Hui Kyong Chun makes a version of this argument in her book *Updating to Remain the Same: Habitual New Media* (Cambridge, MA: The MIT Press, 2016). There, Chun is concerned specifically with the politics that might emerge from an embrace of the public nature of social media. My claim here is a broader one, stemming from the historical existence of Black women. It might be said that social media is dispersing this aspect of the particular historical experience of Black women in the Americas more broadly.

21 Shaviro, "Post-Cinematic Affect," 14.

22 Ibid., 19.

23 Ibid., 31.

24 Ibid., 33, n. 24.

25 Ibid., 33.

26 Stefano Harney and Fred Moten put it this way: "It is not credit we seek nor even debt, but bad debt which is to say real debt, the debt that cannot be repaid, the debt at a distance, the debt without creditor, the black debt, the queer debt, the criminal debt. Excessive debt, incalculable debt, debt for no reason, debt broken from credit, debt as its own principle" (Moten and Harney, "The Undercommons: Fugitive Planning and Black Study," [Wivenhoe, UK: Minor Compositions, 2013], 61).

27 Alessandra Raengo, "Reification, Reanimation, and the Money of the Real," *World Picture 7, Distance* (2012), http://www.worldpicturejournal.com.

28 Grace Jones as told to Paul Morley, *I'll Never Write My Memoirs*, 357.

29 Gilles Deleuze, "Postscript on the Societies of Control," *October* 59 (1992): 4.

30 Wendy Hui Kyong Chun, *Programmed Visions: Software and Memory* (Cambridge, MA: MIT Press, 2013).

31 Fred Moten, "The Case of Blackness," *Criticism* 50, no. 2 (2008): 180.

32 Fatima El-Tayeb, *European Others: Queering Ethnicity in Postnational Europe* (Minneapolis: University of Minnesota Press, 2011).

33 Ruth Wilson Gilmore, "Fatal Couplings of Power and Difference," *Professional Geographer* 54, no 1 (2002): 16.

34 Beth Coleman, "Race as Technology," *Camera Obscura: Feminism, Culture, and Media Studies* 24, no. 1(70) (2009): 201.

35 Snead, "Repetition," 67. The phrase "a succession of accidents and surprises" in Snead's original text appears in quotation marks because it refers to his analysis of Hegel's definition of black culture according to which the African "has no idea of history or progress, but instead allows 'accidents and surprises' to take hold of his fate" (63).

36 Ibid. A recent manifestation of this is the concern in the United States in the mid-2010s about the fact that there is now a generation who cannot expect to be wealthier than their parents.

37 Ibid.

38 Fred Moten and Stefano Harney, *The Undercommons: Fugitive Planning & Black Study* (New York: Autonomedia, 2013), 47.

39 In the prologue to *Antifragile: Things that Gain from Disorder* (New York: Random House), Nassim Nicholas Taleb writes: "Wind extinguishes a candle and energizes fire. Likewise, with randomness, uncertainty, chaos: you want to use them, not hide from them. You want to be the fire and wish for the wind. This summarizes this author's nonmeek attitude to randomness and uncertainty. We just don't want to just survive uncertainty, to just about make it. We want to survive uncertainty and, in addition—like a certain class of aggressive Roman Stoics—have the last word. The mission is how to domesticate, even dominate, even conquer, the unseen, the opaque, and the inexplicable. How?" (Kindle loc. 314–319).

40 See my discussion of this idea in the introduction.

41 Martin Munro, *Different Drummers: Rhythm and Race in the Americas* (Berkeley: University of California Press, 2010), 14.

42 Ibid.

43 Raengo, "Reification," 12. It bears mention that Snead describes Freud's theory of "the return of the repressed" as an exception to the investment in progress and development endemic to European culture.

44 Shaviro, "Post-Cinematic Affect," 11.

45 Grace Jones as told to Paul Morley, *I'll Never Write My Memoirs*, 228.

46 I thank Chandra Ford for this insight.

47 The reference to the "resistance of the object" is to the first chapter of Fred Moten, *In the Break: The Aesthetics of the Black Radical Tradition* (Minneapolis: University of Minnesota Press, 2003).

48 See Shaviro, "Post-Cinematic Affect," for a reading of the title song to "Slave to the Rhythm" that connects it to the themes in "Corporate Cannibal."

49 Grace Jones as told to Paul Morley, *I'll Never Write My Memoirs*, 228.

50 Ibid., 260–261.

51 Ibid., 260.

52 See Daphne Brooks, *Bodies in Dissent: Spectacular Performances of Race and Freedom, 1850–1910* (Durham, NC: Duke University Press, 2006), for a reading of the historical significance of opacity in Black performances.

53 Though it would take me too far afield to fully discuss them, it is worth mentioning here that in various points in her memoir Jones pushes back against the idea that she is a Black woman. These passages in the memoir call attention to a diasporic discourse about race and the politics and potential of Black existence, and the extent to which Jones's errantry is animated by a rejection of received categories and concepts placed upon her by the circumstances of her birth. These passages might enhance analyses of Jones's performance by taking into account her own perspective on it.

54 Royster, *Sounding like a No-No*, 149.

55 Édouard Glissant, *Poetics of Relation*, trans. Betsy Wing (Ann Arbor: University of Michigan Press, 1997), xvi.

56 Ibid., xvi.

57 Grace Jones as told to Paul Morley, *I'll Never Write My Memoirs*, 82.

58 Ibid., 357.

59 See Raengo, "Reification," for an analysis of "Corporate Cannibal" and chattel slavery, and Shaviro, "Post-Cinematic Affect," for a discussion of how "Slave to the Rhythm" critiques the Fordist mode of production.

60 For compelling approaches to cliché, see Rey Chow, *The Protestant Ethnic and the Spirit of Capitalism* (New York: Columbia University Press, 2002), and Meaghan Morris, "Transnational Glamour, National Allure: Community, Change and Cliché in Baz Luhrmann's Australia," in *Storytelling: Critical and Creative Approaches*, ed. Jan Shaw, Philippa Kelly, and L. E. Semler (Basingstoke, UK: Palgrave, 2013), 83–113.

61 On fungibility, see, for example, S. Best, *The Fugitive's Properties: Law and the Poetics of Possession* (Chicago: University of Chicago Press, 2004). I thank Grace Kyungwon Hong for helping me to arrive at this formulation.

62 Coleman, "Race as Technology," 206.

63 Ibid.

64 Ibid., 202.

65 Wendy Hui Kyong Chun, "Race and/as Technology or How to Do Things to Race," in *Race After the Internet*, ed. Lisa Nakamura and Peter A. Chow-White (New York: Routledge, 2012), 38–60. For an earlier version of this essay, see Wendy Hui Kyong Chun, "Race and/as Technology; or, How to Do Things to Race," *Camera Obscura* 70, no. 7 (2009).

66 Chun, "Race and/as Technology" (2012), 38.

67 Ibid., 43.

68 Ibid., 48.

69 Ibid., 57.

70 Ibid., 52.

71 Ibid., 57. As I discussed in chapter 1, the concept of the "transindividual" invoked here is Gilbert Simondon's, for whom it names, according to Muriel Combes, "an impersonal zone of subjects that is simultaneously a molecular or intimate dimension of the collective itself" (*Gilbert Simondon and the Philosophy of the Transindividual*, trans. Thomas LaMarre [Cambridge, MA: MIT Press, 2013], 52).

INTERCESSION

1 Gilles Deleuze, "Bartleby; or, The Formula," in *Essays Critical and Clinical* (Minneapolis: University of Minnesota Press, 1997), 83.

2 Ibid.

3 Ibid.

4 See, for example, relevant artwork by Jay Mark Johnson at http://www.jaymarkjohnson.com/.

5 Mark Rifkin, *Settler Common Sense: Queerness and Everyday Colonialism in the American Renaissance* (Minneapolis: University of Minnesota Press, 2014).

6 See, for example, the books in the Critical Climate Change series co-edited by Tom Cohen and Claire Colebrook (www.openhumanitiespress.orgchange/) and in the New Metaphysics series co-edited by Graham Harman and Bruno Latour (http://www.openhumanitiespress.org) at Open Humanities Press.

7 Deleuze, "Bartleby," 83.

8 Ibid., 75.

9 Ibid., 76. I discuss this in the interlude, "The Sonic Bartleby."

10 William V. Spanos, *Herman Melville and the American Calling* (Albany: State University of New York, 2009), 166.

11 Deleuze, "Bartleby," 87.

12 Ibid., 83, 86; emphasis in original.

13 Ibid., 86.

14 Ibid., 88.

15 Ibid., 89–90.

16 Ibid., 89.

17 The ways that strip photography complicates the cinematic mechanism of mattering is significant here.

18 I use the concept of "survivance" introduced by White Earth Anishinaabe scholar Gerald Vizenor and taken up in subsequent scholarship in Native American and Indigenous Studies. It marks a set of practices that are in excess of mere survival; they grow from and support active and imaginative worldviews. "Survivance" is a form of resistance premised in part on the ongoing adaptation of Native American traditions to changing circumstances. In the introduction to his edited

collection entitled *Survivance: Narratives of Native Presence* (Lincoln: University of Nebraska Press, 2008), Vizenor explains that "the practices of survivance create an active presence, more than the instincts of survival, function or subsistence." For the terms through which "survivance" was introduced into scholarship, see Gerald Vizenor, *Manifest Manners: Postindian Warriors of Survivance* (Middletown, CT: Wesleyan University Press, 1994). For a discussion of the Vizenor's use of the term and its relevance, see Jill Doerfler, "Postindian Survivance: Gerald Vizenor and Kimberly Blaese," in *Gerald Vizenor: Texts and Contexts*, ed. Deborah Madsen and A. Lee (Albuquerque: University of New Mexico Press, 2011), 186–207.

19 See, for example, Audra Simpson, *Mohawk Interruptus: Political Life across the Borders of Settler States* (Durham, NC: Duke University Press, 2014), and Denise Ferreira da Silva, "To Be Announced: Radical Praxis or Knowing (at) the Limits of Justice," *Social Text* 31, no. 1 (2013): 43–62.

20 Giorgio Agamben, *Potentialities: Collected Essays in Philosophy* (Palo Alto, CA: Stanford University Press, 1999), 270.

21 Slavoj Žižek, *The Parallax View* (Cambridge, MA: MIT Press, 2009), 382.

22 Deleuze, "Bartleby," 70.

23 Ibid., 71.

24 It might also be said that in so doing, Bartleby also portends the ways that a nascent American pragmatism will move to make philosophy useful—to give it an agency akin to technology, in the sense of technology as the creation of something useful, a category against which philosophy since Plato had long been defined via the elevation of Being and the Idea.

25 Deleuze, "Bartleby," 88.

26 See Frank Wilderson III, *Red, White & Black: Cinema and the Structure of US Antagonisms* (Durham, NC: Duke University Press, 2010) for a reading of this in relationship to film.

27 Deleuze, "Bartleby," 83, 87.

28 See Katherine McKittrick, *Demonic Ground: Black Women and the Cartographies of Struggle* (Minneapolis: University of Minnesota Press, 2006), as well as Eve Tuck, Allison Guess, and Hannah Sultan, "Not Nowhere: Collaborating on Selfsame Land," *Decolonization: Indigeneity, Education & Society* 26 (June 2014): 1–11.

29 See Gerald Horne, *The Counter-Revolution of 1776: Slave Resistance and the Origins of the United States of America* (New York: New York University Press, 2014).

30 See recent scholarship by Tiffany Lethabo King and Shona Jackson, among others, for analyses and theories of the ways that settler colonialism and chattel slavery function together and separately in the American national project. Tiffany Lethabo King, "The Labor of (Re)Reading Plantation Landscapes Fungible(Ly)," *Antipode* 48, no. 4 (2016): 1022–1039, and S. N. Jackson, "Humanity beyond the Regime of Labor: Antiblackness, Indigeneity, and the Legacies of Colonialism in the Caribbean," *Decolonization: Indigeneity, Education & Society* (2014), https://decolonization.wordpress.com.

31 Saidiya Hartman, *Lose Your Mother: A Journey along the Atlantic Slave Route* (New York: Farrar, Straus and Giroux, 2008), 6.

32 See, for example, among other relevant analyses, Jodi A. Byrd, *The Transit of Empire: Indigenous Critiques of Colonialism* (Minneapolis: University of Minnesota Press, 2011).

33 Deleuze, "Bartleby," 87.

34 See Édouard Glissant, *Poetics of Relation*, trans. Betsy Wing (Ann Arbor: University of Michigan Press, 1997), and Manthia Diawara, "One World in Relation Édouard Glissant in Conversation with Manthia Diawara," *Nka Journal of Contemporary African Art* 28 (March 2011): 4–19.

35 Glissant, *Poetics of Relation*, 62.

36 See Fred Moten, "Black Op," *PMLA* 123, no. 5 (2008): 1743.

37 This phrase itself originates in the Book of Job.

38 C. L. R. James, *Mariners, Renegades, and Castaways: The Story of Herman Melville and the World We Live In* (Hanover, NH: University Press of New England, 1953), 106.

39 Quoted in ibid., 17.

40 Ibid., 40. Scholars have argued about where Queequeg might be from. Lynette Russell explains, "Queequeg, often described as Marquesan (though much more likely to have been Maori), was off selling 'heads' when Ishmael first heard of him. Trade in tattooed Maori heads was relatively common in the nineteenth century and the ship's captain William Dana gave the East Indian Museum in Salem the 'embalmed head of a New Zealand Chief' (Russell, *Roving Mariners: Australian Aboriginal Whalers and Sealers in the Southern Oceans, 1790–1870* [Albany: State University of New York Press, 2012], 138). The above contains a citation to J. Lindgren, "'Let Us Idealize Old Types of Manhood:' The New Bedford Whaling Museum, 1903–1941," *New England Quarterly* 72, no. 2 (1999): 163–202.

41 James, *Mariners, Renegades, and Castaways*, 40.

42 Donald Pease, introduction to James, *Mariners, Renegades and Castaways*, xviii. Spanos also describes Melville in this manner in *Herman Melville and the American Calling*.

43 See Spanos, *Herman Melville*, for a gloss on the changing readings of *Moby Dick* over time and the different interests they serve.

44 James, *Mariners, Renegades, and Castaways*, 53–54.

45 Glissant and Diawara, "One World in Relation."

46 See Deleuze, "Postscript on Control Societies," 5.

47 Anthony Bayani Rodriguez's work on the decolonial intellectual formation of the Atlantic and the importance of Caribbean intellectuals to the Black radical tradition is also an important contribution in that direction; see "Heretical Scripts: Sylvia Wynter & the Decolonial Atlantic" (PhD diss., University of Southern California, 2015).

CHAPTER 5. "WORLD GALAXY"

1 See John E. Drabinski, "'What Is Trauma to the Future?: On Glissant's Poetics," *Qui Parle: Critical Humanities and Social Sciences* 18, no. 2 (2010): 291–307.

2 For a reading of "value" as "contentless and simple," see Gayatri Chakravorty Spivak, "Who Claims Alterity?," in *Remaking History*, ed. Barbara Kruger and Phil Mariani (Seattle, WA: Bay Press), 1989,: 269–292.

3 Édouard Glissant, *Poetics of Relation*, trans. Betsy Wing (Minneapolis: University of Michigan Press, 1997), 27.

4 Ibid., 28.

5 Ibid., 29.

6 Ibid.

7 Ibid.

8 Ibid.

9 Ibid., 32, 30.

10 Ibid., 33.

11 Combes, *Gilbert Simondon*. See chapter 1 for a discussion of transduction.

12 Glissant, *Poetics of Relation*, 32.

13 Ibid.

14 See chapter 4 for a discussion of Nassim Taleb's concept of "antifragile."

15 Glissant, *Poetics of Relation*, 7.

16 Ibid.

17 Manthia Diawara, "One World in Relation: Édouard Glissant in Conversation with Manthia Diawara," *Nka Journal of Contemporary African Art* 28 (March 2011): 34.

18 Glissant and Diawara, "One World in Relation," 7.

19 Franya J. Berkman, *Monument Eternal: The Music of Alice Coltrane* (Middletown, CT: Wesleyan University Press, 2010), Kindle loc. 258.

20 Ytasha L. Womack, *Afrofuturism: The World of Black Sci-Fi and Fantasy Culture* (Chicago: Chicago Review Press, 2013), 9.

21 See Kodwo Eshun for a discussion of Alice (and John) Coltrane in the context of Afrofuturism in his seminal book, *More Brilliant than the Sun: Adventures in Sonic Fiction* (London: Quartet Books, 1999), 164–174.

22 See Luaka Bop, "Luaka Bop Presents: Alice Coltrane Turiyasangitananda," Youtube, 2017, www.youtube.com.

23 See John Scheinfeld (dir.), *Chasing Trane: The John Coltrane Documentary* (Meteor 17, 2016).

24 Jane Iwamura, *Virtual Orientalism: Asian Religions and American Popular Culture* (Oxford: Oxford University Press, 2010), Kindle loc. 173–174.

25 The embrace of jazz musicians and music in Japan and other East Asian countries indicates that the cultural exchanges certainly were not unidirectional. For a brief documentary account of the cultural impact of John and Alice Coltrane's final tour in Japan after the bombing of Nagasaki and Hiroshima, see Scheinfeld, *Chasing Trane*.

26 In *Monument Eternal: The Music of Alice Coltrane* (Middletown, CT: Wesleyan University Press, 2010), Franya J. Berkman writes about Alice Coltrane that "her impulse and ability to create a new musical and spiritual tradition speaks not only to her own vision and means, but also to a historical moment ripe for invention, reinvention, and new modes of self-realization" (Kindle loc. 501–502).

27 H. H. Jun, *Race for Citizenship: Black Orientalism and Asian Uplift from Pre-Emancipation to Neoliberal America* (New York: New York University Press, 2011), 18.

28 John and Alice Coltrane's study of Asian music might also be considered in the political context of the Cold War in which Black leftist activists expressed solidarity with people in Vietnam and China who, like them, were fighting for self-determination in the face of American imperial aggression and the white supremacy embedded in it. See, for example, Vijay Prashad, *Everybody Was Kung Fu Fighting: Afro-Asian Connections and the Myth of Cultural Purity* (Boston: Beacon Press, 2001), and Robeson Taj Frazier, *The East Is Black: Cold War China in the Black Radical Imagination* (Durham, NC: Duke University Press, 2014).

29 For a discussion of Alice Coltrane's relevance to Afrofuturism, see Eshun, *More Brilliant than the Sun.*

30 Glissant and Diawara, "One World in Relation," 8.

31 In *Monument Eternal*, Berkman muses about the music Coltrane composed while leading her ashram:

> What kind of music is this? *Bhajans* at Sai Anantam Ashram are clearly sui generis. While it is common today to hear white Americans singing Indian devotional hymns at yoga centers and at concerts—American artists such as Krishna Das and Jai Utal have major record deals these days, and tickets to hear them sing cost twenty dollars or more—Alice Coltrane's *bhajans* are noncommercial, free to the public, and performed in a predominantly African American, gospel style. Furthermore, for nearly three decades they were played by Alice herself, who infused her arrangements with the diverse genres she explored over the course of her life as a church accompanist, bebop pianist, composer, and avant-garde improviser. What's more, the ritual that one finds at Alice's ashram reflects her own iconoclastic musical and spiritual journey. In the *mandir*, she reproduced the aesthetics of black sacred music characteristic of her formative years in Detroit. She also maintained an approach to musical worship that reflects the theory of her late husband, John Coltrane, that music has a universal, transcendent nature—a theory she synthesized with elements of Hindu practice learned from her gurus and in her travels to India. (Kindle loc. 149–158)

32 Eshun, *More Brilliant than the Sun*, 168.

33 Kodwo Eshun, "Further Considerations on Afrofuturism," *CR: The New Centennial Review* 3, no. 2 (2003): 287–302.

34 In this regard, it could be argued that the digital regime of the image has a privileged relationship within the cinematic to the powers of the false.

35 Lynsey Chutel, "Science Fiction Has Ancient Roots in Africa. Writer Wanuri Kahiu Says It Also Has a Future There," *Quartz: Africa*, 2016, https://qz.com.

36 "Asha" means "no" or "resistance" in Kikuyu. Personal correspondence with Wangui wa Goro, June 30, 2017.

37 "Pumzi" means "breath" or "air" in Kiswahili. Personal correspondence with Wangui wa Goro, January 8, 2018.

38 Personal correspondence with Wangui wa Goro, June 30, 2017.

39 Ibid.

40 Wanuri Kahiu, dir., *For Our Land*, 49 min., in English, Kikuyu, and Swahili (with English subtitles) (Kenya: M-Net, 2009), available at https://vimeo.com.

41 For an announcement of Kahiu and Okorafor's film, see Georg Szalai, "'Pixar of South Africa,' Unveils Film, TV Projects," *Hollywood Reporter*, December 11, 2015, www.hollywoodreporter.com. One of their stories, "Rusties," is available to read online at http://clarkesworldmagazine.com. In July 2017, Nnedi Okorafor announced that HBO is in the early stages of adapting *Who Fears Death* for the small screen. See Lesley Goldberg, "George R. R. Martin Adapting Fantasy Novel 'Who Fears Death' for HBO," *Hollywood Reporter*, July 10, 2017, www.hollywoodreporter.com, and L. Goldberg, "HBO's 'Who Fears Death' Adaptation Adds Writer, Michael Lombardo," *Hollywood Reporter*, September 14, 2017, www.hollywoodreporter.com.

42 Nnedi Okorafor, *Who Fears Death* (New York: Penguin, 2011), 385.

43 Georgio Agamben, *The Time that Remains: A Commentary on the Letter to the Romans*, trans. Patricia Dailey (Palo Alto, CA: Stanford University Press, 2005).

44 Okorafor, *Who Fears Death*, 381.

INDEX

abyss: "after End of the World" and, 77–78; birth out of trauma with, 237n68; Black existence and, 78; Caribbean and, 78–79, 187; jazz issuing from, 203; slavery and, 54, 78, 199, 203
activism, 14
affectivity, 238n5; agency of matter in, 134; capital influencing through, 82; cinema and Black feminism, 246n50
Africa: Afrofuturism as projection of, 205; Black science fiction and, 175, 206; creolization of Asian and, 204; *Pumzi* in Kenya, 206–8; Shell exploiting, 204; speculations on, 204–12; Western philosophy excising, 70–71
Afrofuturism, xii; Africa future projection as, 205; alien and, 141; alternative history, (im)possible future in, 63; Coltrane, A., and, 200, 256n29; cultural production of, 39; definition of, 3–4; digital image and sound in, 114; freedom dreams from, xvi; future speculation on, xv; imagination, technology, future, liberation in, 4; *The Last Angel of History* as, 124; literature, film, video for, 64; masculinization of, 244n22; music for, 57, 64, 69, 74; Shell against future of, 3; speculative fiction strategy in, 74; technology and, 59
Afrofuturism: The World of Black Sci-Fi and Fantasy Culture (Womack), 4
"after End of the World," 75–80
AG. *See* aggressives

Agamben, Giorgio, 46–47, 184
agency, 134, 175–76
aggressives (AG): Black culture and, 96–97; common sense in, 97; demographic of, 98; excessive self-expression as, 96; genderqueer and trans* as, 96; M—becoming invisible as, 100–101; in prison, 99; queer, trans* liberation by, 104–5; trans* as, 240n38
The Aggressives (Peddle), 38–39, 82; AG meaning and milieu in, 97; documentary genre for, 92; Gunn and, 103–4; M— as man and woman in, 96; M—storyline in, 99–100; *Paris Is Burning* compared with, 101; present politics in, 91–92, 104–5; prison, market, queer life cycles in, 99; time and space in, 97–98; transmasculinity and, 241n47
Ahmed, Sara, 86, 239n19
Akomfrah, John, 117–18, 243n10, 247n68; on tyranny of time, 120–21, 136–37. *See also* "Digitopia and the Spectres of Diaspora"; *The Last Angel of History*
algorithmic editing, 124, 137–38, 247n64; definition of, 139; finance of, 214; *The Last Angel of History* with, 125; opacity introduced by, 143
alien, 64, 86, 138, 141, 170, 201, 234n22
America: as afterlife of slavery, 25, 77, 160, 168, 186; Bartleby decoding way of, 177; Black existence as outside, 159; Britain and mugging in, 242n6; colonialism and slavery in, 24, 43, 253n30; imperialism of, 193; manifest destiny of, 179–80, 182, 185;

America (*cont.*)
    nationalism and white supremacy of,
    182, 184; as panoramic and tracking
    shots, 179–80, 183; pragmatism of,
    109–10, 181, 186; racism of, 120; settlers
    lie of, 183
American Revolution, 182–83; settler colo-
    nialism and slavery sustained by, 186
*Antifragile: Things That Gain from Disor-
    der* (Taleb), 21, 163, 250n39
antifragility, 255n14; Black culture as, 162–
    63; decision making and uncertainty
    in, 21; for freedom dreams, 22; as more
    upside than down, 21–22; randomness
    used as, 250n39; unpredictable invest-
    ment in, 32; wind loved as, 163
asha (no, resistance), 257n36
Asian culture: Black Orientalism in, 201–
    2; creolization of, 204; jazz music and,
    200–201, 255n25; music of, 256n28;
    race and, 175–76
atomism, 71–72
autopoiēsis, 69–71, 74, 105

Barad, Karen, 133–34, 246n46
Bartleby: American way decoded by,
    177; death and walls for, 109; eco-
    nomic calculation and, 45; formula of
    withdrawal for, 184; hero alignment
    for, 188–89; imagination and power of,
    111; industry of, xvi, 222n13; "I would
    prefer not to" formula of, 45, 51, 178,
    184; as not civil or useful, 44; opacity
    for, 45–46, 192; organization of things
    unsettled by, 16; as original, 178, 187;
    as other, 186–87; as panoramic shot,
    180; past consigned to potentiality by,
    47–48; political and social philosophy
    and, 182; as pure outsider, 50; as radi-
    cal contingency, 184; as repetition in
    rhythm, 178; as silent, quiet, 107, 116;
    social as unsettled by, 49; sonic and
    visual of, 109; sound wrenched from

vision by, 107–8; as speed and white
    noise, 179; as still, motionless, 108
"Bartleby; or, The Formula" (Deleuze), 178
"Bartleby the Scrivener: A Story of Wall
    Street" (Melville), xvi, 107; American
    pragmatism in, 109–10, 181, 186; class
    struggles and, 231n10; lawyer boss
    choices in, 50–51; opacity, incommen-
    surability, risk in, 43; as radical refusal,
    xvi, 40, 43
Baucom, Ian, 23–24, 48, 228n84
being: beings mattering more than, 74;
    Black existence and white, 36; Blacks
    and conceptualization of, 72–73;
    change process as, 199; as fragments
    of imagination, 102; history and
    concealment of, 129; mutation power
    in, 73–74; Negro, Black, African, Ori-
    ental, Native, Primitive excised from
    Western, 70–71; of technology, flesh,
    imagination, spirit, 71, 76, 102
Benjamin, Walter, 93–94, 125–26
Berardi, Franco, 13–14
The Birth of a Nation (Griffith), 123, 140–
    41, 143–44, 182
Black archive, 142
Black belonging, 33–36, 38, 230n105
Black culture: accidents and surprises for,
    250n35; Afrofuturism and production
    of, 39; AG in, 96–97; as antifragile,
    162–63; *The Last Angel of History* on,
    130–31; repetition admitted by, 147;
    repetition and cuts as equilibrium
    for, 162; space, place, land orientation
    from, 185; unforeseen directions of,
    170; Western civilization critique by,
    188
Black existence, 144; abyss inside, 78;
    being conceptual resisted by, 72–73;
    Blues and, 127; commodity speaks
    as, 79; consciousness and, 233n9;
    control evaded by, 135, 158–59; as
    corrosive, 89; cuts of, 174; digital

chaos, 54

Chun, Wendy Hui Kyong, 125–26, 174–75, 236n58

cinema: alternate histories of, 122–23; Black feminism affecting, 246n50; concepts of, 110; control societies and digital, 123–24; Deleuze on, 112–15, 232n39; digital and Black, 39; digital technologies and, 30–31, 32, 114; image unmoored from material in, 31–32; imagination crisis for, 112; movement-image in, 58–59, 111–12; optical-sound image in, 58, 112; organization of things and, 118, 135; reality in, 111; reason and images of, 113; sonic and visual of, 107–9; temporality of, 238n13; time-image in, 58–59, 111

Cinema 2: The Time Image (Deleuze), 58–59, 112–15

clichés, 173, 251n60

Coleman, Beth, 131, 135–36, 144, 160, 173–74, 175, 236n58

collective individuation, 55

Coltrane, Alice, 39, 199–204, 256n26, 256n28, 256n29, 256n31

Coltrane, John, 64, 200–203, 255n21, 255n25, 256n28

commodity: Black existence as, 79; Jones as, 167–68

computation, 25, 125, 160, 229n86

contingency: Bartleby as radical, 184; human freedom containing, 47

"Corporate Cannibal" (Jones), 147; digital art as, 150; with digital technologies, 151; modulation for, 156; rapid cuts in, 164–65; slavery and, 251n59; "Slave to the Rhythm" connection to, 251n48

corporations: continued existence of, 9; credible future stories by, 4–5; invention, innovation, creativity used by, 13

cosmic perspective: Black consciousness and, 233n9; Coltrane, A., music of, 203–4; dark and, 196; messianic and

apocalyptic times in, 209–11; science and speculative fiction in, 195

counterhegemonic tendencies, xii

credit system, 23–24, 28

creolization, 199–200, 204

cultural studies, 226n49; Britain and American mugging in, 242n6; financial speculation and, 225n30, 225n33; interdisciplinarity of, 10–11; repetition and, 147, 161

cuts, 231n23; for Black antifragility, 162–63; Black existence and, 174; "Corporate Cannibal" with rapid, 164–65; digital technologies and irrational, 114, 161–62, 242n19; modulation mechanism as, 162; rhythm repetition role in, 163

Dash, Julie, 119, 138

Daughters of the Dust (Dash), 119

decolonization, 77, 235n40, 237n66

Deleuze, Gilles, 55, 58–59, 82, 178; on American nationalism and white supremacy, 182, 184; on American pragmatism, 181–82; on American Revolution, 182–83; on cinema, 232n39; on cinematic image, 112–15; on irrational cuts, 114, 242n19; on originals, 110–11

difference, 132–33

digital technologies, 229n86, 243n7; alternate cinema histories from, 122–23; Black bodies surveillance in, 102, 245n37; Black cinema and, 39; Black culture archive in, 142; as cinematic, 32, 114; control societies and, 59, 115, 123–24, 132; "Corporate Cannibal" with, 150–51; derivatives need of, 30; elsewhere and, 233n20; Hooker using, 149–51, 156–57, 164–65; image in, 114–16, 118, 137; irrational cuts in, 114, 161–62, 242n19; *The Last Angel of History* made with, 124; media, cinema and, 30–31; modulation potentials in, 155, 158; perception and thought in, 59;

Sun Ra, 38, 53–55, 59–61, 67, 200; Black consciousness and, 233n9; digital sound images of, 234n22
surprises: Black culture and, 250n35; Europeans insuring against, 162; queerness inviting, 214
surrealism: poetry for, xiii; "the Marvelous" and, xii–xiii; as vibrant matter, xv
survivance, 183, 252n18
sympoiesis, 74

Taleb, Nassim Nicholas, 20–22, 162–63, 250n39
El Tayeb, Fatima, 159–60
technē: Black existence and, 123, 125, 130–31; Black history intersection with, 125; as bringing forth, 134; *The Last Angel of History* and, 130–31, 136; race as, 131; technology as art, poetry in, 128; as tool, 39, 74–75
technological mediation, 29; Black existence relationship with, 123; queer times, Black futures and, 38; race and, 135–36; sound and audio in, 59
technology: Afrofuturism with, 4, 59; Blackness as, 173; Jones association with, 148; living beings and, 71; racism rise and, 129; slavery undergirded by, 26; technē and art, poetry as, 128. *See also* race as technology
temporality: of cinema, 238n13; dark of, 53; as linear, 92–93; queer times, Black futures and, 38; theories of, 226n52
"the Marvelous": magic perceived in, xii; surrealism encountering, xii–xiii
"thinking of thought": collective possibilities from, 15
A Thousand Plateaus (Deleuze and Guattari), 55
time and space: *The Aggressives* in, 97–98; cosmic perspective and, 195

"time as officially ended": without memory of possessing as, 79; *Space Is the Place* and, 56, 77–78
time-image: in cinema, 58–59, 111; in film, 113–14; irrational cuts and, 114
time travel, 42
tracking shots, 179–80, 183
trans*, 19, 97; AG as, 96, 104–5, 240n38; looking for and after, 103; studies of, 17; transmasculinity and, 241n47; violence against, 103–4
transduction, 255n11; of consciousness, 68–69; definition of, 72; of entangled matter, 211
transindividual being, 248n12, 248n14, 252n71; new insights with, 176; self-creation of, 69
transnational citizenship, 193–94
Trump, Donald, 242n3
tyrannies, 117, 120–22, 136–37

unaccountability, 32; Bartleby in, 50; dominant standards refusal as, 46–47
United States (U.S.), 250n36
universal exchange, 37
U.S. *See* United States
utopian vision, 86, 88, 90, 117

"Venus in Two Acts" (Hartman), 51
violence: Black women and sexual, 249n17, 249n18; of finance capital, 214; old organization of, 210; poetry for repelling, 104; queer suffering of, 18, 88, 103–4; race as technology and, 135; racist, misogynist, transphobic, homophobic, 103–4; as sexual, 249n17; slavery and sexual, 249n18; straight times imposed as, 104; of white supremacy, 78. *See also* quotidian violence
visibility: gay marriage and queer, 19; of M—, 100–101; politics of, 91–92; surveillance inherent in, 102, 245n37; unequal calculuses of, 99–101; of valued persons, 101–2

ABOUT THE AUTHOR

Kara Keeling is Associate Professor of Cinema and Media Studies at the University of Chicago. Keeling is the author of *The Witch's Flight: The Cinematic, the Black Femme, and the Image of Common Sense* (2007).